Painless Windows

A Handbook for SAS® Users

Windows 95
Windows NT

Jodie Gilmore

 SAS Institute Inc.

Comments or Questions?

The author assumes complete responsibility for the technical accuracy of the content of this book. If you have any questions about the material in this book, please write to the author at this address:

> SAS Institute Inc.
> Books by Users
> Attn: Jodie Gilmore
> SAS Campus Drive
> Cary, NC 27513

If you prefer, you can send e-mail to sasbbu@sas.com with "comments for Jodie Gilmore" as the subject line, or you can fax the Books by Users program at (919) 677-4444.

The correct bibliographic citation for this manual is as follows: Gilmore, Jodie, *Painless Windows: A Handbook for SAS® Users*, Cary, NC: SAS Institute Inc., 1997. 332 pp.

Painless Windows: A Handbook for SAS® Users

Copyright © 1997 by SAS Institute Inc., Cary, NC, USA.

ISBN 1-58025-054-8

SAS Institute Inc., SAS Campus Drive, Cary, North Carolina 27513.

1st printing, September 1997

The SAS® System is an integrated system of software providing complete control over data access, management, analysis, and presentation. Base SAS software is the foundation of the SAS System. Products within the SAS System include SAS/ACCESS®, SAS/AF®, SAS/ASSIST®, SAS/CALC®, SAS/CONNECT®, SAS/CPE®, SAS/DMI®, SAS/EIS®, SAS/ENGLISH®, SAS/ETS®, SAS/FSP®, SAS/GRAPH®, SAS/IMAGE®, SAS/IML®, SAS/IMS-DL/I®, SAS/INSIGHT®, SAS/IntrNet™, SAS/LAB®, SAS/MDDB™, SAS/NVISION®, SAS/OR®, SAS/PH-Clinical®, SAS/QC®, SAS/REPLAY-CICS®, SAS/SESSION®, SAS/SHARE®, SAS/STAT®, SAS/TOOLKIT®, SAS/TRADER®, SAS/TUTOR®, SAS/DB2™, SAS/GEO™, SAS/GIS™, SAS/PH-Kinetics™, SAS/SHARE*NET™, SAS/SPECTRAVIEW®, and SAS/SQL-DS™ software. Other SAS Institute products are SYSTEM 2000® Data Management Software, with basic SYSTEM 2000, CREATE™, Multi-User™, QueX™, Screen Writer™, and CICS interface software; InfoTap® software; JAZZ™ software; NeoVisuals® software; JMP®, JMP IN®, JMP Serve® software; SAS/RTERM® software; and the SAS/C® Compiler and the SAS/CX® Compiler; Video Reality™ software; VisualSpace™ software; Budget Vision™, Campaign Vision™, CFO Vision™, Compensation Vision™, Enterprise Miner™, HR Vision™, and IT Service Vision™ software; Scalable Performance Data Server™ software; SAS OnlineTutor™ software; Emulus® software. MultiVendor Architecture™, MVA™, MultiEngine Architecture™, and MEA™ are trademarks of SAS Institute Inc. SAS Institute also offers SAS Consulting®, and SAS Video Productions® Services. *Authorline*®, Books by Users℠, The Encore Series®, *ExecSolutions*™, *JMPer Cable*®, *Observations*®, *SAS Communications*®, *SAS OnlineDoc*™, *SAS Professional Services*™, *SAS Views*®, the SASware Ballot®, and SelecText™, and Solutions@Work™ documentation are published by SAS Institute Inc. The SAS Video Productions logo, the Books by Users SAS Institute's Author Service logo, the SAS Online Samples logo, and the Encore Series logo are registered service marks or registered trademarks of SAS Institute Inc. The Helplus logo, the SelecText logo, Samples logo, the Video Reality logo, and the Quality Partner logo, the SAS Business Solutions logo, the SAS Rapid Warehousing Program logo, the SAS Publications logo, the Instructor-based Training logo, the Online Training logo, the Trainer's Kit logo, and the Video-based Training logo are service marks or trademarks of SAS Institute. All trademarks above are registered trademarks or trademarks of SAS Institute Inc. in the USA and other countries. ® indicates USA registration.

The Institute is a private company devoted to the support and further development of its software and related services.

Other brand and product names are registered trademarks or trademarks of their respective companies.

Table of Contents

3 Editing and Working with Files

4 Submitting SAS® Code

5 Printing

6   Adjusting Your Windows Environment

7   Managing SAS® Files

8   Customizing Your Start-up Files

Appendix 1   Troubleshooting

Appendix 2   Creating a Print File

Glossary

Index

Welcome to the SAS® System for Windows 95 and Windows NT

What This Book Is

Painless Windows is a task-oriented book about the SAS System under Microsoft Windows 95 and Windows NT that does not assume the user grew up using Windows.

Note: The term "Windows" refers to both Windows 95 and Windows NT in the rest of this book. Where there is a difference between the two systems, the specific system is mentioned.

Two other books specific to using the SAS System under Windows are

- *SAS Companion for the Microsoft Windows Environment, Second Edition*
- *Painless Windows 3.1: A Beginner's Handbook for SAS Users.*

While the Companion is an excellent reference book, it is not primarily task-oriented. Nor does it supply much information on getting around in Windows itself. And *Painless Windows 3.1* does not address the needs of Windows 95 and Windows NT users.

This book assumes you are familiar with the SAS System but not with Windows. It also acknowledges that you may not even like Windows but that you have to use SAS software under Windows to do part of your job. In this book, you learn to use key features of base SAS software to accomplish certain tasks under Windows. Example tasks include

- opening a file that contains SAS code

- submitting SAS code

- saving changes to your SAS code

- printing output from your SAS code.

The book also touches briefly on some other components of the SAS System, including SAS/AF and SAS/CONNECT software.

You also learn how to get around in Windows. For example, the first chapter shows you how to slow down your mouse and how to redisplay an application you want to use after it has disappeared behind several other applications. The chapters include many screen shots, showing what your display should look like while you are filling out dialog boxes and using menus.

What Software You Need

The information in this book assumes you have Microsoft Windows 95 or Microsoft Windows NT (Version 4.0). These environments are significantly different from Windows 3.1—if you need information on using SAS under Windows 3.1, refer to *Painless Windows 3.1*.

Also, the examples and discussion throughout this book assume you have Release 6.12 of the SAS System for Windows. Much of the book applies as well to Release 6.11 and previous releases, but not all.

What This Book Is Not

This book is not a comprehensive guide to using Windows. For example, it does not discuss how to tune Windows performance or discuss using the Control Panel to add serial ports to your system. Nor is this book a guide to SAS software itself. It assumes you know what a DATA step is, that you have used PROC PRINT, and that you know the difference between a system option and a statement option. If you need a guide to using SAS software in general or need more information on Windows, refer to "Further Reading" later in this chapter.

This book is not meant to replace SAS Institute reference documentation. It does not show you every nuance of the tasks it discusses, nor does it show you every way to perform a task. Also, there are aspects of Release 6.12 of the SAS System that this book does not cover. For example, it does not cover using e-mail or advanced OLE features. For nitty gritty details, turn to SAS Institute's reference guides.

Finally, this book is not an installation guide. SAS Institute provides comprehensive installation instructions along with the software. If you need installation assistance, contact your on-site SAS System consultant, ask your company's help desk, or review the documentation that came with your SAS software.

Book Overview

This book contains 12 chapters and two appendices. The chapters are task-oriented and progress from simple tasks such as opening and closing files to more complicated tasks such as using SAS/CONNECT software to connect your PC to other computers. The first appendix gives some pointers for solving common problems you may encounter; the second appendix discusses creating print files. In addition, this book contains a main table of contents, individual chapter tables of contents, and an index. Use these tools to quickly find what you are looking for. If you encounter a term with which you are unfamiliar, check the glossary.

Graphics: This book contains many pictures of menus and screens. Because Windows is a highly-customizable operating system, your menus and screens may not look exactly like those shown in this book. However, you should still be able to use the graphics to orient yourself.

FasTip and HelpPath Sections: Many sections begin with a FasTip that gives bare-bones information on performing a task. If you have performed the task before and need a quick reminder, check these first. FasTips do not appear in Chapters 8-12 and the appendices, as these chapters cover complex tasks that cannot be summarized in a few words.

Also, for many topics a HelpPath is provided. HelpPaths tell you how to get online information about the topic. All HelpPaths are from the SAS System help, unless otherwise noted.

Typographical Conventions

This book uses several typefaces to convey particular information. For example, menu items are in one typeface, while SAS code is in another. The following list gives the purpose of each typeface used:

Bold: Bold face is used to set off elements in windows and dialog boxes, such as menu choices and field names.

`monospace:` Monospace is used for SAS code and operating system commands.

italics: Italics are used in SAS code to indicate user-supplied values.

What You Should Read

If you are a neophyte Windows user, you should read Chapters 1 and 2 thoroughly. They give you a survival kit of information that you need to understand the rest of the book. If you have used Windows 3.1, but are new to Windows 95 or NT, read the first section in Chapter 1. Then, read the chapters that describe the tasks you want to do.

If you have used SAS for Windows before but cannot remember how to perform a certain task, turn to the appropriate chapter for a refresher.

Further Reading

Because this book is a beginner's guide, it does not contain information on complex tasks, nor does it cover all features of either the SAS System or Windows. Check the following list for books you may want to have on hand for further research. The list is by subject.

SAS System Documentation: The following books are about the SAS System. This is not a complete list; check the SAS Institute Publications Catalog or the SAS Institute's World Wide Web page (http://www.sas.com) for additional titles. Books with (SUP) after their titles are published through the SAS Institute's SAS User Publishing program.

Base SAS Software:

SAS Applications Programming: A Gentle Introduction (SUP)

A Quick Start to Data Analysis Using SAS (SUP)

The Little SAS Book: A Primer (SUP)

100 Essential SAS Software Concepts (SUP)

Introducing the SAS System, Version 6, First Edition

SAS Language and Procedures: Introduction, Version 6, First Edition

SAS Language and Procedures: Usage, Version 6, First Edition

SAS Language and Procedures: Usage 2, Version 6, First Edition

SAS Language: Reference, Version 6, First Edition

SAS Procedures Guide, Version 6, Third Edition

SAS/AF Software:

Getting Started with the FRAME Entry: Developing Object-Oriented Applications, Version 6, First Edition

SAS Screen Control Language: Reference, Version 6, Second Edition

SAS Screen Control Language: Usage, Version 6, First Edition

SAS/AF Software: Usage and Reference, Version 6, First Edition

Other Useful SAS System Books:

SAS Software: Abridged Reference, Version 6, First Edition

SAS Companion for the Microsoft Windows Environment, Version 6, Second Edition

Microsoft Windows Environment: Changes and Enhancements to the SAS System, Release 6.10

> *Microsoft Windows Environment: Changes and*
> *Enhancements to the SAS System, Release 6.11*
> *SAS Software: Changes and Enhancements, Release 6.10*
> *SAS Technical Report P-242, SAS Software: Changes and*
> *Enhancements, Release 6.08*
> *Master Index to SAS System Documentation, Version 6,*
> *Fourth Edition*
> *SAS/CONNECT Software: Usage and Reference, Version 6,*
> *Second Edition*

Note: You can find changes and enhancements documentation for Release 6.12 in the online help under the **What's New** topic, and also at the Institute's Web page (http://www.sas.com).

Microsoft Windows Documentation: The following books, listed in alphabetical order, are about Windows. Check your local bookstore and library for additional titles.

Windows 95 Books:

> *Alan Simpson's Easy Guide to Windows 95*
> *The Complete Idiot's Guide to Windows 95*
> *Denny Goodman's Windows 95 Handbook*
> *Field Guide to Microsoft Windows 95*
> *Inside Windows 95*
> *Introducing Microsoft Windows 95*
> *Learn Windows 95* (a video)
> *The Little Windows 95 Book*
> *Mastering Windows 95*
> *The Mother of All Windows 95 Books*
> *PC Guide for Windows 95*
> *The Ultimate Microsoft Windows 95 Book*
> *Voodoo Windows 95: Mastery Tips and Masterful Tricks*
> *Windows 95 for Dummies*
> *Windows 95 Made Easy*

Windows NT Books:

> *The ABCs of Windows NT Workstation 4*
> *The Complete Idiot's Guide to Windows NT Workstation 4.0*
> *Inside Windows NT*
> *Keys to Learning Windows NT*

Learn Windows NT in a Day
Microsoft Windows NT Step by Step
Teach Yourself... Windows NT
Using Windows NT Workstation 4.0
Windows NT: A Practical Guide
Windows NT Answer Book
Windows NT 4 for Dummies
Windows NT: Inside and Out
Windows NT Quick Reference Guide
Windows NT: The Complete Reference
Working with Windows NT

1 Learning to Do Windows

Introduction

This chapter teaches you the basics of using Windows 95 or Windows NT. If you have used a previous version of Windows (such as 3.1), all you may need to read is the first section, "Migrating from Windows 3.1." If you have never used Windows before, skip the migrating section, and begin reading with "Making the Mental Adjustment."

Migrating from Windows 3.1

If you are moving from Windows 3.1 (or Windows 3.11 for Work Groups), you may find that many of the features of Windows 95 or NT are confusing and that many of the features of Windows 3.1 are missing or changed. This section helps you make the transition more smoothly by describing some of the correlations between Windows 3.1 and Windows 95 or NT features.

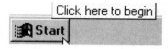

To use this section, scan the headings for the Windows 3.1 feature you are interested in, and read that section. Or, read the entire section—it is pretty short—for an overall view of how Windows 3.1 features relate to Windows 95 or NT features.

Program Manager: With Windows 3.1, you used the Program Manager to organize your Windows applications. In Windows 95 or NT, the Program Manager is unnecessary because the Windows desktop lets you perform the same tasks. For example, the **Start** button provides access to all your program groups, and the Taskbar shows you what applications are running and enables you to switch to any application.

Main Program Group: Instead of having a **Main** program group, Windows 95 or NT shows you all the program groups at a glance when you click on the **Start** button and then on **Programs**.

Start Up Program Group: Windows 95 or NT still has a **Start Up** program group. Click on the **Start** button, then on **Programs**. Now click on **StartUp**. The menu lists the applications that execute immediately when Windows starts up.

To move an application to the **StartUp** program group, follow these steps:

1. Right-click on the **Start** button, then click on **Explore** to open the Windows Explorer.

2. Display the folder that contains the program you want to put in the **StartUp** folder.

3. Right-click on the program icon, then click on **Create Shortcut**.

4. Click on **Edit→Cut**.

5. Display the **StartUp** folder. This folder has the pathname C:\WINDOWS\PROGRAMS\STARTUP for Windows 95 users, or C:\WINNT\PROGRAMS\STARTUP for Windows NT users.

6. Click on **Edit→Paste**.

The next time you start Windows, the new application runs immediately.

File Manager: The Windows Explorer, accessed by right-clicking on the **Start** button and then clicking on **Explore**, replaces the File Manager. In general, the two are similar. See "Becoming Familiar with the Windows Explorer" later in this chapter for more information.

Print Manager: Windows 95 or NT still spools your printer output to the various available printers, but it uses a Printers window instead of the Print Manager. Most of the menu choices are the same. To access the Printers window, click on the **Start** button, then on **Settings**, then on **Printers**. Now double-click on the name of the printer you want to see. A window very similar to the old Print Manager window appears.

Control Panel: Windows 95 or NT still has the Control Panel, and many of its features are similar to the 3.1 version. To access the Control Panel, click on the **Start** button, then on **Settings**, then on **Control Panel**. The Control Panel window appears. Double-click on the aspect of your system you want to adjust, such as **Mouse**, **Display** (where you can set the desktop colors), or **Fonts**.

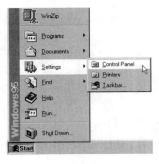

Control-Menu: In Windows 3.1, the Control-menu and window-close button occupied the same space; clicking once on the button opened the menu (which gave choices such as **Close** and **Minimize**), while double-clicking on the button closed the window. The button was located at the top left of the window.

In Windows 95 or NT, the Control-menu and the window-close button occupy separate places in a window:

- The Control-menu is accessed by clicking once on the icon in the top left corner of the title bar.

- The window-close button is located in the top right corner of the title bar, and clicking once on it closes the window. The window-close button is a large X.

Notepad Editor: The Notepad editor still exists under Windows 95 or NT. To access it, click on the **Start** button, then on **Programs**, then on **Accessories**. Now click on **Notepad**.

DOS Editor: You can still use the DOS editor if you prefer it to the many editors available under Windows (including the WordPad and Notepad editors that ship with Windows). To start the DOS editor, first start a DOS session by clicking on the **Start** button, then on **Programs**, then on **MS-DOS Prompt**.

Now type the following at the DOS prompt:

```
EDIT filename
```

where *filename* is the name of the file you want to edit.

To save a file, click on **File** in the DOS editor menu, then on **Save**. To close the editor, click on **File** then on **Exit**.

To close the DOS session, type EXIT at the DOS prompt.

Task List: In Windows 95 or NT, the Taskbar along the bottom edge of the window replaces the Windows 3.1 Task List.

Run Dialog Box: In Windows 95 or NT, the Run dialog box is accessed by clicking on the **Start** button, then on **Run**.

DOS Prompt: Windows 3.1 was a "layered" environment, where Windows ran on top of DOS, and the Program Manager organized your Windows desktop. Windows 95 or NT is an "integrated" environment—there is no DOS separate from Windows. However, you can still run DOS applications in a DOS prompt window.

To open a DOS prompt window, click on the **Start** button, then on **Programs**, then on **MS-DOS Prompt**.

Making the Mental Adjustment

If you are used to a command-line-driven environment like MVS or CMS, the mouse- and menu-driven Windows environment can be overwhelming. Instead of typing a command, you now have to point and click or remember some obscure key sequence. Instead of an uncluttered screen, you now have to worry about scroll bars, icons, colors, and layered windows.

This chapter helps you make the mental adjustment to the Windows environment by defining some common terms, showing you how to take control of your mouse, explaining how files are stored on the PC, and demonstrating how the Windows desktop and the Windows Explorer help keep your screen and files organized.

How Windows Works

Windows is an operating system, like VMS or CMS. But instead of issuing commands at a prompt, you work with files and start applications using a "graphical user interface" (GUI). This interface includes windows, dialog boxes, icons, buttons, and other items. Usually, you use a mouse to interact with the GUI, although you also use the keyboard.

Windows supports a "DOS mode," where you can run older, DOS-based applications from the DOS prompt. However, Windows 95 and Windows NT are not themselves DOS-based applications.

To work with applications under Windows, you use the Windows desktop, and in particular, the **Start** button. The **Start** button is a Windows component that organizes all your Windows applications into groups and makes interacting with the operating system easier. Some applications, such as Microsoft Paint and Microsoft Write, come with Windows; other applications you install separately—such as the SAS System.

Note: It is possible to use alternatives to the Windows desktop and even use a version of the Windows 3.1 Program Manager. However, this book assumes you are using the standard Windows desktop.

Unlike many operating systems, Windows can do several things at once. For example, in DOS, if you submitted a command, you had to wait for that command to finish before you could do anything else. With Windows, you can submit a command, and that command operates in the background—enabling you to start another process.

In particular, you can have several "instances" of a program open at once. Therefore, you can start multiple SAS sessions, all running at the same time.

Note: Only the first SAS display manager session started uses the SASUSER.PROFILE catalog. Subsequent display manager sessions use a temporary profile catalog called WORK.PROFILE.

Terms You Should Know

Every operating system has its own jargon, and Windows is no exception. If you have used a different windowing environment, such as X Windows under UNIX, some of the terms are familiar. But you should scan this section anyway, to see if there are discrepancies between how you understand a term and how this book uses it.

The glossary at the end of this book provides a more complete list of terms used with the SAS System under Windows. The following alphabetical list gives you a head start so you can read this chapter without referring to the glossary constantly. The terms are explained here, as they are used in the rest of this chapter.

active window: the application or part of an application that is ready to accept input.

application: a program with its attendant windows. Examples include the SAS System, Microsoft Word, and Lotus 1-2-3.

click: to press a mouse button once. Unless otherwise stated, click means to press the left mouse button.

Clipboard: a Windows component that is like an online pegboard—a place to store something until you need it again. Typically, the Clipboard is used to store text and graphics that you want to copy somewhere else.

close: to shut down an individual window or an entire application.

dialog box: a type of window that solicits information from you. Usually, you must supply this information before you can continue using an application.

double-click: to quickly press a mouse button twice in a row.

desktop: your screen, where all applications appear.

icon: a pictorial representation of something, such as a window or file.

mouse: the hand-held device you use to select and manipulate applications and text. The mouse activates the mouse pointer on the screen.

point: to move the mouse pointer over an item on the screen, such as a menu choice, a word, or an icon.

popup menu: a context-sensitive menu that appears when you click the right mouse button.

program group: a collection of applications available from the **Programs** selection of the **Start** button. Examples of program groups include **Accessories** and **The SAS System**.

right-click: to press the right-hand mouse button once. Usually, right-clicking displays a context-sensitive menu called a popup menu.

Start button: The button in the lower-left corner of the screen labeled "Start". Clicking on this button enables you to launch applications, alter configuration settings, access Windows help files, and perform other tasks.

Taskbar: A list of all open applications, located across the bottom of the desktop.

Windows Explorer: A Windows application that helps you manage your files.

Becoming Familiar with the Windows Desktop

When you start Windows, the Windows desktop appears. That may be all that happens, or other applications may start, depending on how your system is configured. The Windows desktop keeps a list of all open applications. This list is displayed across the bottom of the screen and is called the Taskbar. The active application's name is highlighted; to move to a different application, click on the application's name in the Taskbar.

Figure 1.1 shows a sample Windows desktop; the Taskbar indicates that two applications are open: SAS and Microsoft Word. Your desktop may look slightly different than the one in Figure 1.1.

Figure 1.1
Sample Windows Desktop
with Taskbar

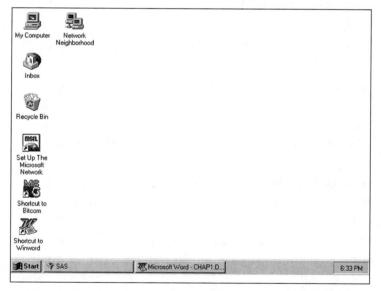

Besides the Taskbar, two more useful components of the Windows desktop are the **Start** button and the **Recycle Bin**.

- The **Start** button is located in the lower-left corner of the Windows desktop. You use it to start applications and manage your Windows session. See "Starting Applications" later in this chapter.

- The **Recycle Bin** is a temporary storage area for files deleted (when you use the Windows Explorer to delete them). See "Restoring Deleted Files" later in this chapter for more information.

Recycle Bin

Windows Geography

The applications and windows you see as you work with Windows have many things in common. This section familiarizes you with the "lay of the land" under Windows. Figure 1.2 shows the LOG and PROGRAM EDITOR windows of the SAS System, which contain some of the standard window elements.

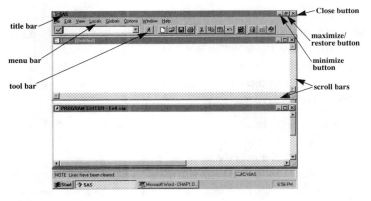

Figure 1.2
Standard Window Elements

Here is a brief description of each element in Figure 1.2.

Title Bar: Each window has a title bar that tells the name of the window. In this case, the title bar at the top tells you the application is SAS. Each individual window also has a title bar, such as the LOG window and the PROGRAM EDITOR window. As well as providing the title of the application, the title bar is also the "handle" for moving windows, as discussed later in this chapter.

Menu Bar: If you are used to nonwindowing environments, you are familiar with giving operating system commands. In Windows, you often use the menu bar to issue these commands. For example, instead of typing "save example1.sas" on a command line, you click on **File**, then on **Save**. While this may seem awkward at first, it does provide the advantage of not having to remember command syntax.

Use the following guides as you browse the menus:

- If a menu choice has an arrow after it, that means there is another layer of choices.

- If a menu choice has an ellipsis after it, that means clicking on it opens a dialog box.

- If there is no symbol after the menu choice, clicking on that choice executes a command, such as SAVE.

- Shortcut keys are listed to the right of menu choices. Instead of using the menus, you can press the shortcut key to achieve the same result. For example, CTRL-S is the shortcut key for SAVE.

Tool Bar: Another method of issuing commands under Windows is to use the graphical tool bar. For example, to save a file in the SAS System, click on the icon that looks like a computer disk. Most applications, including the SAS System, allow you to define your own tools; this enables you to customize your environment and work efficiently.

Scroll Bars: Most windows provide both horizontal and vertical scroll bars. These enable you to move left, right, up, and down in the window. Clicking on the up arrow moves the view up, clicking on the down arrow moves the view down. Similarly, clicking on the left arrow moves the view left, clicking on the right arrow moves the view right. To move larger distances, click in the scroll bar area instead of on the arrows. "Scrolling" in Chapter 3 provides more detailed information on using scroll bars.

Minimize Button: Click on the minimize button (the left-most of the three buttons in the top-right corner of a window) to cause the window to shrink to an icon. If you minimize an entire application, the window disappears from the desktop; to restore the application, click on its name in the Taskbar.

Maximize/Restore Button: The middle button in the top of the window does double duty. If it is two layered boxes (as it is in Figure 1.2), clicking on it causes the window to take up the whole screen (that is, maximize). If it is a single box, clicking on it causes the window to restore to whatever size it was before it was maximized.

Close Button: The Close button is the right-most button in the top-right corner of a window, and is an X. Clicking on it closes the application or window.

Taking Control of Your Mouse

While using Windows with only a keyboard is possible, it is more efficient to also use a mouse. But often, people unfamiliar with the mouse are frustrated by having the pointer move too quickly, not being able to double-click properly, and other problems caused by lack of practice. However, using the mouse does not have to be a rat race! Windows provides a way to slow the mouse down, adjust the double-click rate, and in general let you take control of your mouse.

Using the Mouse Buttons: Most mice have two or three buttons. The left button is used to "click" on things—icons, filenames, options, etc. The right mouse button is reserved for special tasks, such as opening popup menus. If your mouse has a middle button, you can pretty much ignore it, although some software applications (including the SAS System) let you associate commands with the middle mouse button. Figure 1.3 shows the standard, right-handed definition of the mouse buttons.

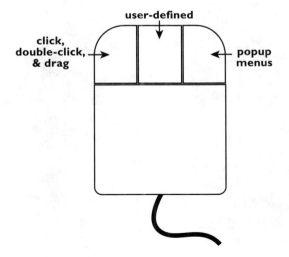

Figure 1.3
Using the Mouse Buttons

Note: If your mouse is a left-handed mouse, the left and right buttons are switched. The "left button" is always the button under your index finger.

Adjusting How Your Mouse Works: To adjust how your mouse works, follow these steps:

1. Click on the **Start** button, then on **Settings**. When the second-level menu appears, click on **Control Panel**.

2. When the Control Panel appears, double-click on the **Mouse** icon. The Mouse Properties dialog box opens. Figure 1.4 shows a sample Mouse Properties dialog box.

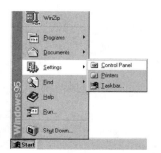

Figure 1.4
Sample Mouse Properties
Dialog Box

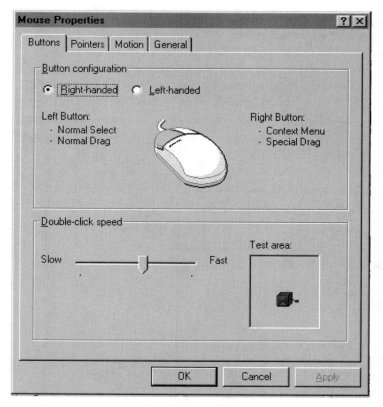

3. There are four tabs in the Mouse Properties dialog box. The top tab is **Buttons**. On this tab, you can adjust the mouse's double-click speed and the left-or right- handed configuration of your mouse.

4. New Windows users usually prefer a slower double-click speed. In the **Double-click speed** area, place your mouse pointer over the slider, hold the left mouse button down, and drag the mouse pointer so the slider moves to the left (toward **Slow**). Release the mouse pointer and double-click on the jack-in-the-box icon in the **Test area** to see if you like the new speed. If your double-click is successful, the icon shows a jack-in-the-box pop out. Double-clicking again closes the jack-in-the-box.

5. If you are left-handed, click next to **Left-handed** in the **Button configuration** area. The text next to the mouse explains what function each mouse button has—if you choose this option, the button under your left index finger (originally the "right" mouse button) becomes the "left" mouse button and vice versa.

6. To slow your mouse down so you can follow it more easily with your eyes, click on the **Motion** tab at the top of the Mouse Properties dialog box. In the **Pointer speed** area, place your mouse pointer over the slider, hold the left mouse button down, and drag the mouse pointer so the slider moves to the left (toward **Slow**). Release the mouse pointer; now move the mouse pointer, to see if you like the new speed.

7. To make the mouse pointer easier to find on the screen when you move the mouse, you may want to use "pointer trails." To enable this feature, click on **Show pointer trails** in the **Pointer trail** area. Now when you move your mouse pointer, the mouse leaves a brief trail of pointers behind.

Depending on your mouse driver (the software that controls your mouse), you may also see other options, such as changing the mouse pointer to a larger size.

When you are happy with your selections, click on **OK**. This closes the Mouse Properties dialog box. To close the Control Panel, click on **File** in the Control Panel menu, then click on **Close**.

As you become more adept with your mouse, return to the Mouse
Properties dialog box and adjust the settings again to fit your new
skill level.

Using Your Mouse to Communicate with Applications: Your
mouse is the primary method of communicating with Windows
applications, although you also use function keys and keyboard
sequences. You need to master several skills with the mouse:

pointing

Pointing involves moving the mouse pointer until it is directly on
top of something, such as an icon or a menu choice. In some
cases, pointing causes Windows to take an action. For example,
in the **Start** button menu, simply pointing (without clicking) to a
menu item opens the submenu.

clicking

Clicking involves pressing and releasing the left mouse button
once. Usually, you click on something to select (that is,
highlight) it.

right-clicking

Right-clicking involves pressing and releasing the right mouse
button once. Usually, you right-click on something to display a
context-sensitive menu.

double-clicking

Double-clicking involves pressing the mouse button twice in
rapid succession. Usually, you double-click on something to activate it (such as starting an application from an icon).

dragging

Dragging involves holding the mouse button down while you
move the mouse around. Usually, you drag an object to move it
(such as moving window borders or text in a text editor).

Practice Using Your Mouse: One way to practice using your
mouse is to use the tutorial that comes with Windows. To access
this tutorial, click on the **Start** button, then click on **Help** in the
Start button menu. In the window that appears, double-click on

Tour: **Ten minutes to using Windows**. You must have your Windows CD-ROM to use this tutorial.

Learning the Basic Survival Kit

There are several things you should know before you start using Windows extensively. For example, how do you start applications? When you are done with them, how do you close them? What if you want to use a new application but do not want to close the others? Learning the answers to these and a few other questions helps you work more efficiently under Windows.

Starting Applications: An easy way to start an application is by clicking on its name in the **Programs** menu and submenus, accessed by clicking on the **Start** button.

When you click on the **Start** button, a menu appears, as shown in Figure 1.5.

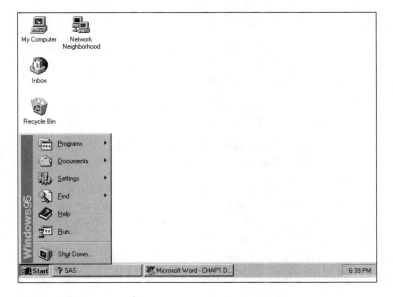

Figure 1.5
Start Button Menu

To start an application, such as the SAS System, click on the **Programs** item in the **Start** button menu. A second menu appears, as shown in Figure 1.6.

Figure 1.6
Programs Menu from the
Start Button

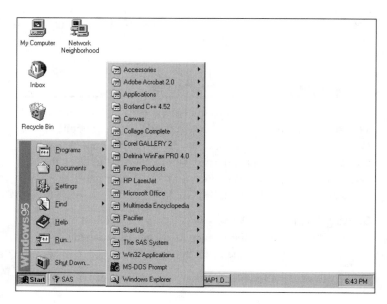

This menu shows the program groups available on your system, such as **Accessories** and **StartUp**.

* **Accessories** contains handy applications supplied by Microsoft and installed with Windows. Example accessories include Paint (a drawing program) and WordPad (a text editor).

* **StartUp** contains applications you want to start automatically every time you start Windows.

Your desktop may show other groups, such as **The SAS System** and **Microsoft Office**, depending on what software is installed on your PC.

Note: Most of the time merely placing the mouse pointer over the text is sufficient to select it in a menu, but not always. And clicking doesn't hurt anything. Therefore, in many places, this book says "click on **Programs**" or gives other similar instructions.

Program groups in the **Programs** menu that are followed by a right arrow contain subgroups. Clicking on the main group displays the subgroup. Take a moment to investigate all program groups on your desktop, to see what applications are available to you. To close the **Programs** menu system without starting an application, click outside of the menus.

Closing Applications: The easiest way to close applications is to click on the Close button. This is the X in the upper-right corner of an application's main window. Sometimes, you also have to confirm that you really want to exit the application. (For example, by default the SAS System prompts you with the question "Are you sure you really want to terminate the SAS session?")

Two other methods of closing an application include

• clicking on the **File** choice in the application's menu bar and then clicking on **Exit** or **Close**

• right-clicking on the application's name in the Taskbar and clicking on **Close**.

Managing Several Open Applications at Once: One of the nice things about Windows is that you can use several applications at the same time. But you have only one screen, so the open windows are layered. The window that is "on top" is usually the active window. To make another window active, you must somehow get to it.

Suppose you have started the SAS System, but now want to open Microsoft Word as well, without ending your SAS session. Follow these steps to start Word:

1. Click on the **Start** button.

2. Click on **Programs** in the **Start** button menu, then on **Microsoft Office**. When the third-level menu appears, click on **Microsoft Word**.

Now two applications are open at once: the SAS System and Word.

Here are some ways you can return to your SAS session:

• Click on **SAS** on the Taskbar.

• press ALT-ESC to toggle through all open applications.

Using Dialog Boxes: To communicate with most Windows applications, you must use dialog boxes. These are interactive ways to give commands and information to an application. When you adjusted your mouse settings, you were using a dialog box. Dialog boxes have many features in common, such as the following:

• Clicking on **OK** or **Close** applies your changes and closes the dialog box.

- Clicking on **Cancel** closes the dialog box without having any other effect.

- Sometimes you can type a value into a field—this is called a text-entry field.

- If there are several choices for a field value, clicking on a down arrow displays a list of choices—click on one of the choices to change the field value. This is called a drop-down list box.

- Other times, the entire list of choices is displayed in a list box; use the scroll bars to navigate the list. Click on a choice to select it.

- If there are options that can be on or off, clicking in the box or button by the option toggles its value. If a box has an 'x' in it, or if a round button is filled in, the option is on. The difference between check boxes (square boxes) and radio buttons (round buttons) is as follows:

    - you can choose several options in a list of check boxes

    - options with radio buttons are mutually exclusive.

- Many dialog boxes offer a context-sensitive help button near the upper-right corner of the dialog box. Clicking on this button changes the mouse pointer to a question mark/arrow. Now click on the part of the dialog box you want more information on. The help information is displayed in a window. Click again anywhere to close the instructions. Occasionally, instead of the context-sensitive help button, you may see a button labeled **Help**.

- In dialog boxes that list files, you may see four useful icons. Click on the icon to activate it.

    -    Move up a level in the folder hierarchy.

    -    Create a new folder.

- List folders and files with no details.

- List folders and files with details such as file description, creation date, etc.

Figure 1.7 shows an example dialog box that displays many of these features.

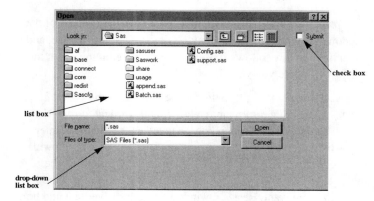

Figure 1.7
Some Standard Dialog Box Features

Figure 1.8 shows another dialog box with more features.

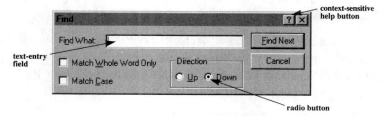

Figure 1.8
More Standard Dialog Box Features

Controlling How Programs Work: The icons you see on the desktop are not magic. They are pictorial representations of operating system commands and command options. When you install an application such as the SAS System, the installation utility adds the icon to the appropriate program group in the **Programs** menu, and associates certain commands and options with the icon. These commands control the location of the program's executable file (such as SAS.EXE) and other aspects of running the program. This collection of commands constitutes the application's "properties".

You can change an application's properties by using the Properties dialog box. "Altering the Properties of the SAS System Icon" in Chapter 8 gives some examples of how to change SAS System properties.

Moving and Resizing Windows: Sometimes the default size or position of a window is not satisfactory. You've already learned about the minimize and maximize buttons, but you can also move windows or cause them to shrink and grow.

To move a window, place the mouse pointer in the title bar of the window. Now hold the mouse button down. Drag the mouse, and the entire window follows it. Release the mouse button when the window is where you want it.

To resize the window, place the mouse pointer on the edge of the window. The pointer turns into a horizontal, vertical, or diagonal double-headed arrow (depending on whether the mouse pointer is positioned on a side, the top or bottom, or a corner of the window, respectively). Hold the mouse button down and drag the mouse—the window edge follows the pointer—until the window is the size you want. Resize a window in both the vertical and horizontal directions at once by placing the mouse pointer over a corner of the window. In this case, the pointer turns into a diagonal double-headed arrow.

To practice resizing windows, double-click on the **Recycle Bin** icon on the Windows desktop. Now make the Recycle Bin window narrow, then tall, then back to its original size. Close the Recycle Bin by clicking on its Close button.

Note: You cannot resize a maximized window.

Shutting Down Windows: You can choose to leave Windows running all the time, even when you are away from your desk. Or, you may want to turn your computer off. Never turn off your computer without properly shutting down Windows.

To shut down Windows, click on the **Start** button, then click on **Shut down** (at the bottom of the **Start** button menu). A dialog box appears, asking what type of shut-down you want to use. Click on **Shut down the computer?** and press Enter. Windows shuts down, and the screen displays a message that it is now safe to turn your computer off.

Handy Keyboard Shortcuts

Table 1.1 provides a list of handy keyboard shortcuts for perform-ing tasks in the Windows environment. Refer to this table as you read the rest of the book—if you do not want to use the mouse for a task, use the keyboard shortcut listed in the table.

Table 1.1
Keyboard Shortcuts

KEYBOARD SHORTCUT	ACTION
ALT-Enter	Opens the Properties dialog box for an icon
CTRL-ESC	Opens the **Start** button menu
ALT-ESC	Toggles through all open applications
ALT-TAB	Toggles between the two last-used applications
TAB	Moves the cursor from field to field in dialog boxes
SHIFT-TAB	Moves the cursor backward through fields in dialog boxes

The menus also provide a type of keyboard shortcut, called hotkeys. These are the underlined letters you see in each of the menu choices. If the menu is open, pressing the hotkey is equiva-lent to clicking on a menu choice.

To open a menu without using the mouse, press the ALT key. This highlights the first item in the menu bar. Once the highlight is in the menu bar, use your arrow keys to move to the menu item you want and press Enter to execute the command. Or, type the letter that is underlined in the menu.

Note: The hotkey is not always the first letter of the menu choice.

Understanding How Files Are Stored and Named

If you are coming from a UNIX or VMS background, you are familiar with the hierarchical structure of folders, subfolders, and files under Windows. But if you are familiar with MVS, CMS, or VSE, you may be used to a different file structure. It is important to understand how Windows files are stored and named before you begin to use SAS software to create and manage files.

Note: The terms *folder* and *directory* are synonymous.

Understanding the Windows File Structure: Under Windows, individual files have a filename and an extension. Think of a file as a collection of information, where the filename describes the information and the extension describes the format of the information. For example, MEMO.TXT is a memo and is in plain ASCII text format. HOUSE.TIF is a picture of a house in the TIFF bitmap format.

Windows supports long filenames—that is, you can use a total of 255 characters for the filename, plus three characters for the extension. In addition, filenames and extensions can contain spaces, quotation marks, and other characters not allowed in filenames under many other operating systems.

Examples of valid filenames are CONFIG.SYS, DECEMBER'S REPORT.TXT and JOAN & TOM.DOC. The following characters are not allowed in filenames: / \ : ; ? " < > | *.

Note: Although an external file can have a long name, currently SAS names such as data set names must be eight characters or less.

Understanding Truncated Filenames: If you intend to use files under Windows and other operating systems that do not support long filenames, be aware that the long filename is truncated to eight characters, replacing certain characters (such as commas and spaces) with underscores (_) and extra characters with a tilde (~) and a numeral. For example, suppose you had the following files in a folder:

DECEMBER'S REPORT.TXT
DECEMBER'S BILLS.TXT
THAT'S ALL.TXT
X,Y.TXT

The truncated names are as follows:

DECEMB~1.TXT
DECEMB~2.TXT
THAT'S~1.TXT
X_Y~1.TXT

Note that the last file, X,Y.TXT, has the ~1 added, even though the filename is short. This is because of the substitution of the underscore for the comma.

Understanding Files and Folders: Files are grouped together in *folders*. (In previous versions of Windows and DOS, the term *directory* was used. Directory and folder are synonymous.) Folders can contain subfolders as well as files. For example, you might have a folder called BILLS, and within that folder you have some miscellaneous files along with two subfolders, PAID and OVERDUE. In turn, these subfolders contain files for each individual bill.

Your root folder is the top-level folder that contains all other subfolders and files. Usually, this is called C:\ and is the default folder when you boot your PC. The C:\ folder can contain many subfolders, which can contain other subfolders, etc.

Figure 1.9 shows a sample folder hierarchy.

Figure 1.9
Example Folder Hierarchy

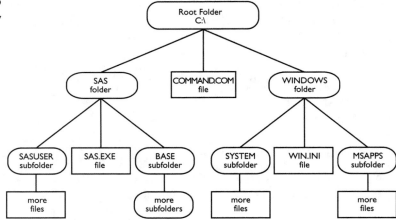

Understanding Drives: Another concept you need to understand is drive. While the root folder is referred to as C:\, the drive is referred to as C:. Your computer may have several drives—the hard drive might be C:, the 3 1/2" floppy drive might be A:, and if you have a CD-ROM drive, it might be designated D:. If you are on a network, you probably have access to many drives. To find out how your system is organized, use the Windows Explorer, which is discussed later in this chapter.

Understanding Common File Extensions: Some file extensions are associated with particular applications. For example, files with an extension of .SAS are SAS programs, while files with a .DOC extension are usually Word files. Table 1.2 gives some common file extensions.

Table 1.2
Common File Extensions

TEXT FILES		SAS FILES	
EXTENSION	FILE TYPE	EXTENSION	FILE TYPE
SAS	SAS code	SD2	SAS data file
DAT	raw data files	SI2	SAS data file index
TXT	ASCII text files	SC2	SAS catalog
LST	SAS output	SS2	SAS stored program
LOG	SAS log files	SV2	SAS data view
		SA2	SAS access descriptor

Using Wildcard Characters: Like most operating systems, Windows accepts wildcard characters in filenames when you are performing file maintenance (such as deleting, moving, or searching). Table 1.3 lists the wildcard characters Windows accepts.

Table 1.3
Wildcard Characters

CHARACTER	MEANING
*	replaces any number of characters
?	replaces a single character

To show how these wildcard characters work, here are a few examples:

PROG*.SAS	finds PROG1.SAS and PROGRAM2.SAS
PROG?B.SAS	finds PROG1B.SAS but not PROG11B.SAS
REVENUE.*	finds REVENUE.SAS and REVENUE.DAT

Understanding How SAS Files Are Stored under Windows: As a SAS user, you already know about the various types of SAS files and that these files are stored in SAS data libraries. Under Windows, the concept of a SAS data library is loosely analogous to that of a folder, with the addition of the concept of SAS engines. An example will help illustrate this.

Suppose you have two folders, C:\REPORTS and C:\INCOME. In the REPORTS folder, there are some Release 6.12 SAS data sets. In the INCOME folder, you also have Release 6.12 SAS data sets but also some Release 6.04 data sets. To access these three categories of data sets, you would set up three SAS data libraries. Two of the data libraries would point to the INCOME folder, but each of these libraries would contain only those data sets accessed by the appropriate SAS engine.

You can also concatenate several folders into one SAS data library, using either the LIBNAME statement or the Libraries dialog box. See Chapter 7 for more information on using the Libraries dialog box; "Defining Filerefs and Librefs" later in this chapter gives an example of the LIBNAME statement.

For more information on SAS data libraries under Windows, follow this help path:

HelpPath: **Help→SAS companion→SAS Companion for Microsoft Windows→Running the SAS System under Windows→Using SAS Files→Using Data Libraries**

Knowing the Important Files and Folders: Certain files, folders, and subfolders are important to you as a SAS software user. The following list gives some of these and briefly describes their purpose:

SAS.EXE — is the executable program that runs the SAS System.

CONFIG.SAS — contains the configuration options for your SAS session.

AUTOEXEC.SAS — contains startup statements you want to execute when you begin a SAS session.

SASUSER subfolder — corresponds to your SASUSER SAS data library, and contains your SAS profile catalogs, key definitions, tool definitions, and so on.

SASWORK subfolder — contains your WORK SAS data library.

Using Filenames in SAS Statements and Commands: When you type the name of folders, subfolders, and files in SAS statements and commands, such as on the Command bar or in dialog boxes, separate the folder, subfolder, and filename with a backslash. For example, the following INCLUDE command references a file named MEDICAL.DAT in a folder called MYDATA, which is a subfolder of the root folder on the C: drive:

```
INCLUDE 'C:\MYDATA\MEDICALREPORT.DAT'
```

This is called the *full pathname* for the file, which states explicitly
where the file is stored. When in doubt, specify the full pathname
for files; while there are rules for how the folder and file extension
default, it is always safe to specify the full pathname.

Defining Filerefs and Librefs: One of the most common uses of the
full pathname is when you use the FILENAME and LIBNAME
statements to define filerefs and librefs in your SAS programs.
Here is an example of each of these statements, using the full pathname for the file or folder:

```
filename misc 'c:\misc\qtr1.dat';
libname inv 'c:\sas\invoices';
```

Note: If the filename contains spaces or other punctuation such as a
single quotation mark, use double quotation marks in SAS statements such as FILENAME and LIBNAME.

Becoming Familiar with the Windows Explorer

While you can use the SAS System to rename, delete, copy, and
move files, you may also want to use the Windows Explorer, which
is a Windows application for managing files. One advantage of
using the Windows Explorer is that it gives you a pictorial view of
the available drives and folders on your PC. For example, Figure
1.10 shows the Windows Explorer displaying the SAS folder with
its files and subfolders.

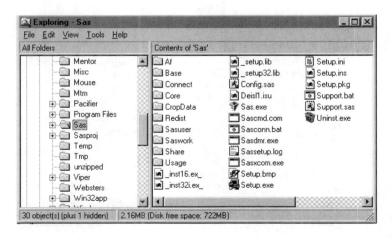

Figure 1.10
**The Windows Explorer
Listing the Contents of the
SAS Folder**

Your display may look different from this, depending on what SAS products you have installed.

To start the Windows Explorer, right-click on the **Start** button, then click on **Explore**. To see the contents of a particular folder, use the scroll bar in the center of the window to get to the folder you want to see. Click on the folder name—the contents of that folder are displayed in the right half of the window.

If you double-click on a folder in the left half of the window, any subfolders in that folder are displayed underneath the folder. This is called "expanding" the folder. Double-clicking on the folder again "collapses" the folder so that the subfolders are not shown.

The Windows Explorer uses different icons to indicate various file types. Some executable files have rectangular icons with a bar across the top; other executable files use a special icon associated with the program. If the file can be edited (such as a text file), the icon has fake text on the page. Folders and subfolders are indicated by little file folders.

To see the contents of a subfolder in the right half of the window, double-click on the subfolder name. The view changes accordingly. To change drives, scroll to the top of the left-hand Windows Explorer window and click on the drive you want to see.

Copying and Moving Files: You can use the Windows Explorer menus to copy and move files. For example, look at Figure 1.11.

Figure 1.11
Preparing to Copy a File Using the Windows Explorer

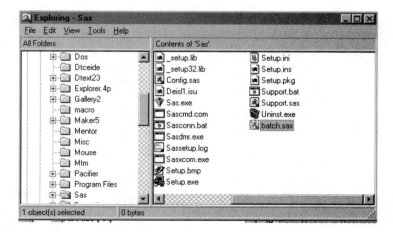

The file BATCH.SAS (a file in the SAS folder) is highlighted. Remember, to highlight a file, click on its name. To copy this file to a different folder, click on **Edit** in the Windows Explorer menu, then on **Copy**. The file is copied to the Windows Clipboard. Now display the folder to which you want to copy the file, and highlight the folder name by clicking on it. Once the target folder is highlighted, click on **Edit** in the Windows Explorer menu, then on **Paste**. The file is copied to the target folder.

Moving a file works exactly the same except choose **Cut** from the Windows Explorer **File** menu instead of **Copy**.

Renaming Files: To rename a file using the Windows Explorer, highlight the file by clicking on it. Click on **File** in the Windows Explorer menu, then on **Rename**. A box appears around the filename. Type the new name, and press Enter.

Deleting Files: To delete a file using the Windows Explorer, highlight the file by clicking on it. Click on **File** in the Windows Explorer menu, then on **Delete**. A dialog box asks you if you are sure you want to send the file to the **Recycle Bin**. Click on **Yes** to complete the file deletion.

Note: Files deleted to the **Recycle Bin** are not deleted from the system. To completely delete a file, double-click on the **Recycle Bin** icon on the desktop, highlight the file in the file list, and press the Delete key. A dialog box asks you if you are sure you want to completely delete the items. Click on **Yes** to complete the deletion.

Warning: Be careful when you move, rename, or delete files–some files, such as the SASUSER.PROFILE catalog, must have a particular name in order to work. In general, it is safe to move, rename, or delete catalogs and other files you have created; do not move, rename, or delete files created automatically by the SAS System. Nor is it a good idea to rename SAS data sets using the Windows Explorer because the data set name is also stored in the data set's header information.

Restoring Deleted Files: You can use the Recycle Bin to restore a file you have recently deleted from a Windows Explorer window.

Here are the basic steps for restoring a deleted file:

1. Double-click on the **Recycle Bin** icon on the Windows desktop.

2. When the Recycle Bin opens, click on the file you want to restore.

3. Click on **File** in the Recycle Bin menu, then on **Restore**. The file is restored to whatever folder it was originally stored in.

Warning: Files deleted from within the SAS System are not sent to the Recycle Bin–they are deleted completely from the hard disk. To recover these files, you must have a third-party file restoration utility, such as Norton Utilities.

Creating Folders: You may want to create new folders and subfolders to store the files associated with your work with the SAS System. For example, you might need separate folders for SAS programs, SAS logs, SAS output, and miscellaneous files.

To use the Windows Explorer to create a folder or subfolder, click on **File** in the Windows Explorer menu, then on **New**. When a list of choices appears, click on **Folder**. A new folder icon appears in the right half of the window, ready for a new name. Type the name and press Enter. The folder is now ready to store files.

To close the Windows Explorer, click on its Close button.

Testing Your Survival Kit

Now that you understand a little bit about how Windows works, you are ready to see if you can "do Windows." Try the next chapter, which walks you through most of the fundamental tasks involved in using base SAS software. After you've done the first two or three exercises, you'll see that "doing Windows" is not that hard after all. And even if you never like Windows, at least you will not feel like you're looking through frosted glass while you work.

2 Performing the Basic SAS® Software Tasks under Windows

Getting Ready for the Tutorial

Now that you understand Windows' file-naming conventions, can double-click, and can open and close applications, you are ready to apply these skills to using the SAS System. Most of this chapter is a tutorial. You should try each exercise so that you get a feel for how the SAS System works under Windows.

Because of the tutorial nature of this chapter, it does not show you every aspect of every task—there are many ways to edit a file, for example; this chapter shows only a few techniques. But if you master the techniques in this chapter, you can then learn new techniques as you go along, using the online help, other manuals, etc.

The sections "Getting Oriented" and "Getting Help" are not tutorial, but they do provide important information. If you are new to Windows, you should read these sections.

Before you begin the exercises in this chapter, you should close Windows and bring it up again, so you have a "pristine" environment to work in. (For more information on closing Windows, see "Shutting Down Windows" in Chapter 1.)

Starting Your SAS Session

FasTip: Click on the **Start** button. Click on **Programs**, then on **The SAS System**. Now click on **The SAS System for Windows v6.12**.

HelpPath: Help→How to→How to... with the SAS System→Get Started with the SAS System→Starting SAS, then choose **From the Start menu** or **From the Run Command**

Help→SAS System→SAS System Help: Main Menu→SAS Windows→PROGRAM EDITOR→ SAS Text Editor→SAS Global Commands

To start the SAS System, click on the **Start** button, then on **Programs**, then on **The SAS System**. Now click on **The SAS System for Windows v6.12**. Figure 2.1 shows a sample **Start** menu, with the pointer over **The SAS System for Windows v6.12**. Your display should look similar to this before you start this exercise. (Your display may not be identical to Figure 2.1 because you may have different software installed.)

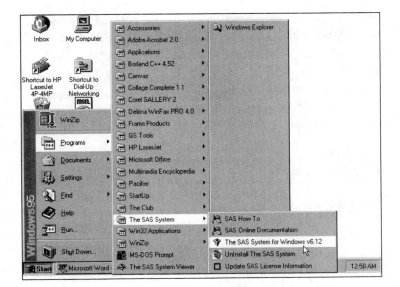

Figure 2.1
Starting the SAS System

The SAS System logo appears, followed by the LOG and PRO-
GRAM EDITOR windows. Figure 2.2 shows how these SAS windows look. Typically, there are some notes in the LOG window that
state your site number, version number, and other site-specific
information.

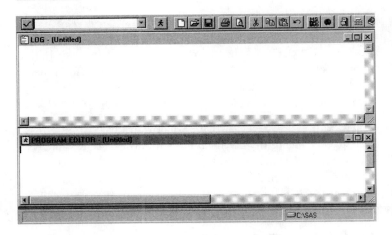

Figure 2.2
Initial LOG and PROGRAM
EDITOR Windows

While you can proceed directly with the rest of the tutorial, starting with "Accessing the SAS Sample Library," you may prefer to read the next two sections before proceeding.

Note: Under Windows 95 and Windows NT, you can have more than one SAS session running at once. The number of sessions is limited only by the amount of RAM (Random Access Memory) your computer has.

Getting Oriented

HelpPath: Help→SAS companion→SAS Companion for Microsoft Windows→Running the SAS System under Windows→Using Graphical Interface Features of the SAS System→Overview of the SAS System Interface

While the basic geography of the SAS System, such as the LOG, PROGRAM EDITOR, and OUTPUT windows, is the same across operating systems, you need to know some windowing terminology to fully understand the SAS System for Windows. Here is a brief orientation session.

Note: Many aspects of the appearance and behavior of the SAS System are configurable. The discussion that follows assumes you are using the defaults for the various features. If you are using someone else's system, and it has been configured to differ from the defaults, ask the machine's owner to reset the features to the default behavior before you read the rest of this chapter.

Application Workspace: The large window that has "SAS" across the top and contains the LOG and PROGRAM EDITOR windows is called the AWS–the Application Workspace. The AWS is like a container for your SAS session—in general, everything you do in your SAS session—opening new windows, interacting with dialog boxes, etc.—occurs inside the AWS.

Title Bar: Across the top of the AWS is the title bar. Every window inside the AWS also has a title bar.

Scroll Bars: Down the right side of the windows are scroll bars that enable you to move up and down in the windows. The scroll bars at the bottom of windows let you move left and right across the screen.

Menus: Just under the title bar is the SAS System main menu. Here you find commands to open and save files, print, submit code, change system options, invoke other parts of the SAS System, and ask for help.

Command Bar: Under the menu bar, on the left, is a white box— this is the Command bar, and it is where you type display manager commands. If you are coming from MVS or CMS, use the Command bar like the command line in those operating systems. To activate the Command bar, point to it with the mouse and click. To return to a SAS window, click in the window. (Alternatively, you can press F11 to move the cursor to the Command bar; press ESC to return the cursor to the active SAS window.)

The Command bar remembers the commands you have issued in your SAS session and keeps a list of them. If you want to repeat a command, click on the down arrow by the Command bar to display a reverse order list of recently issued commands. Click on the command you want. This copies the command to the Command bar. Once the Command bar contains the command you want to issue, click on the check mark to the left of the Command bar to execute the command, or press Enter.

Tool Bar: To the right of the Command bar is the tool bar—this is a graphical menu, where clicking on an icon executes a command (such as save, print, or help). Each window in the SAS System has its own tool set (except for the LOG, PROGRAM EDITOR, and OUTPUT windows, which all use the same tools). The tool bar icons change when you make a new window active.

Minimize and Maximize/Restore Buttons: There are three buttons in the upper-right corner of most SAS windows. The left-most and middle buttons control the size of the window:

The left-most button is the minimize button. Click on this to shrink the window to an icon. To get the window back, click **Window** in the SAS System main menu, then click on the name of the minimized window.

The middle button is the maximize/restore button. It's action depends on the button's shape:

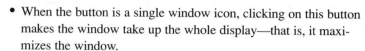

- When the button is a single window icon, clicking on this button makes the window take up the whole display—that is, it maximizes the window.

- When a window is maximized, the maximize button becomes the restore button. In this case, the button shows two layered windows. Clicking on the restore button makes the window return to its original size.

Close Button: You learned about the Close button in Chapter 1; it is the X icon in the upper-right corner of an application's AWS. Not only does the SAS System AWS have a Close button, but so do most windows inside the AWS, like the LOG and PROGRAM EDITOR windows. Click on the Close button to close a window.

Context-Sensitive Menus: Notice that the LOG and PROGRAM EDITOR windows do not have menu bars. That is because the selections available in the main menu change, depending on which window is active. If you click in the LOG window, its title bar is highlighted. It is now the active window. If you click on **Edit** in the main menu, you see that, for example, **Undo** is grayed out—this is not a valid command in the LOG window. But if you click in the PROGRAM EDITOR window and then look at the **Edit** menu, **Undo** is available.

Popup Menus: Another way to see the menus for a particular window is to click the right mouse button in the window. The menu that appears is called a popup menu. For example, Figure 2.3 shows the first layer of the popup menu for the LOG window.

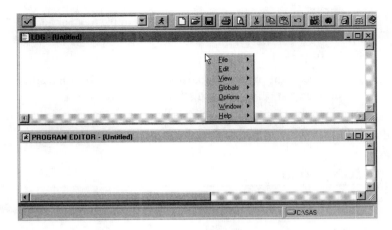

Figure 2.3
Popup Menu for the LOG
Window

If you activate a menu by mistake, click outside the menu, anywhere in the SAS AWS. This closes the menu; now try again.

Practice Using the SAS Menus: Use the following exercise to practice using the menus:

1. Make the PROGRAM EDITOR window active by clicking anywhere within it.

2. Click on **Window** in the SAS System main menu.

3. Click on **OUTPUT.** This takes you to the OUTPUT window.

4. Click the right mouse button in the OUTPUT window. The popup menu appears.

5. Click on **Window**, then on **PROGRAM EDITOR.** Now both the OUTPUT and PROGRAM EDITOR windows are visible.

6. To return to the default appearance, right-click in the PROGRAM EDITOR window, click on **Window**, then on **LOG**.

Other SAS System AWS Features: At the bottom of the SAS AWS are some useful items:

• In the lower-left corner is a status bar, which displays brief help messages about various tools and the results of display manager commands.

- If you place your mouse pointer over a tool in the tool bar and wait a bit, a "tool tip" appears below the tool that tells you what the tool does.

- In the lower-right corner is a folder icon with a folder name after it. This tells you which folder the SAS System is using as its working folder. "Changing the SAS Working Folder" in Chapter 3 provides more information.

Getting Help

FasTip: Click on the Help icon on the SAS AWS tool bar.

HelpPath: Help→**SAS companion**→**SAS Companion for Microsoft Windows**→**Running the SAS System under Windows**→**Using Graphical Interface Features of the SAS System**→**Accessing Online Help and Documentation**

While this book only scratches the surface of using the SAS System for Windows, all the information you could possibly want is at your fingertips—or at least at your mouse pointer. So, before continuing with the tutorial, read this section to familiarize yourself with the SAS Help system.

The main method of obtaining help while using the SAS System is to click on **Help** in the SAS System main menu, or click on the help icon on the tool bar:

 Also, many dialog boxes offer context-sensitive help. To access it, click on the help icon located in the upper-right corner of the dialog box. Click on this icon, then click on a field or button in the dialog box to display an explanation of the dialog box feature. To close the explanation, click anywhere outside the explanation. A few dialog boxes also contain a **Help** button.

Note: Some of the help topics and explanations in the SAS Help system are not applicable to the Windows 95 and Windows NT operating systems. Rather, these topics and explanations pertain to the Windows 3.1 environment. If a help topic refers to features such as "the Program Manager" or "the File Manager," ignore these topics.

Using the Help Menu: If you click on the **Help** menu item in the SAS System main menu, you see the choices illustrated in Figure 2.4.

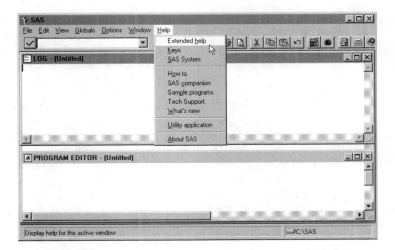

Figure 2.4
SAS System Help Menu

Here is an explanation of the **Help** menu choices you may use most often:

Extended help is useful when you want help for a specific window, like the CATALOG window or PROC BUILD window.

If you choose **Extended help** from the primary SAS windows, such as the LOG and PROGRAM EDITOR, it opens the Help Topics: SAS System Help window, which lists several avenues of help.

SAS System is identical to choosing **Extended help** from one of the main SAS System windows, such as the LOG or PROGRAM EDITOR.

How to opens the Help Topics: How to... window. From here, double-click on **How to... with the SAS System**, then choose a task-oriented topic like **Get Started with the SAS System** or **Access Data with the SAS System**.

SAS companion opens help specific to the SAS System for Windows. This includes reference material on system options, statement options, and so on.

Sample programs contains many examples that you can copy to the Clipboard and submit or paste into the PROGRAM EDITOR window as a boilerplate for your own program. For more information, see "Accessing the SAS Sample Library" later in this chapter.

Practice opening the various **Help** menu items by clicking on them, then close the resulting windows by clicking on their Close buttons.

How the SAS Help System Is Organized: The information in the SAS Help system is organized from general to specific. By making choices in the Help windows, you progress through the layers toward the specific topic or task you are interested in (this is sometimes referred to as "drilling down").

Types of Help Windows: There are two types of windows in the SAS Help system: topic list windows and topic windows.

- Topic list windows display available topics. In these windows, topics are represented by book icons, and the hierarchy of the information is indicated by indents. For example, the third level of information is indented farther than the second level.

- Topic windows display the information or steps you are looking for. If the information is longer than the window size, the window has scroll bars. Use the scroll bars to see the rest of the information.

Navigating Topic List Windows: Topic lists include two types of icons:

 Topics represented by book icons expand when you double-click on them, and list that topic's subtopics. The book icon you double-clicked on "opens." If you double-click on the book icon again, the book icon closes and the list of subtopics disappears. (This expand/collapse technique is similar to how you display and collapse folders in the Windows Explorer.)

 Question marks display the topic information when you double-click on them.

Figure 2.5 shows a sample topic list that illustrates both types of icons.

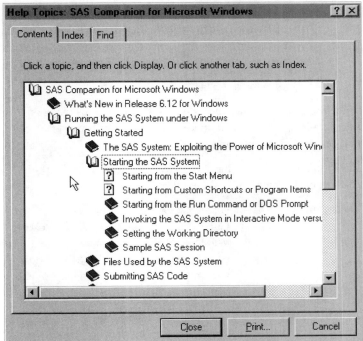

Figure 2.5
Sample Topic List

Navigating Topic Windows: The windows that display topic information have various titles, depending on what part of the Help system you are in. For example, if you chose **SAS companion** in the SAS System **Help** menu, the topic window's title is SAS Companion for Microsoft Windows. If you chose **How to** in the SAS System **Help** menu, the topic window's title is How to... .

In the topic information, you may see highlighted text. These highlighted text strings are called "links." When you move the mouse pointer over a link, the pointer turns into a hand. Clicking on a link takes you to more information on that topic.

All topic windows contain the following buttons:

Help Topics   takes you to the list of topics from which you chose the current topic. In some topic windows, this button is labeled **Contents**.

Back	takes you back one link.
Print	sends the current topic to the default printer.
<<	takes you to the topic preceding the current topic in the topic list.
>>	takes you to the topic succeeding the current topic in the topic list.

Some topic windows also include an **Index** button. Clicking on this button takes you to the help index, which is described later in this chapter in "Using the Help Index."

Each topic window also has a menu bar. Some of the most useful features of this menu bar are the following:

Edit→Copy	copies the text of the topic to the Clipboard; then you can paste it into any Windows application that accepts text (such as the SAS PROGRAM EDITOR window or a word-processing application).
Bookmark→Define	enables you to create a bookmark. Bookmarks are shortcuts to specific topics in the Help system. Once you define a bookmark, it is listed in the **Bookmark** menu. Clicking on a bookmark name jumps you directly to that help topic.
Options→ Display History Window	displays the Windows Help History window, which lists all the help topics you have accessed during your current SAS session.

Some topic window menu bars also include an **Online Book** choice. Use this choice to access the SAS System online documentation.

To close a topic window, click on its Close button. This also closes the topic list window.

Note: Remember to use the **Help Topics** button if you want to close the topic but return to the topic list.

Using the Help Index: All topic list windows provide access to the help index. To open the index, click on the **Index** tab in the topic list window. Type the topic you want to look up into the text entry field or at least the first few letters of the topic. As you type, the list box that contains all the topics scrolls to match what you type.

To return from the index to the topic list, click on the **Contents** tab.

When you find a topic in the index that you want to see, double-click on the topic. This opens the topic window.

Performing a Text Search: You can search the SAS Help system for text strings. This is useful if you do not know what the topic is called, but you know the information for that topic contains a certain word. To perform a text search, click on the **Find** tab in the topic list window.

The first time you perform a text search, the SAS System builds a list of search words before performing the search. Follow the directions in the dialog boxes that appear to build this word list. Building the minimal word list (recommended) takes about two to eight minutes. This minimal word list contains only certain search words and is not truly a full text search database. You can, however, choose to build a word list that contains virtually every word in the SAS Help system–this makes your searches more effective, but takes longer to create and uses quite a bit more hard disk space. You can even customize the word list to suit your needs and reach a happy medium between the minimized and maximized word lists.

Note: To create a master word list, create it from the **Find** tab accessed by clicking on **Help→SAS System**. If you create the word list from other help topics (such as **SAS companion**, **How to**, etc.), the word list applies to only that help topic.

If you have already created the word list, fill in the information on the **Find** tab. Type the search string in the text entry field at the top of the **Find** tab and choose matching words to narrow your search. Once the topic list on the **Find** tab shows the topic you want, double-click on the topic to display it.

Clicking on the **Options** button from the **Find** tab lets you set the following search parameters:

- By default the search looks for words beginning with the letters you type. But you can also search for words that end in those letters, for words that contain those letters anywhere in the word, or for words that consist only of those letters.

- If you type more than one word to search for, you can control whether the search results should contain all those words or any one of the words.

- Normally, the matching word list and topic list are updated immediately after each keystroke. But you can also cause the search to wait for you to click on the **Find Now** button.

Accessing the SAS Sample Library

FasTip: Click on **Help→Sample programs**. Now double-click on **SAS Sample Library**, then choose a topic and a program.

A nice feature of the SAS System for Windows is that it comes with an extensive set of sample programs. By copying a sample program to the PROGRAM EDITOR window, modifying it, and saving it to a new file, you make your code development process easier. This section shows you how to access a sample program and copy it to the PROGRAM EDITOR window.

Note: You can also open existing files and edit them. Chapter 3 provides information on opening files.

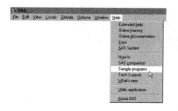

To access the SAS Sample Library, click on **Help** in the SAS System main menu, then on **Sample programs**. The Help Topics: SAS Sample Library window appears, as shown in Figure 2.6.

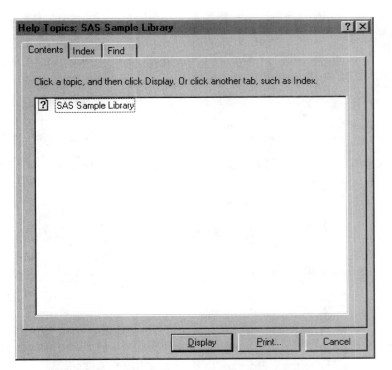

Figure 2.6
Help Topics: SAS Sample
Library Window

Now double-click on **SAS Sample Library**. The SAS Sample
Library window appears, as shown in Figure 2.7. If the window is
too small to read, resize it using the mouse.

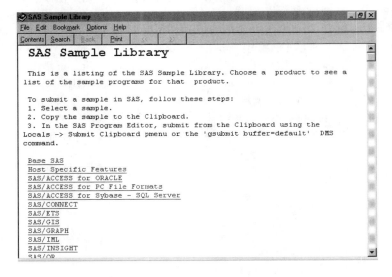

Figure 2.7
SAS Sample Library
Window

From this window, choose the topic that interests you. For this example, click on **Base SAS**. When the list of contents appears, click on **Adding New Observations to a SAS Data Set**. The sample program appears, as shown in Figure 2.8.

Figure 2.8
A Sample Program

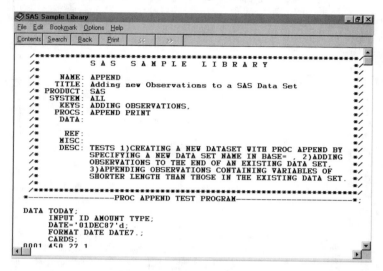

Copying a Sample Program to the PROGRAM EDITOR Window: To copy this program to the PROGRAM EDITOR, click on **Edit** in the SAS Sample Library window's menu, then on **Copy** (or press CTRL-C). This copies the text to the Clipboard. Now close the SAS Sample Library by clicking on its Close button. When the PROGRAM EDITOR window reappears, make it active (click on its title bar). Be sure the cursor is at the beginning of the top line in the PROGRAM EDITOR window. Now click on **Edit** in the SAS System main menu, then on **Paste** (or press CTRL-V). The file appears in the PROGRAM EDITOR window. To see more of the program, click on the PROGRAM EDITOR's maximize button. Figure 2.9 shows what the display looks like when you do this.

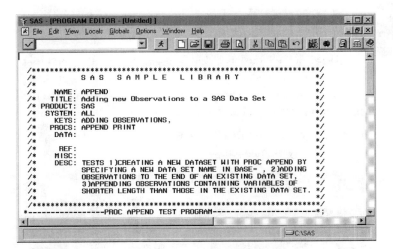

Figure 2.9
Maximized **PROGRAM EDI-
TOR** Window with the
APPEND Program

Note: Before you press CTRL-V, make sure the cursor is at the
beginning of the top line in the PROGRAM EDITOR window.

To return the PROGRAM EDITOR window to its default size,
click on its restore button (which has replaced the maximize button).

Editing a File

HelpPath: Help→SAS companion→SAS Companion for
Microsoft Windows→Running the SAS System
under Windows→Using Graphical Interface
Features of the SAS System→Working within Your
SAS Session→Using the SAS Text Editor Windows

Help→SAS System→SAS System Help: Main
Menu→SAS Windows→PROGRAM EDITOR→
SAS Text Editor→SAS Global Commands

Now that you have the sample file in the PROGRAM EDITOR
window, you can make changes. For example, suppose you do not
want all that header information. To delete a large chunk of text,
mark it with your mouse.

To begin the mark, click on the first letter of the first line (in this
example, a space). Now hold the mouse button down while you
drag the mouse pointer over the text. As you move the mouse, each

succeeding line of text is highlighted. When all the header information is highlighted, release the mouse button.

Dragging with the mouse is a skill, and you may need several tries until you feel confident. If you have trouble highlighting, click anywhere in the text to discontinue the mark, scroll back up to the top using the vertical scroll bar, and try again.

Figure 2.10 shows the PROGRAM EDITOR with the header information properly highlighted.

Figure 2.10
Highlighting Text in the
PROGRAM EDITOR
Window

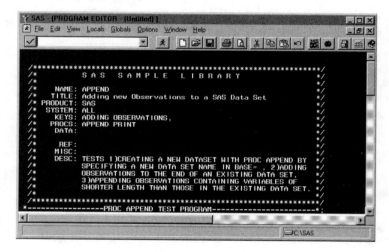

To delete the highlighted text, press the Delete key. The text disappears.

If you accidentally delete something, undo the change by clicking on **Edit** in the SAS System main menu, then clicking on **Undo** (or press CTRL-Z).

There are many other editing features of the PROGRAM EDITOR window. You can toggle between insert mode (the default) and overstrike mode, search for and replace text, do a spell check, etc. Chapter 3 goes into more detail on editing files.

Submitting a File

FasTip: Click on **Locals→Submit**.

HelpPath: **Help→How to→How to... with the SAS System→Get Started with the SAS System→Submitting SAS Code**, then choose a topic

Help→SAS companion→SAS Companion for Microsoft Windows→Running the SAS System under Windows→Getting Started→Submitting SAS Code, then choose a topic

Now that you have the code looking the way you want, submit it. Methods of submitting code abound—you can use a function key, the tool bar, the menus, or commands.

For this exercise, we'll use the menus. To submit the code, click on **Locals** in the SAS System main menu, then on **Submit**. The code is submitted, the PROGRAM EDITOR window clears, notes appear in the LOG window, and the OUTPUT window appears. Figure 2.11 shows what the last page of the output looks like.

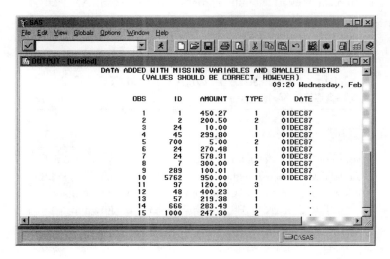

Figure 2.11
Last Page of Output from the APPEND Program

Note: If your code contains an error, the OUTPUT window may not appear. If this happens, examine the notes in the LOG window to see where the error is.

To return to the PROGRAM EDITOR window, click on **Window** in the SAS System main menu, then on **PROGRAM EDITOR** (or press F3, which by default is defined as END).

Note: The action of the F3 key differs between the PROGRAM EDITOR and OUTPUT windows. In the PROGRAM EDITOR window, pressing F3 submits your code. In the OUTPUT window, pressing F3 returns you to the PROGRAM EDITOR and LOG windows.

Chapter 4 provides more information on submitting SAS code in a variety of ways.

Recalling Code to the PROGRAM EDITOR

FasTip: Click on **Locals→Recall text**.

If your output is not correct, recall your code, edit it, and resubmit it. To recall the last submitted program to the PROGRAM EDITOR, click on **Locals** in the SAS System main menu, then click on **Recall text** (or press F4).

Looking at the Output with the OUTPUT MANAGER Window

FasTip: Issue the MANAGER command.

If your code generates a lot of output, you may want to use the OUTPUT MANAGER window to view your output. To open this window, issue the MANAGER command from the Command bar. The OUTPUT MANAGER window appears, as shown in Figure 2.12.

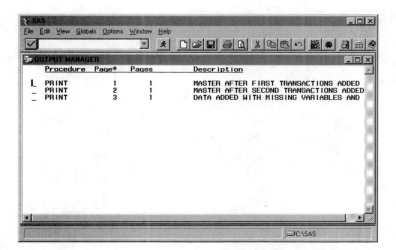

Figure 2.12
OUTPUT MANAGER
Window

In this case, three pages of output are listed, because the APPEND program issued three PROC PRINT statements. Each submission is listed with its beginning page number, number of pages, and title. To view the output, double-click on the line you want to see. The OUTPUT window appears with the chosen output displayed. To return to the PROGRAM EDITOR window, click on **Window** in the SAS System main menu, then on **PROGRAM EDITOR** (or press F3).

Printing the Output

FasTip: Click on the Print icon on the SAS AWS tool bar.

HelpPath: Help→SAS companion→SAS Companion for
Microsoft Windows→Running the SAS System
under Windows→Managing SAS Output→Printing

Help→How to→How to... with the SAS
System→Get Started with the SAS
System→Printing with the SAS System,
then choose a topic

Figure 2.13
Print Dialog Box

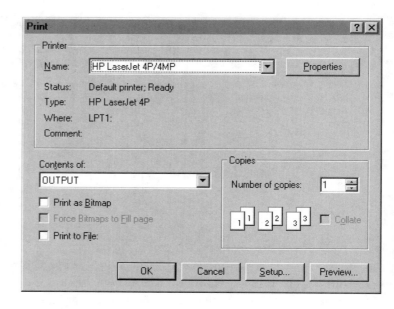

To print what is displayed in the OUTPUT window, click on
Window in the SAS System main menu, then on **OUTPUT**. This
makes the OUTPUT window active. Now click on **File** on the SAS
System main menu, then on **Print** (or press CTRL-P). The Print
dialog box appears, similar to the one shown above in Figure 2.13.

Click on **OK** to send the contents of the window to your default printer.

Chapter 5 provides more detail about printing.

Saving a File

FasTip: Click on the Save icon on the SAS AWS tool bar.

Besides printing your output (or code, or log results), you
also might want to save the contents of the window to a file.

Because you have not saved the APPEND program before, you
must give the file a name. Make the PROGRAM EDITOR window
active. (If it does not contain your code, recall it by pressing F4.)
Now click on **File** on the SAS System main menu, then on **Save as**.
The Save As dialog box opens. Figure 2.14 shows a sample Save
As dialog box.

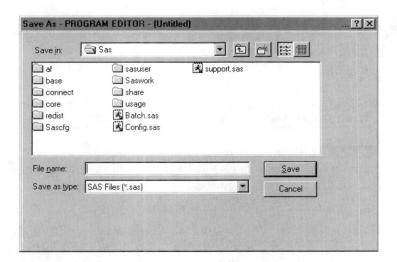

Figure 2.14
Save As Dialog Box

The title bar of the dialog box lists the active window title and filename. In this case, the program has never been saved, so the dialog
box lists it as **Untitled**. Type the name you want to use for the file
in the **File name** field—we'll use APPEND.SAS. If you do not
specify the full pathname, the file is stored in the SAS working
folder. In this case, the working folder is C:\SAS (as indicated by
the **Save in** field). If you'd rather save the file in the SASUSER
folder, type the following in the **File name** field:

```
C:\SAS\SASUSER\APPEND.SAS
```

Now click on **Save**; the file is saved and the dialog box closes.

"Saving an Existing File" and "Saving a New File" in Chapter 3
explain further how to use the Save As dialog box.

Ending Your SAS Session

FasTip: Click on the SAS AWS Close button.

HelpPath: Help→SAS companion→SAS Companion for
Microsoft Windows→Running the SAS System
under Windows→Getting Started→Ending Your
Display Manager Session

To end your SAS session, click on the SAS AWS Close button. When a dialog box asks if you really want to end the session, click on **OK**. The SAS System shuts down, and you are returned to the Windows desktop.

Placing the SAS System on the Desktop

HelpPath: Help →How to→How to... with the SAS System→Get Started with the SAS System→Setting Up Icons for Specialized SAS Sessions→For an Interactive SAS Session

Although not strictly necessary, you may find it useful to have a **SAS System** icon on the desktop. That way, you can simply double-click on the icon to start the SAS System instead of having to use the **Start** button menus. A copy of a program icon is called a *shortcut*.

To place a SAS System shortcut on the desktop, follow these steps:

1. Right-click in a blank area of the desktop.

2. When the popup menu appears, click on **New**, then on **Shortcut**.

3. The Create Shortcut dialog box appears. In the **Command line** field, type the following:

```
c:\sas\sas.exe system-options
```

where *system-options* are any SAS System options you want to use (such as CONFIG and AUTOEXEC).

4. Click on **Next**.

5. In the next dialog box that appears, type a name for the shortcut you are creating. For example, you could type

```
Shortcut to SAS
```

6. Click on **Finish**. Figure 2.15 shows how the desktop looks after the shortcut is created—the mouse pointer is on the SAS System shortcut.

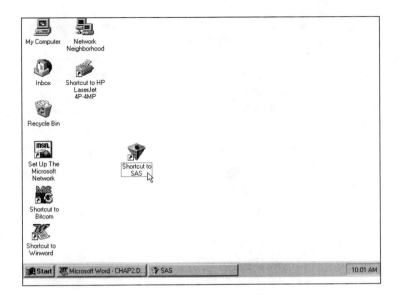

Figure 2.15
Windows Desktop with a
SAS System Shortcut

7. Use the mouse to drag the **Shortcut to SAS** icon on the desktop so it is positioned where you want it.

Now you can double-click on the **Shortcut to SAS** icon on the desktop to start the SAS System, without having to navigate the **Start** button menus.

Note: Each shortcut you create has its own properties, such as command line and working directory. When you change one shortcut's properties, the changes do not apply to other shortcuts to the same program.

Deciding Where to Go from Here

If you use the SAS System for Windows only occasionally and all you do is submit a file, look at the output, and print or save it, you may not need to read much more of this book. However, this chapter has scratched only the surface of Release 6.12 of the SAS System—it is a powerful, flexible tool if you are willing to explore it. You can create your own tool bar icons, use the SAS System to access data in other applications, and so on.

Why not be adventuresome? Read Chapter 3, which explains more about using the SAS PROGRAM EDITOR window, and perhaps Chapter 5, about printing. Or, read Chapter 12 if you'd like to download some files from your mainframe. Take another look at the Table of Contents at the beginning of this book, and see what topics interest you—each chapter opens another panoramic view on Release 6.12 of the SAS System for Windows.

3 Editing and Working with Files

Introduction

This chapter shows you how to use the SAS Text Editor to edit files and how to perform other tasks involving files such as opening and saving files. Becoming familiar with the shortcuts and capabilities of the SAS Text Editor makes your work more efficient and less frustrating. While this chapter uses the PROGRAM EDITOR window to illustrate file editing techniques, you can use these techniques in any SAS Text Editor window (such as the NOTEPAD window and the SOURCE window in SAS/AF software).

Note: You do not have to use the SAS Text Editor to edit your files—you can use a different Windows text editor. See "Using a Different Text Editor" later in this chapter for more information.

Moving the Cursor

HelpPath: Help→SAS companion→SAS Companion for Microsoft Windows→Running the SAS System under Windows→Using Graphical Interface Features of the SAS System→Working within Your SAS Session→Using the SAS Text Editor Windows→Moving the Cursor

The basic tools for moving the cursor are your arrow keys. Keyboards differ, but you should have at least one set of arrow keys—up, down, left, and right. If your keyboard has a numeric keypad, you can use the arrow keys on the pad as well.

Note: To use the keypad arrow keys, NumLock must be off. Check your keyboard for a NumLock key, and see if the NumLock indicator light is on. If so, press the NumLock key once to turn it off.

The basic increments of cursor movement are

• by character

• by line

• by word

• by page.

Moving Character by Character: The left and right arrow keys move the cursor one character at a time to the left and right.

Moving Line by Line: The up and down arrow keys move the cursor up and down one line.

The Home key moves your cursor to the beginning of a line of text; the End key moves your cursor to the end of a line of text.

Moving Word by Word: Use the Control key with the left and right arrow keys to move the cursor from word to word.

CTRL-LeftArrow moves the cursor one word to the left; CTRL-RightArrow moves the cursor one word to the right.

Moving Page by Page: The PageUp and PageDown keys scroll the active window one full page up and down respectively. The size of the page is relative to the size of the window.

Moving to the Top and Bottom of a File: Using the Control key with the PageUp and PageDown keys moves your cursor to the first and last characters of your file:

- To move to the first character, press CTRL-PageUp.

- To move to the last character, press CTRL-PageDown.

Note: CTRL-Home is equivalent to CTRL-PageUp, and CTRL-End is equivalent to CTRL-PageDown.

Undoing Changes

FasTip: Click on the Undo icon on the SAS AWS tool bar.

Before you start editing a file, it is good to know how to undo your changes, especially while you are learning to use the mouse and the editing commands.

To undo a change, such as a line deletion or insertion of text in the wrong place, click on **Edit** in the SAS System main menu, then on **Undo** (or press CTRL-Z). This undoes the last thing you did (except for irreversible actions, such as saving or printing a file). Choosing **Undo** several times in a row undoes recent changes in reverse order.

Another way of undoing changes is to clear the PROGRAM EDITOR (click on **Edit** in the SAS System main menu, then click on **Clear text**) without saving the file. Now open the file again—the changes you made were not saved, so the original file is the same as it was.

You may want to keep backup files, in case you make a mistake that you cannot fix, like overwriting a file.

Note: No change that you make to your file is permanent until you save the file. See "Saving a File" in Chapter 2 and "Saving Files" later in this chapter for more information on how to save your file.

Marking Text

HelpPath: Help→SAS companion→SAS Companion for
Microsoft Windows→**Running the SAS System
under Windows→Using Graphical Interface
Features of the SAS System→Working within
Your SAS Session→Using the SAS Text Editor
Windows→Selecting Text**

Help→SAS companion→SAS Companion for
Microsoft Windows→**What's New in Release 6.12
for Windows→Enhanced Text Selection**

To mark text means to highlight one or more characters, usually in
preparation for moving, copying, or deleting the text.

Clearing a Mark: Before you become adept at marking text, you
may highlight too much or too little. Clicking the mouse button
anywhere in the window clears the mark so that you can start over.
(This is different than in some other Windows applications such as
Notepad and Word, where moving the cursor with the arrow keys
clears the mark. With the SAS Text Editor, moving the arrow keys
without the Shift key held down has no effect on the mark.)

You can also use the menus to clear a mark. Click on **Edit** in the
SAS System main menu, then click on **Deselect**.

Using the Mouse to Mark Text: You can use either your mouse or
the keyboard to mark text. You had a little practice at using the
mouse to mark text in Chapter 2. Here is the basic procedure:

1. Click on the first character of the section you want to highlight.

2. Hold down the mouse button and drag the mouse until all the
   text you want to include is highlighted.

3. If you need to go beyond the edge of the window, drag the
   mouse pointer over the edge of the window, and the window
   scrolls. However, it scrolls quite quickly—you may have to practice a bit before you get it to stop exactly where you want.

4. Release the mouse button when all the text you want to mark is
   highlighted.

More techniques you may find helpful include

* Double-clicking in the middle of a word highlights that word.

* Holding down the CTRL key while double-clicking on a line of text highlights the entire line.

* Holding down the ALT key while dragging the mouse pointer highlights a rectangular block (column) of text.

Using the Keyboard to Mark Text: If you prefer to use the keyboard to mark text, place the cursor over the first character of the section you want to mark. Now hold the Shift key down, and use the cursor movement keys to extend the mark. For example, pressing Shift-CTRL-LeftArrow extends the mark one word to the left, Shift-CTRL-PageDown extends the mark to the end of the file.

Marking All Text: If you want to select all text in the window, click on **Edit** in the SAS System main menu, then click on **Select all**.

Deleting Text

FasTip: Mark the text, then press the Delete key.

To clear an entire window (even the LOG), click on the New icon.

HelpPath: Help→**SAS companion**→**SAS Companion for Microsoft Windows**→**Running the SAS System under Windows**→**Using Graphical Interface Features of the SAS System**→**Working within Your SAS Session**→**Using the SAS Text Editor Windows**→**Deleting Text**

As with moving the cursor, you can delete by character, by word, or by line. You can also delete all the text in the window. In addition, you can choose to delete text by using keys on the keyboard or by using the menus.

Deleting a Single Character: To delete a single character, press Backspace or Delete. Here is the difference between the two:

- The Backspace key deletes the character immediately before the cursor position.

- The Delete key deletes the character under the cursor.

Deleting a Word: To delete a word, double-click on the word, then press Delete.

Deleting Lines of Text: To delete an entire line of text, including the carriage return, first click in the line you want to delete. Now press CTRL-Delete.

To delete all the characters in the line after the cursor position (except the carriage return), press ALT-Delete.

To delete a large chunk of text, first mark the text, then press Delete.

Using the Menus to Delete Text: Instead of pressing the Delete key, you can use the menu. Click on **Edit** in the SAS System main menu, then click on **Clear selected text**.

Be careful—if you select **Clear text** instead, the entire window is cleared. If this happens to you, immediately click on **Edit**, then on **Undo**. The text reappears.

Clearing an Entire Window: You can clear the text from a window in several ways. Here are two methods:

- For text-editing windows, such as the PROGRAM EDITOR, click on **File** in the main SAS System menu, then click on **Clear text**.

- For any SAS window, including the LOG and OUTPUT windows, click on the **New** icon in the tool bar:

If you are clearing a text-editing window, you are prompted to save before the window is cleared.

Cutting Text

FasTip: Mark the text, then press CTRL-X.

Cutting text is not exactly the same as deleting it. When you delete text, it is gone. If you cut the text, it is placed on the Clipboard for future use. You can then paste the text somewhere else in a SAS window or in another application such as Excel or Word.

To cut text, first mark it. Then click on **Edit** in the SAS System main menu, then click on **Cut** (or press CTRL-X). The text disappears from the SAS window and is placed on the Clipboard.

The Clipboard can hold only one section of text at a time. That is, if you cut one portion of text, then cut a second portion of text, the Clipboard contains only the second portion of text.

Copying Text

FasTip: Mark the text, then press CTRL-C.

If you want to reuse text but do not want to delete it from its original position, copy it instead of cutting it. First, mark the text. Now click on **Edit** in the SAS System main menu, then click on **Copy** (or press CTRL-C). The text is placed on the Clipboard but remains in its original position as well. A side effect of copying text is that the mark is cleared.

The Clipboard can hold only one section of text at a time. That is, if you copy one portion of text, then copy a second portion of text, the Clipboard contains only the second portion of text.

Pasting Text

FasTip: Place the cursor at the insertion point and press
CTRL-V.

If you have cut or copied text, you can paste it elsewhere in a SAS window or even in another Windows application such as WordPad. To paste text into a SAS window, position your cursor where you want the new text to appear—the text appears after the cursor. Now click on **Edit** in the SAS System main menu, then click on **Paste**

(or press CTRL-V). The text is pasted into the SAS window. The text is not deleted from the Clipboard, so you can paste it several times in a row if you want.

Inserting Text

FasTip: Position the cursor and type.

If you want to type new text in a file, position your cursor where you want the new text to appear. If you are in insert mode, the text appears in front of the existing text. If you are in overstrike mode, the text replaces the existing text.

The shape of the cursor indicates whether you are in insert or overstrike mode:

• A block cursor indicates overstrike mode.

• A thin cursor indicates insert mode.

To switch between the two modes, press the Insert key.

If you want to replace a chunk of text with new text, mark the text, then start typing. When you type, the marked text is deleted and the new text replaces it.

If you want to append text to a file without opening it, type the new text in the PROGRAM EDITOR window, then use the Save As dialog box to append to the file as described in "Saving an Existing File" later in this chapter.

Scrolling

The scroll bars on the right side and bottom of the window can help you scroll. You control how much the window scrolls by how you use the scroll bars.

Scrolling Line by Line or Character by Character: To scroll line by line, click repeatedly on the up and down arrows. To scroll character by character horizontally, click repeatedly on the left and right arrows.

Scrolling by Larger Amounts: To smoothly scroll vertically or horizontally, drag (that is, hold the mouse button down and move the mouse) the square block inside the scroll bar. Release the mouse button when you have scrolled to where you want to be.

To jump vertically through a file, click in the vertical scroll bar. Clicking above the square block jumps your cursor toward the top of the window; clicking below the square block jumps your cursor toward the bottom of the window. Use the horizontal scroll bar in the same way to move left and right by large amounts.

Remember that you can also use the PageDown and PageUp keys alone and in combination with the Control key to scroll your file.

Dragging and Dropping Text between SAS Windows

FasTip: Use the left-button drag for the default action.

Use the Control key plus the left mouse button for copying.

Use the right mouse button to get a move/copy prompt.

HelpPath: **Help→SAS companion→SAS Companion for Microsoft Windows→Running the SAS System under Windows→Using Graphical Interface Features of the SAS System→Working within Your SAS Session→Using the SAS Text Editor Windows→Dragging and Dropping Text**

After you mark some text, you can drag it to another place in the same window or to another SAS window. As you recall, dragging is done by holding down the mouse button and moving the mouse. Dropping is when you release the mouse button when the pointer is in the destination window.

Why Drag and Drop?: Why would you want to drag and drop text? Suppose you have some code in the NOTEPAD window that you want to submit. By using drag and drop, you can move the text to the PROGRAM EDITOR window without opening any menus.

How to Drag and Drop Text: Here is the basic procedure for dragging and dropping text:

1. Mark the text you want to move and release the mouse button.

2. Place the mouse pointer over the marked text and hold the mouse button down.

3. Drag the pointer to the destination window and release the mouse button.

You must hold the mouse button down for a second or so before you begin dragging. Otherwise, the mark is changed instead of the text being dragged.

Note: It is also possible to move text from your SAS session to another Windows application and vice versa. Both the SAS window and the target application must be visible at the same time. To accomplish this, resize the SAS AWS as described in "Moving and Resizing Windows" in Chapter 1.

Interpreting the Mouse Pointer: You can drag text from any SAS window to any SAS window that supports text input. For example, you can drag and drop text from the OUTPUT window to the PROGRAM EDITOR window but not to the LOG window. The mouse pointer indicates which windows accept dropped text:

• If the pointer is over a window that accepts text, the pointer turns into a little box (with or without a + sign over it).

• If the pointer is over a window that does not accept text, the pointer turns into a "no" icon—a circle with a bar through it.

Whether or not the pointer has a + sign over it tells you that the text is moved or copied:

• If the pointer has a + sign over it, the text is copied from one window to the other.

• If the pointer has no + sign over it, the text is moved (that is, deleted) from the original window.

Controlling Whether the Text is Copied or Moved: To control whether the text is copied or moved, use the Control key and either the left and right mouse button, as follows:

- If you hold the Control key down while dragging, the text is always copied. Be sure you release the Control key after you release the mouse button.

- If you use the right mouse button to drag the text, you are prompted whether you want to move or copy the text when you release the mouse button at the insertion point.

Use Table 3.1 to help you determine how to control the copying and moving of text.

Table 3.1
Controlling Whether Text Is Copied or Moved During Drag-and-Drop

KEY AND/OR BUTTON	HAS THE FOLLOWING RESULT
Left Mouse Button	moves text from text-editing window to text-editing window
	copies text from non-text-editing window to text-editing window
Control + Left Mouse Button	copies text
Right Mouse Button	prompts you with a dialog box with **Move** and **Copy** choices. If the destination window is the PROGRAM EDITOR, the dialog box also offers a **Submit** choice.

Searching for Text

FasTip: Click on **Edit→Find**.

Press CTRL-R for repeat find.

If you have a long program in the PROGRAM EDITOR window and want to find some text, it may be faster to use the Find feature than to scroll through the window. To search for text, click on **Edit** in the SAS System main menu, then click on **Find**. The Find dialog box appears, as shown in Figure 3.1.

Figure 3.1
Find Dialog Box

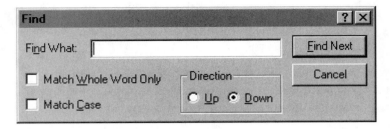

Controlling the Search Parameters: Type the word you want to find (such as an option name, a data set name, or some other key-word) in the **Find What** field. The search is case insensitive unless you click on the **Match Case** option.

If the **Find What** field contains the word data, by default the search finds both lines containing DATA A and proc datasets. If you want to find only the whole word "data", use the **Match Whole Word Only** option.

Controlling the Search Direction: By default, the search starts at the cursor position and continues forward (down) through the file. If you want to search backward from the cursor position, click on the **Up** option.

Performing the Search: When you have the options set to your satisfaction, click on **Find Next**. The cursor jumps to the next instance of the word you wanted to find, and the dialog box closes. If no such word is found, the message area at the bottom of the SAS AWS displays a message: WARNING: No occurrences of "*word*" found.

Note: The search function does not find the occurrence of a word that the cursor is in.

Repeating a Search: If you want to repeatedly search for a word, either open the Find dialog box again–it remembers the last search you performed–or click on **Edit** in the SAS System main menu, then click on **Repeat find** (or press CTRL-R).

Replacing Text

FasTip: Click on **Edit→Replace**.

Replacing one string of text with another works similarly to finding text. Click on **Edit** in the SAS System main menu, then click on **Replace**. The Replace dialog box appears, as shown in Figure 3.2.

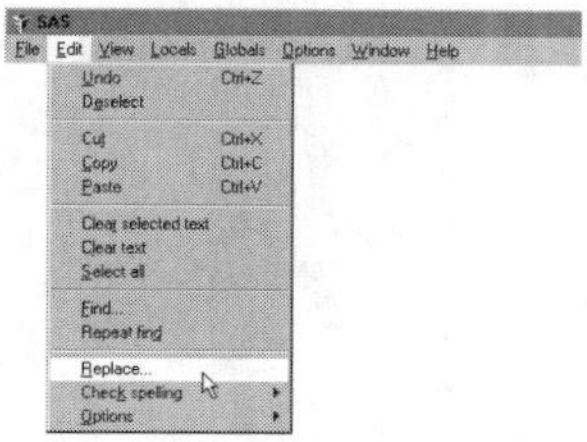

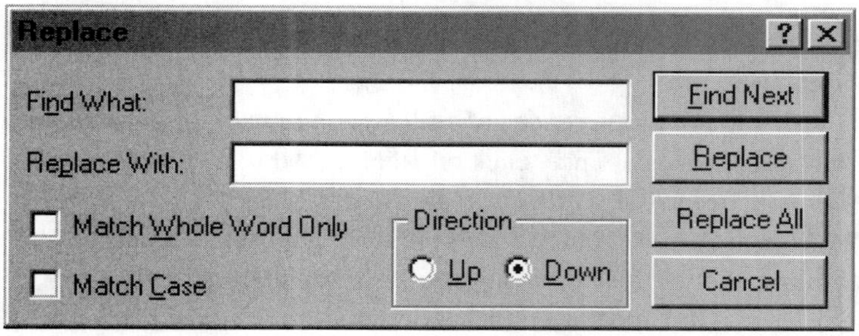

Figure 3.2
Replace Dialog Box

Type the search string in the **Find What** field, and the replacement string in the **Replace With** field.

Controlling the Search and Replace Parameters: Many of the options in the Replace dialog box are similar to the ones in the Find dialog box. For example, the replacement is case insensitive unless you click on the **Match Case** option. The default direction of the search is down; to change this, click on the **Up** option. The Replace dialog box remembers this direction and retains it for the remainder of your SAS session, unless you change it again. If you want to ensure only entire instances of the search string are replaced, click on the **Match Whole Word Only** option.

Performing the Replacement: When you have the options set to your satisfaction, click on **Replace**. The SAS System finds the first instance of the search string and replaces it.

Caution: The SAS System does not prompt you for the replacement. Undo an erroneous replacement by clicking on **Edit** in the SAS System main menu, then click on **Undo** (or press CTRL-Z).

Repeating Replacements: The Replace dialog box does not stay open after it replaces the text. To replace the next instance, open the Replace dialog box again and click on **Replace**. The Replace dialog box does remember what search you performed last time and retains the text strings in the text entry fields.

If you prefer, use the RCHANGE command from the Command bar to repeat replacements. You are not prompted for the replacement.

Getting Prompted for Replacements: There is no "prompt before replace" option in the Replace dialog box. To simulate a prompt, press CTRL-R to perform the repeat-find operation. To do the actual text replacement, open the Replace dialog box again and click on **Replace**.

Replacing All Occurrences of a String: To replace all instances of the search string at once, click on **Replace All** in the Replace dialog box, instead of on **Replace**. Be careful when using **Replace All**—you are not prompted for the replacements, so you might replace a lot of things accidentally if the original string occurs in places you did not expect. If you find that you've used the **Replace All** feature unadvisedly, click on **Edit** in the SAS System main menu, then on **Undo** to reverse all the changes at once.

Spell Checking Your Program

FasTip: Click on **Edit**→**Check spelling**→**Spell all suggest**.

HelpPath: Help→**SAS System**→**SAS System: Main Menu**→**Utilities**→**SPELL**→**WINDOWS**

The SAS System includes a spell checker. To access this feature, click on **Edit** in the SAS System main menu, then on **Check spelling**. This opens another menu, as shown in Figure 3.3.

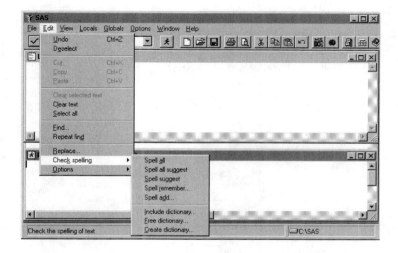

Figure 3.3
Spell Check Menu

Generating a Misspelled Word List: To generate a list of unrecognized words and their corresponding line numbers, click on **Spell All** in the second-level spell-check menu. The SPELL: Unrecognized Words window opens with the list. Figure 3.4 shows a sample SPELL: Unrecognized Words window.

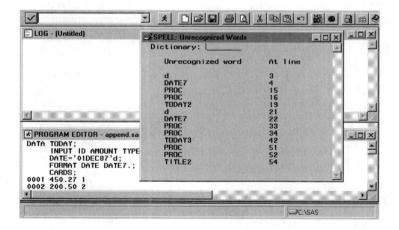

Figure 3.4
SPELL: Unrecognized Words Window

To close the SPELL: Unrecognized Words window, click on its Close button.

Letting the SAS System Make Spelling Suggestions: If you click on **Spell all suggest** instead of **Spell all** in the second-level spell-check menu, the SPELL: Suggestions window appears. This window lists the first unrecognized word, the dictionary being used, and the suggestions for the misspelled word. Figure 3.5 shows a sample SPELL: Suggestions window.

Figure 3.5
SPELL: Suggestions Window

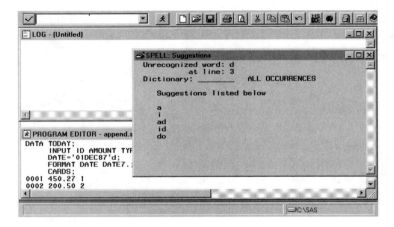

To implement one of the suggestions, click on the word with the correct spelling. Then click on **Locals** in the SAS System main menu, then click on **Replace**. Alternatively, use the TAB key to move the cursor to the correct spelling, then press Enter to highlight your choice. Issue the REPLACE command from the Command bar. Only that occurrence is corrected.

If you want all occurrences of that misspelling corrected, highlight the correct spelling, then click on **ALL OCCURRENCES** before you do the replace. The message area of the SAS AWS tells you how many occurrences were replaced.

Ignoring Suggestions: If you do not want to take action on a word, click on the Close button of the SPELL: Suggestions window. It moves to the next word.

Canceling the Suggestion Process: To cancel the whole process of spell checking and suggesting corrections, click on **File** in the SAS System main menu, then click on **Cancel**. Or, issue the CANCEL command from the Command bar.

Adding Words to the Dictionary: You can add words to the default dictionary so that they are not flagged as misspelled in future spell checks. You can also create auxiliary dictionaries. These techniques work in both the SPELL: Unrecognized Words window and the SPELL: Suggestions window.

To add a word to the default dictionary, click on the word, or use the TAB key to move the cursor to the word and press Enter to highlight it in the SPELL: Unrecognized Words window. This step is not necessary in the SPELL: Suggestions window. Now click on **Locals** in the SAS System main menu, then on **Remember**. Or, issue the REMEMBER command from the Command bar. From now on, that word is not flagged as misspelled.

To create an auxiliary dictionary, place your cursor in the **Dictionary** field and type a dictionary name. If one does not exist, create a new name, such as MYDICT. The name must be a valid SAS name. This creates an entry MYDICT.DICTIONARY in your SASUSER.PROFILE catalog. In the SPELL: Unrecognized Words window, all REMEMBER commands now affect the auxiliary dictionary, not the default dictionary. In the SPELL: Suggest window, you must set the dictionary for each change; otherwise the REMEMBER command affects the default dictionary.

To return to using the default dictionary, click in the **Dictionary** field and use your Delete and Backspace keys to clear this field. Now press Enter. The field is blank, and all REMEMBER commands now affect the default dictionary.

Changing the SAS Working Folder

FasTip: Double-click on the folder icon in the lower-right corner of the SAS AWS.

HelpPath: **Help→SAS companion→SAS Companion for Microsoft Windows→Running the SAS System under Windows→Using Graphical Interface Features of the SAS System→Working within Your SAS Session→Changing the SAS Working Directory**, then choose a topic

Help→How to...with the SAS System→Customize Your SAS Session→Changing the SAS Working Folder, then choose a topic

When you start a SAS session, the SAS System uses a default folder called the SAS working folder. This folder is where the SAS System looks for files, stores files, etc. Usually, this is the folder that contains your SAS.EXE file—in this book, this folder is C:\SAS. You can use the folder lists in dialog boxes such as Open and Save As to change folders when you open and close files. But if all your files reside in a particular folder, it may be more efficient to change the working folder instead of changing the folder in the dialog boxes.

The working folder is displayed in the lower-right corner of the SAS AWS. For example, in Figure 3.6 the mouse pointer is near the working folder name (C:\SASPROJ).

Figure 3.6
Working Folder Displayed
in the SAS AWS

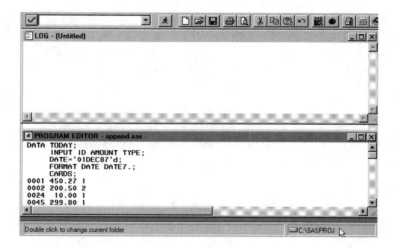

Changing the Working Folder During Your SAS Session: To change the working folder, double-click on the folder name in the lower-right corner of the SAS AWS. The Change Folder dialog box appears, similar to Figure 3.7.

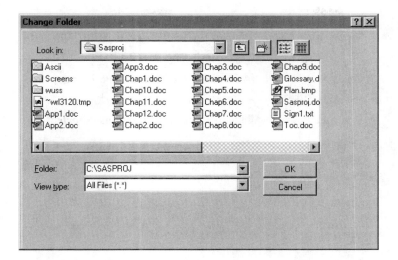

Figure 3.7
Change Folder Dialog Box

You can change the folder in a number of ways. You can type the full pathname of the folder in the **Folder** field. Or, you can use the mouse to navigate the list of folders and double-click on the folder you want to use. To move up in the folder hierarchy, click on the icon showing a folder with an up arrow, to the right of the **Look in** field.

Once the **Folder** field contains the name of the folder you want, click on **OK**. If you change the folder more than once during a single SAS session, the **Folder** field remembers all the folders you have used. To select a previous working folder, click on the down arrow by the **Folder** field and select the correct folder. Then click on **OK**.

Note: Changing the working folder using the Change Folder dialog box is not a permanent change. The next time you invoke the SAS System, the working folder defaults to C:\SAS (or wherever the SAS.EXE file is stored).

Changing the Working Folder Permanently: To permanently change the working folder, you must do it outside of the SAS System. Follow these steps:

1. Open the Windows Explorer by right-clicking on the **Start** button and clicking on **Explore**.

2. By default, the Windows Explorer shows you the contents of the **Start Menu** folder. Double-click on **Programs** in the right half of the window, then double-click on **The SAS System** folder.

3. Right-click on **The SAS System for Windows v6.12**, then click on **Properties**.

4. When the Properties dialog box appears, click on the **Shortcut** tab.

5. Double-click in the **Start** in field, and type the name of the folder you want to use as the SAS working folder. Be sure to include the full pathname of the folder.

6. Click on **OK**.

The next time you start the SAS System, the new folder is used as the working folder.

Note: This change applies only to the shortcut to the SAS System accessed from the **SAS System** program group. If you have created additional shortcuts to the SAS System (such as on the desktop), you must change each shortcut's properties individually.

Opening Files

FasTip: Click on the Open icon on the SAS AWS tool bar.

This section provides details about opening files into the PRO-GRAM EDITOR window.

Using the Open Dialog Box: To open this dialog box, click on **File** in the SAS System main menu, then click on **Open**. Figure 3.8 shows a sample Open dialog box.

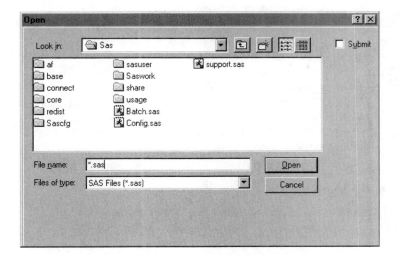

Figure 3.8
Open Dialog Box

You can type the name of the file you want to open in the **File name** field. Or, use the **Look in** and folder list to navigate to the folder where the file is stored. To move up in the folder hierarchy, click on the icon showing a folder with an up arrow, to the right of the **Look in** field. To open a subfolder, double-click on it in the folder list.

You may want to "filter" the files listed. If a folder contains many files, you can control which extensions are listed. Click on the down arrow by the **Files of type** field. You can choose to show only files with .SAS, .LOG, .LST, or .DAT extensions, or to show all files (*.*). Click on your choice to change the value in the field.

When you have found the file you want to open, click on its name, then click on **Open**. The file is copied to the window from which you opened the dialog box (usually the PROGRAM EDITOR).

If you click on **Submit** in the Open dialog box before you click on **Open**, the file is immediately submitted. Use this option only with files that contain SAS code.

Using the Command Bar: If you prefer, you can issue the INCLUDE command from the Command bar to open a file into the PROGRAM EDITOR window. The syntax of the INCLUDE command is as follows:

INCLUDE *filename*

For example, the following command opens a file named APPEND.SAS:

```
INCLUDE APPEND.SAS
```

If the file is not in the working folder, you must type the full path-name of the file.

The INCLUDE command copies a file to the PROGRAM EDITOR but does not submit it.

Using the Most Recently Used File List: Like many Windows applications, the SAS System remembers the files you have used most recently and lists them in the **File** portion of the SAS System main menu. To see these files, click on **File**. To open a listed file, click on its name. For example, Figure 3.9 shows the File menu with three files listed. Clicking on **c:\sas\sasuser\append.sas** opens that file in the PROGRAM EDITOR window.

Figure 3.9
File Menu Showing the
Three Most Recently Used
Files

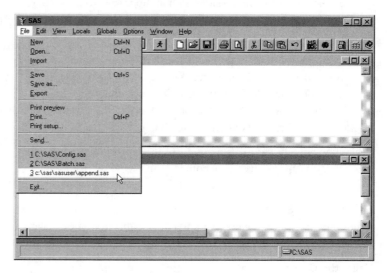

Note: If you already have a file open and click on its name again, you end up with two copies in the PROGRAM EDITOR window.

Saving Files

FasTip: Click on the Save icon on the SAS AWS tool bar.

Saving files works similarly to opening files. In Chapter 2, you learned a little about using the Save As dialog box to save a file. This section provides more details about saving files.

Saving an Existing File: If you have a file open in the PROGRAM EDITOR or other SAS window, the name of the file is listed in the window title bar. For example, in Figure 3.10, the mouse pointer is positioned in the PROGRAM EDITOR title bar, near the filename (**append.sas**).

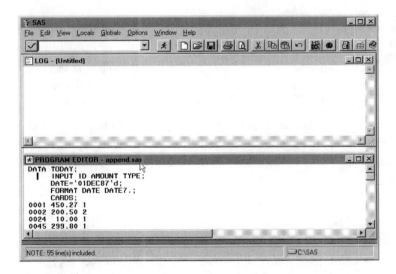

**Figure 3.10
PROGRAM EDITOR
Window Showing the Open
Filename**

If you have made changes and want to save them to the same file, click on **File**, then click on **Save**. The file is immediately saved.

You can also use the Save As dialog box to save an existing file. Click on **File**, then click on **Save as**. When the Save As dialog box appears, double-click on the filename in the list of files, then click on **Save**. Now another dialog box appears, as shown in Figure 3.11.

Figure 3.11
Append or Replace Dialog Box

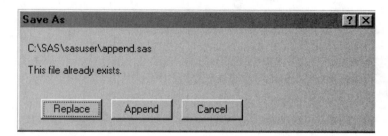

This dialog box tells you that the file already exists and gives you the choice of overwriting (replacing) the file or appending new data to it. Because you want to save your changes, choose **Replace**. Choose **Append** only if you are adding new data to the end of your file.

Saving a New File: To save a previously unsaved file, click on **File**, then click on **Save as**. This opens the Save As dialog box, as shown in Figure 3.12.

Figure 3.12
Save As Dialog Box

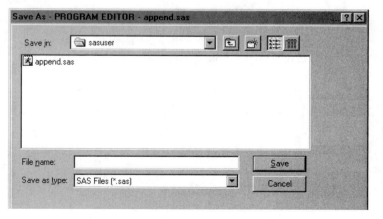

Besides typing the name of the file you want to save in the **File name** field, you can also use the folder list field to control where the file is stored. The **Save in** field shows the current folder. If you want to save the file in a subfolder of that folder, double-click on the subfolder's name in the folder list. To move up in the folder hierarchy, click on the icon showing a folder with an up arrow, to the right of the **Save in** field.

If you specify a filename that already exists in the folder you've chosen, you are prompted about replacing or appending the file. If you typed the wrong filename by mistake, click on **Cancel** and type a different filename.

Using the Command Bar: If you prefer, you can issue the FILE command from the Command bar. The syntax of the FILE command is as follows:

FILE *filename*

For example, the following command saves a file named APPEND.SAS to the working folder:

```
FILE APPEND.SAS
```

If you do not want the file saved to the working folder, you must type the full pathname of the file. As in using the Save As dialog box, if the file already exists, you are prompted about replacing or appending.

The FILE command copies the contents of the SAS window (e.g., the PROGRAM EDITOR) to the file but does not clear the text from the window.

Using a Different Text Editor

Although the SAS System provides the PROGRAM EDITOR, NOTEPAD, and other SAS Text Editor windows, you do not have to use them to develop your SAS code if you prefer another text editor. This is one of the major advantages of using the SAS System under Windows–the ability to share information (including text) between applications.

Earlier in this chapter, you learned to cut, copy, and paste text in the SAS System. Most other Windows applications, including text editors and word processing applications, also support cutting, copying, and pasting text. So, you can type your SAS code in the text editor you prefer to use. Then, copy the code to the Clipboard, and paste it into any SAS Text Editor window (such as the PROGRAM EDITOR, NOTEPAD, or SOURCE window). Examples of applications that you may prefer to use instead of the SAS Text Editor include WordPad (which is shipped with Windows), Microsoft Word, WordPerfect, and WordPro.

Transferring Formatted Text: Formatting, such as bold, underlining, or different font sizes, is not preserved when you paste text into a SAS window. The pasted text in the SAS window is plain unformatted text. (The converse is not true—text copied from the SAS System to another application retains all formatting except color, providing that the target application supports the Rich Text Format.)

Submitting Code from Another Editor: You do not even have to paste code into the SAS System—you can submit it directly from the Clipboard. See "Submitting Code Stored on the Clipboard" and "Using Drag and Drop" in Chapter 4.

Using the SAS System Viewer

HelpPath: Help→What's New→SAS System Viewer

The SAS System Viewer enables you to view and print files created with the SAS System without starting the SAS System—you can even use the SAS System Viewer without having the SAS System installed on your computer.

Note: The SAS System Viewer is freely redistributable.

The SAS System Viewer can show you the contents of the following types of files:

- SAS programs (.SAS)

- SAS data sets (.SD2)

- SAS output (.LST)

- SAS logs (.LOG)

- SAS catalogs (.SC2).

Once you have a file open in the SAS System Viewer, you can print it, search for text, subset your data, format your data, sort your data, and many other useful tasks. Also, you can have several files open at once. Figure 3.13 shows the SAS System Viewer with two files open—a data set and a SAS program.

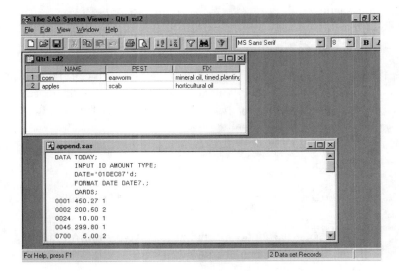

Figure 3.13
SAS System Viewer

For further information on the SAS System Viewer, start the Viewer up and click on **Help** in the Viewer menu. Now click on **Help Topics** and select a topic that interests you.

You can start the SAS System Viewer in several ways.

Starting the SAS System Viewer from the Windows Explorer:
To start the SAS System Viewer from the Windows Explorer, follow these steps:

1. Right-click on the file you want to view.

2. Click on **SASView**.

This opens the SAS System Viewer as well as the file on which you right-clicked.

Starting the SAS System Viewer from the Desktop: To start the SAS System Viewer from the Windows desktop, follow these steps:

1. Click on the **Start** button.

2. Click on **Programs→The SAS System Viewer**.

This opens the SAS System Viewer but does not open any particular file. Use the SAS System Viewer's **File** menu to open the file you want to see.

Starting the SAS System Viewer from the DOS Prompt: You can start the SAS System Viewer from the DOS prompt.

Note: The "DOS prompt" referred to in this chapter is called the "command prompt" under Windows NT. Other than this difference in terminology, all the examples and explanations are the same for both Windows 95 and Windows NT users.

Use the following syntax to start the SAS System Viewer from the DOS prompt:

```
sasview SAS-file </p | /pt printer-name>
```

- *SAS-file* is the name of one of the supported types of SAS files (such as a SAS program or a SAS data set).

- /p prints the SAS file to the default printer.

- /pt *printer-name* prints the SAS file to the specific printer named by *printer-name*. See "Discovering What Printers Are Available" in Chapter 5 for more information. Use quotes around a printer name that contains spaces or special characters.

The /p and /pt options are mutually exclusive.

Note: Unless you have added the folder that contains the SASVIEW.EXE program to your Windows system variable PATH, you must specify the full pathname for the SASVIEW program at the DOS prompt. By default, the full pathname for the SASVIEW program is as follows:

```
C:\PROGRA~1\THESAS~1\SASVIEW.EXE
```

The folder names in this path look odd because they contain more than eight characters, but DOS prompt commands recognize only eight-character or shorter filenames. The long names for the folders are PROGRAM FILES and THE SAS SYSTEM VIEWER.

4 Submitting SAS® Code

Introduction

Now that you have learned how to use the PROGRAM EDITOR window to open a file and edit it, your next logical step is to submit the code. You learned one way in Chapter 2, using the **Submit** item in the **Locals** menu. But there are many other ways to submit code. Which method you choose depends on the following:

- where your code is (it does not have to be in the PROGRAM EDITOR window)

- your preferences for using menus, function keys, tool bars, and Command bar/command line.

This chapter also presents information on stopping a SAS job and on managing your SAS log and output files.

Note: This chapter and the ones preceding it have focused on using the interactive features of the SAS System. The SAS System also supports batch processing, where you do not interact at all with it and no display manager windows appear on your screen. See Chapter 9 for information on submitting batch SAS programs.

Submitting Code from the PROGRAM EDITOR Window

FasTip: Click on the Run icon in the SAS tool bar.

HelpPath: Help→SAS companion→SAS Companion for Microsoft Windows→**Running the SAS System under Windows→Getting Started→Submitting SAS Code→Submitting Code from the PROGRAM EDITOR**

Help→How to→**How to... with the SAS System→ Get Started with the SAS System→Submitting SAS Code→From the PROGRAM EDITOR**

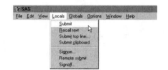

In Chapter 2, you submitted your code using the menus. This is one of the ways to submit code from the PROGRAM EDITOR window. Two shortcut methods are to use the tool bar and function keys:

• To submit code via the tool bar, click on the Run icon.

• To submit code via the function keys, press F3.

Note: Before you use any of these methods, be sure the PROGRAM EDITOR window is the active window.

Submitting a Certain Number of Lines

FasTip: Click on **Locals→Submit top line**.

Highlight text, then press F3.

Instead of submitting a whole block of code, you can submit a certain number of lines, choosing between two methods:

• the Submit top line dialog box

• highlighting text.

Submitting a portion of your code is useful if you want to test the first few lines of a program (like a group of FILENAME or LIBNAME statements) without running the entire program. Or perhaps the code you want to run is the top portion of an existing file. Use one of these techniques to submit only the portion of code you need.

Using the Submit Top Line Dialog Box: If the code you want to submit is located at the top of your program, you can use the Submit top line dialog box. Click on **Locals** in the SAS System main menu, then click on **Submit top line**. The Submit top line dialog box appears, as shown in Figure 4.1.

Figure 4.1
Submit Top Line Dialog Box

Either click on the number of lines (1-8) you want to submit, or click on the **N** option and specify the number of lines to submit, then click on **OK**.

Submitting Highlighted Text: To submit a section of code in the middle of your program, you cannot use the Submit top line dialog box. However, you can highlight the code, then submit the high-lighted text (press F3, click on **Locals→Submit**, click on the Run icon, or issue the SUBMIT command.)

Submitting Code from the Open Dialog Box

FasTip: Click on **File→Open**, then choose the filename, click on the **Submit** option, and click on **OK**.

If you know you want to submit a file, not edit it, when you open it, click on the **Submit** option in the Open dialog box before you click on **OK**. When you do click on **OK**, the file is immediately submitted.

Submitting Code Stored on the Clipboard

FasTip: Click on **Locals→Submit Clipboard**.

HelpPath: Help→SAS companion→SAS Companion for Microsoft Windows→Running the SAS System under Windows→Getting Started→Submitting SAS Code→Submitting Code from the Clipboard

Help→How to→How to... with the SAS System→ Get Started with the SAS System→Submitting SAS Code→From the Clipboard

If you are familiar with a mainframe environment such as MVS, the SAS System's PROGRAM EDITOR window was your only choice for submitting code. That is, the code you wanted to submit had to be in the PROGRAM EDITOR window before you could run it. Not so for Windows SAS users. Under Windows, you can develop your code using some other tool than the SAS System and submit the code without ever using the PROGRAM EDITOR window. For example, perhaps your code is in the NOTEPAD window. Or, as discussed in "Using a Different Text Editor" in Chapter 3, maybe you prefer editing text in Word or some other word processing application.

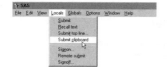

To use this technique, copy your SAS program to the Clipboard while in the other application. Now switch to your SAS session and click on **Locals** in the SAS System main menu, then click on **Submit Clipboard**. The text stored on the Clipboard is submitted to the SAS System. The messages associated with your program appear in the SAS LOG window, but the PROGRAM EDITOR window remains empty.

Using Drag and Drop

HelpPath: Help→SAS companion→SAS Companion for Microsoft Windows→**Running the SAS System under Windows→Getting Started→Submitting SAS Code→Submitting SAS Code by Dragging and Dropping**, then choose a topic

Help→**How to→How to... with the SAS System→ Get Started with the SAS System→Submitting SAS Code→From a File Object in Explorer**

In Chapter 3, you learned how to drag and drop text. You can use this technique to submit code. You can also drag and drop file icons to submit code.

Dragging and Dropping Text: By default, when you highlight a section of text, drag it, and drop it into the PROGRAM EDITOR window, the text is included—but not submitted. You cannot drop text over a non-text editing SAS window, such as the LOG window.

If you use the right mouse button instead of the left mouse button to drag and drop the text, a dialog box asks whether you want to include or submit the code. To submit the code, click on **Submit** in the dialog box. This technique works only for text dragged from one SAS window to another and from applications that support right mouse button dragging. For example, trying to drag text from Microsoft Word using the right mouse button does not work because Word does not support right mouse button dragging.

Dragging and Dropping File Icons: When you look at the contents of a folder in the Windows Explorer, each file is represented by an icon. To submit a file that contains SAS code, drag the icon and drop it onto your SAS session.

Note: The SAS System must be running to use this technique.

To use this drag and drop technique, open the Windows Explorer, and display the folder that contains the file you want to submit. Also, make sure your SAS session is visible—either the entire session or a minimized one. For example, Figure 4.2 shows the Windows Explorer displaying the contents of the SASUSER folder. Both the Windows Explorer and the SAS session have been resized to share the display.

Figure 4.2
The Windows Explorer and
the SAS System Resized for
File Icon Submit

Whether the text of the file is only copied to the SAS System or submitted immediately depends on where you drop the file icon:

- To submit the file immediately, drop the icon the LOG or OUT-PUT window.

- To copy the text of the file to the SAS System without submitting the code, drop the icon on the PROGRAM EDITOR window or another text editing window such as the NOTEPAD window.

If your SAS session is minimized, drag the file icon onto the **SAS** icon on the Taskbar and hold it there. After a few seconds, the SAS session maximizes and you can then drop the icon where you want it.

Submitting Several Files at Once: If you select two or more files in the Windows Explorer and drop them on your SAS session, the files are submitted or included sequentially. However, you cannot predict the order in which the programs are submitted or included.

You select several files by using the Shift and Control keys when you click on the files, as explained here:

- To select a contiguous block of files in the Windows Explorer, click on the first file. Now hold the Shift key down and click on the last file.

- To select several non-contiguous files in the Windows Explorer, click on the first file. Now hold the Control key down and click on the other files.

Dropping File Icons on the SAS.EXE Icon: You can also drop SAS program file icons on the SAS.EXE file icon. Unlike other techniques discussed in this chapter, this technique runs the program in batch mode and is not suitable for programs that require interaction (such as SAS/GRAPH procedures, PROC REPORT windows, or other interactive SAS System components).

To use this technique, follow these steps:

1. Start the Windows Explorer by right-clicking on the **Start** button, then clicking on **Explore**.

2. Click on the file you want to submit, to highlight it.

3. If necessary, open another Windows Explorer window, and display the SAS System folder, where the SAS.EXE file is stored.

   This step is not necessary if the file you want to submit is stored in the same folder as the SAS.EXE file. However, if the file is in a subfolder of the SAS System folder (e.g., the SASUSER folder), you cannot display both the SAS System folder and its SASUSER subfolder at once in one Windows Explorer window. So, you need two windows.

   To open a second Windows Explorer window, right-click on the **Start** button, and click on **Explore**. Use the mouse to resize and move the new window as necessary.

4. Drag the program file icon over to the SAS.EXE file icon and release it. As you drag the file icon, a plus sign follows your mouse pointer. When the plus sign is over the SAS.EXE file icon, release the mouse pointer. Figure 4.3 shows how your display might look right before you release the mouse pointer.

Figure 4.3

Dropping a File Icon on the
SAS.EXE Icon

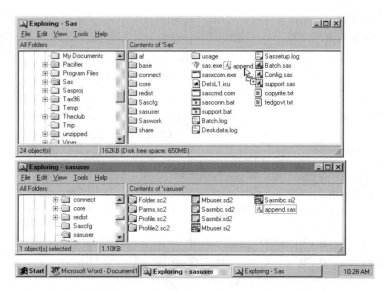

Note: If the SAS System is running when you drop a file icon on the SAS.EXE icon, a second SAS session is started.

6. When you release the mouse pointer, you see a dialog box, asking the following question:

```
Are you sure you want to start executable
using dropped-file as the initial file?
```

Click on **Yes** to continue; click on **No** if the executable or dropped filename is incorrect. If you click on **Yes**, the SAS System starts in batch mode and runs the file you selected. Log and list files are created as for any batch program. See "Understanding Where Batch Logs and Output Go" in Chapter 9.

Also refer to Chapter 9 for additional methods of submitting batch SAS jobs.

Right-Clicking on File Icons

By right-clicking on a SAS program file icon, you can choose to submit the code in several different ways. Open the Windows Explorer, and display the folder that contains the SAS program file you want to submit. Right-click on the file—a menu opens as shown in Figure 4.4.

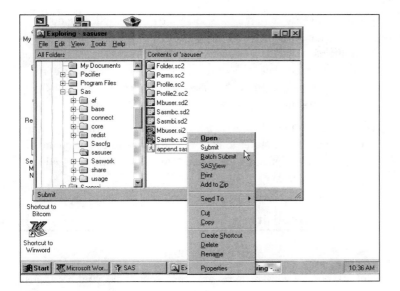

Figure 4.4
**Popup Menu for Submitting
a SAS File from the
Windows Explorer**

You can choose one of three ways to submit your code:

• Clicking on **Submit** starts a SAS session and immediately submits the code.

• Clicking on **Open** starts a SAS session and copies the program to the PROGRAM EDITOR window, but does not submit the code. This is useful if you want to edit the program before submitting it.

• Clicking on **Batch Submit** submits the code in batch mode; see Chapter 9 for more information on using batch mode.

Double-Clicking on File Icons

If you do not want to hassle with resizing applications so you can drag and drop file icons from the Windows Explorer, you can double-click on files with .SAS and .SS2 extensions. This technique includes the file into the PROGRAM EDITOR window—it does not submit the code.

Note: By default, the Windows Explorer does not show file extensions in the file list. To make the extensions visible, click on **View** in the Windows Explorer menu, then on **Options**. In the dialog box that appears, be sure the check box next to **Hide MS-DOS file extensions for file types that are registered** is not checked.

If you've already started a SAS session by double-clicking on a SAS program file icon, then double-click on another, the same SAS session is used for the second file. However, if the first SAS session was started in another manner (e.g., clicking on the **SAS System** icon or double-clicking on the SAS.EXE file icon), double-clicking on a SAS program file icon starts a second SAS session.

By default, double-clicking on a file icon starts a SAS display manager session. If you prefer to have the programs run in batch mode when you double-click on them, see "Double-Clicking on a File Icon" in Chapter 9.

Recalling Submitted Code

FasTip: Click on **Locals→Recall Text**.

Unless you're a whiz-bang programmer, sometimes your programs contains errors. (Dang those tricky semicolons!) To recall submitted code to the PROGRAM EDITOR window, click on **Locals** in the SAS System main menu, then click on **Recall text**. If you have submitted three blocks of code, clicking on **Recall text** three times recalls the text in the opposite order it was submitted, inserting the recalled text before whatever text is already in the PROGRAM EDITOR window.

(F4 is the keyboard shortcut for the **Recall text** menu choice).

Note: Even if you have submitted text via the Clipboard, the **Submit** option in the Open dialog box, or drag-and-drop, the **Recall text** menu choice still recalls your programs.

Interrupting a Submit

HelpPath: Help→SAS companion→SAS Companion for Microsoft Windows→**Running the SAS System under Windows**→**Getting Started**→**Interrupting Your SAS Session**

If you submit a long program or a program that contains an infinite loop, you may want to abort the program. You can stop a program in two ways:

- stop only the program

- cancel the entire SAS session.

Stopping a Program: To stop a SAS program, press CTRL-Break. The Break key may say "Pause" on it—it is usually located on the upper-right side of your keyboard.

When you press CTRL-Break, the BREAK dialog box asks you if you want to cancel the submitted statements or continue. To cancel the statements, press Enter. (If you pressed CTRL-Break by accident and do not want to cancel the submitted statements, click on the **N to continue** line.) Figure 4.5 shows the BREAK dialog box.

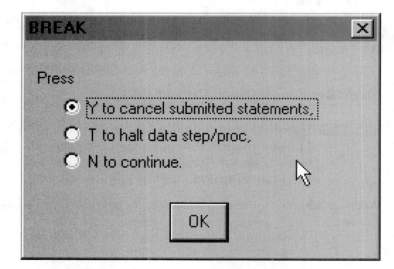

Figure 4.5
BREAK Dialog Box

Note: It may take several seconds for the BREAK dialog box to appear—do not press CTRL-Break more than once.

Canceling the Entire SAS Session: If your program has created problems and you think the best thing to do is to start over, cancel the entire SAS session: click on the SAS System Close button. Any unsaved work is lost when you do this, so use it only as an emergency measure, or save your work first.

When All Else Fails...: If things are really bad, your display is locked up, and the mouse does not work, try pressing CTRL-ALT-DEL. The results differ between Windows 95 and Windows NT:

- For Windows 95, pressing CTRL-ALT-DEL once displays a list of tasks and shows you which are not responding. Click on any task that is listed as not responding, then click on **End Task**. If this has no effect, press CTRL-ALT-DEL a second time to reboot your computer.

- For Windows NT, pressing CTRL-ALT- DEL displays a dialog box. Click on the **Task Manager** button, then click on the **Applications** tab. End any task that is listed as not responding. If this has no effect, press CTRL-ALT-DEL a second time to reboot your computer.

If CTRL-ALT-DEL has no effect, you may have to turn your system off—but this is a last-ditch choice and may cause you to lose a lot of work if you have several applications open and have not saved recently.

Managing Your Log and Output Files

HelpPath: Help→**SAS companion**→**SAS Companion for Microsoft Windows**→**Running the SAS System under Windows**→**Managing SAS Output**→**Routing Procedure Output and the SAS Log to a File**

When you submit code, the LOG window tracks the creation of data sets, setting of options, procedure statements, and other items. The OUTPUT window may contain the results of your program. If you want to save the log or output of a program, click in the appropriate window to make it the active window. Then, use the Save As dialog box or the FILE command to save the file, as described in "Saving Files" in Chapter 3. Usually, log files are saved with an extension of .LOG and output files have an extension of .LST.

5 Printing

Introduction

If you are familiar with a mainframe environment like MVS, you are used to printing by setting system options such as PAGESIZE and LINESIZE and issuing the PRINT command. While the system options and the command still work under Windows, you can also use dialog boxes to set the page and line size. Not only that, but the dialog boxes also enable you to choose fonts, typesizes, and other features. You can even print files, such as SAS programs and SAS output, without starting the SAS System.

SAS System print jobs are managed by Windows. The dialog boxes you see when printing from SAS are standard dialog boxes for selecting printer options. This chapter explains a bit about how printing works in Windows in general, then addresses printing issues specific to the SAS System.

Although the discussion in this chapter uses the OUTPUT window (because often you want to print the output from your code), the principles are the same for any SAS window (such as the LOG and SOURCE windows).

Note: This chapter deals primarily with printing from a display manager session. For information on printing in batch mode, see "Printing in Batch Mode" in Chapter 9. Appendix 2, "Creating a Print File," discusses how to create files that contain printer codes.

Discovering What Printers Are Available

FasTip: Click on the **Start** button, then click on **Settings**, then click on **Printers**.

Your computer may be connected to several printers—perhaps a PostScript printer, a plotter, and a network printer. To see what printers are available to your Windows applications, click on the **Start** button, then click on **Settings**, then click on **Printers**. The Printers window appears, similar to the one shown in Figure 5.1.

Figure 5.1
Using the Printers Window to See What Printers Are Available

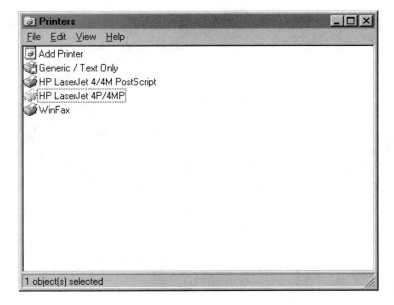

Even though you may have several printers, only one is the *default* printer—the printer used for a print job if you do not explicitly change the printer. To see which printer is the default printer, click on a printer's icon, then click on **File** in the Printers window menu. If there is a check mark next to **Set As Default**, that printer is the default printer.

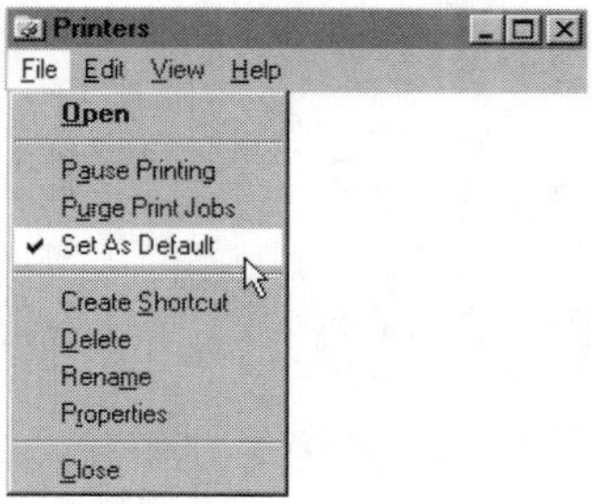

To change the default printer, first click on the name of the printer you want to use as the default. Then click on **File** in the Printers window menu, then click on **Set As Default**.

Understanding How Windows Manages Print Jobs

By default, Windows manages all print jobs submitted from Windows applications, including from the SAS System. Windows routes the jobs to the appropriate printers, monitors the status of the printers, and controls when each job prints. In mainframe terms, this process is similar to a printer spool, except that in the PC environment, you typically have more control over the print jobs.

As print jobs accumulate, Windows creates a print queue. Use this print queue to change the order and priority of print jobs, temporarily stop printing a job (pause), resume printing a job, or delete a print job.

Listing Your Print Jobs: To list your print jobs, click on the **Start** button, click on **Settings**, then click on **Printers**. When the Printers window appears, double-click on the icon for the printer you want to access. A window similar to Figure 5.2 appears.

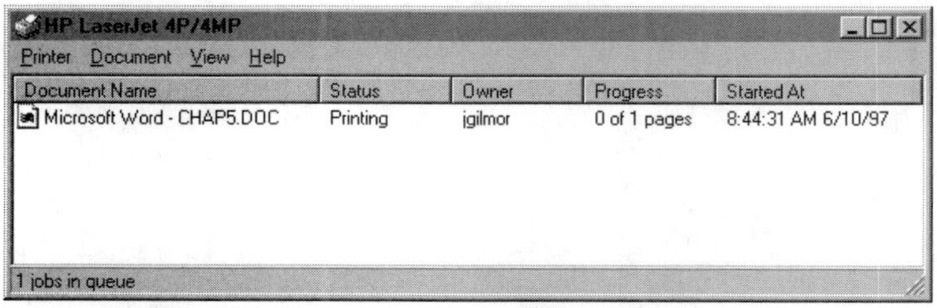

Figure 5.2
Listing the Jobs for a Printer

When you send a print job from the SAS System or another Windows application, the job is listed in the appropriate printer window. From this window you can pause or rearrange the print jobs; see "Delaying Printing," "Resuming Printing," and "Changing the Order of Print Jobs" later in this chapter.

Configuring Your Printer

FasTip: Click on **File**→**Print setup**.

HelpPath: Help→**SAS companion**→**SAS Companion for Microsoft Windows**→**Running the SAS System under Windows**→**Managing SAS Output**→**Printing**→**Changing the Print Options**

You may want to configure your printer before you use it with the SAS System. For example, you may decide that you want to print a particular piece of output in landscape mode instead of the default portrait mode.

In general, you'll use the Print Setup dialog box to configure your printer, although you can also use the Print dialog box.

Selecting a Printer: Click on **File** in the SAS System main menu, then click on **Print setup**. The Print Setup dialog box appears, similar to Figure 5.3.

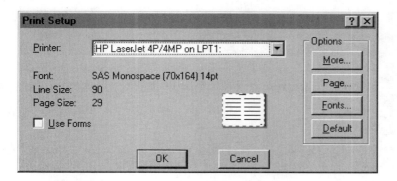

Figure 5.3
SAS System Print
Setup Dialog Box

In this dialog box, use the **Printer** field to specify which printer to use (click on the down arrow to display the list of available printers).

Changing Your Page Orientation: To change the page orientation, click on **Page** in the Print Setup dialog box. The Page Setup dialog box appears, as shown in Figure 5.4.

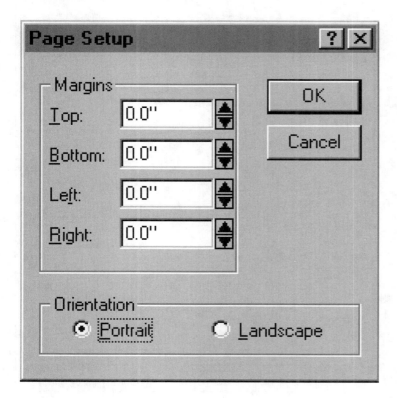

Figure 5.4
Page Setup Dialog
Box

In this dialog box, adjust the margins and the page orientation. To use landscape mode, click on **Landscape**. To change the various margins, either click on the up and down arrows by each value or double-click in the margin's box and type the new value. The SAS System automatically adjusts the page size and line size to fit the new margins.

When you are finished, click on **OK** to return to the Print Setup dialog box.

Changing Other Aspects of Your Output: If you want to change other aspects of the printer setup, explore available options for your printer by clicking on **More** in the Print Setup dialog box. When you click on this button, a printer-specific setup dialog box appears. For example, Figure 5.5 shows the printer options dialog box for the HP LaserJet 4P.

Figure 5.5
Example Printer Options
Dialog Box

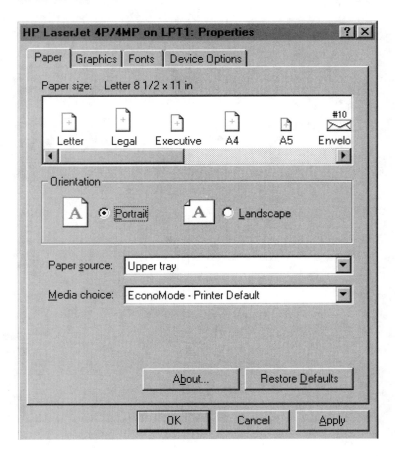

Your printer manual can help you decipher the available choices.
Depending on the printer, there may be even more dialog boxes
available. For example, clicking on **Options** in the HP LaserJet 4P
setup dialog box opens yet another dialog box with more advanced
options.

Click on **OK** (several times if necessary) to return to the Print
Setup dialog box.

Choosing a Printer Font: Clicking on **Fonts** in the Print Setup dialog box opens the Font dialog box, where you can choose the font
and typesize you want to use for a particular job. Figure 5.6 shows
the printer Font dialog box.

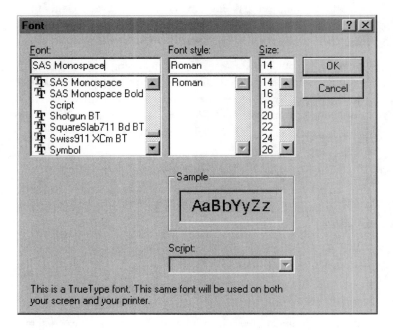

Figure 5.6
**Font Dialog Box for Setting
the Printer Font**

By default, the SAS System uses a 10-point SAS Monospace font
for your output. To change the font, use the **Font**, **Font style**, and
Size fields to choose a font you like (scroll if necessary).

Only monospace fonts (such as Courier and SAS Monospace) work
well with SAS output. Proportional fonts (such as Times Roman
and Helvetica) do not produce satisfactory results. This is because

with monospace fonts each character uses the same amount of space, so columns of data align exactly. Proportional fonts use different amounts of space for different characters, so columns of data do not align correctly.

Note: The fonts the SAS System uses for output and the fonts used in SAS windows are separate. The font you choose using the **Fonts** button in the Print Setup dialog box does not affect the font used in SAS System windows. Use the screen Font dialog box to set the screen fonts. This dialog box is accessed through the **Options** choice in the SAS System main menu.

Resetting Printer Options to the Default: If you have explored the various printer setup dialog boxes and made some changes that produce results you did not expect, return all printer options to their default settings by clicking on **Defaults** in the Print Setup dialog box.

Configuring Your Printer from the Print Dialog Box: You can configure your printer directly from the Print dialog box. Click on **File** in the SAS System main menu, then click on **Print**. When the Print dialog box appears, click on **Setup**. This opens the Print Setup dialog box, just as if you had clicked on **File→Print setup**.

When you're finished setting print job parameters, click on **OK** until you return to the Print dialog box. Then, you can click on **Print** to print the job or on **Preview** to see how the output will look before printing. See "Previewing a Print Job" later in this chapter for instructions on previewing.

The **Properties** button in the Print dialog box also lets you set print job characteristics. Clicking on **Properties** opens a printer-specific dialog box (the same one opened by clicking on **More** in the Print Setup dialog box).

If the Print Setup and the printer's Properties dialog boxes contain the same parameter (such as landscape versus portrait mode), setting the parameter in one dialog box updates that parameter in the other dialog box.

**Understanding How the Changes You Make Affect Your
Windows Environment:** The changes you make via the SAS
System Print Setup dialog box are permanent. That is, they last,
even if you exit the SAS System, until you change them again.

However, the changes you make via the SAS System's Print Setup
dialog box do not affect other Windows applications' (such as
Microsoft Word) printer settings.

Printing the Contents of a Window

FasTip: Click on the Print icon on the SAS AWS tool bar.

HelpPath: Help→SAS companion→SAS Companion for
Microsoft Windows→**Running the SAS System
under Windows→Managing SAS Output→
Printing→Printing from the SAS AWS**

Help→How to→How to... with the SAS System→
Get Started with the SAS System→Printing with
the SAS System→The Current Window as Text

Suppose you have submitted your SAS code, and now the OUT-
PUT window contains the results of your data analysis. To print the
results, click on **File** in the SAS System main menu, then click on
Print (or press CTRL-P). The Print dialog box appears, as shown
in Figure 5.7.

Figure 5.7
Print Dialog Box Invoked
from the OUTPUT Window

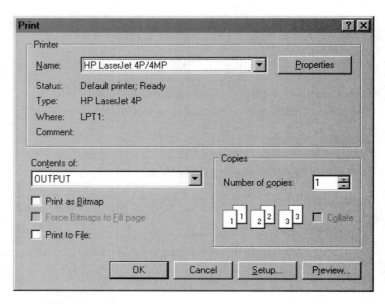

The **Contents of** field displays the title of the active window (in this case the OUTPUT window). To print, click on **OK**. If you've forgotten to configure the printer for this job, click on **Setup**, which opens the Print Setup dialog box.

When you click on **OK** in the Print dialog box, the print job is sent to the Windows print queue.

Printing the Contents of a Window as a Bitmap

FasTip: Click on **File**→**Print**→**Print as Bitmap**.

HelpPath: **Help**→**SAS companion**→**SAS Companion for Microsoft Windows**→**Running the SAS System under Windows**→**Managing SAS Output**→**Printing**→ **Printing from the SAS AWS**

Help→**How to**→**How to... with the SAS System**→**Get Started with the SAS System**→**Printing with the SAS System**→**The Current Window as a Bitmap**

In the previous section, you printed the contents of the OUTPUT window as plain text. You can also print the whole window— including the scroll bars, maximize and minimize buttons, title bars, etc. That is, you create a bitmap of the window.

Bitmap files are useful when you want a picture. For example, the screen dumps in this book, such as Figure 5.8, are bitmaps. If you are developing a full-screen application, you may want to print some SAS windows as bitmaps to accompany your documentation. Or, if you are teaching a class, you may want to show what a window looks like.

To print a window as a bitmap, click on **File** in the SAS System main menu, then on **Print**. Now click on **Print as Bitmap**. As Figure 5.8 shows, now the **Contents of** field indicates that you are going to print the OUTPUT window as a bitmap.

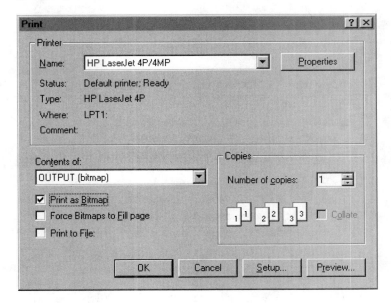

Figure 5.8
Print Dialog Box Ready to Print the OUTPUT Window as a Bitmap

When you have the bitmap option checked, you can choose to print one of several bitmaps. Click on the down arrow by the **Contents of** field. The choices include the following:

- *active-window* (**bitmap**) - prints the active window as a bitmap

- **SAS AWS window** (**bitmap**) - prints the whole SAS Application Workspace as a bitmap

- **Entire screen** (**bitmap**) - prints the entire screen (including all other visible Windows applications and icons) as a bitmap

- **Clipboard** (**bitmap**) - prints whatever is stored on the Clipboard as a bitmap.

The last choice, the **Clipboard**, is discussed in the next section, "Printing the Contents of the Clipboard."

When you click on the bitmap option, another option appears: **Force Bitmaps to Fill page**. If you select this option, the SAS System scales the output so that it takes up the entire page.

Printing the Contents of the Clipboard

FasTip: Copy the text to the Clipboard, then click on **File→Print→**down arrow of **Contents** of field→ **Clipboard** (**text**) or **Clipboard** (**bitmap**).

HelpPath: Help→**SAS companion→SAS Companion for Microsoft Windows→Running the SAS System under Windows→Managing SAS Output→Printing→Printing from the SAS AWS**

Printing from the Clipboard is handy when you do not want to print your whole output but rather only a section of it.

Printing Text: Use your mouse to highlight the section of text you want to print. Now click on **Edit** in the SAS System main menu, then click on **Copy** (or press CTRL-C) to copy the text to the Clipboard. Now click on **File** in the SAS System main menu, then click on **Print** (or press CTRL-P), and click on the down arrow by the **Contents of** field. Click on **Clipboard** (**text**), then click on **OK**. The only text that is printed is the section you highlighted.

Printing Bitmaps: You can also print the Clipboard as a bitmap, to print portions of your screen that are valid bitmaps. You have to be able to select and copy these bitmaps from the screen. For example, if you select and copy to the Clipboard an icon that appears in the SAS Graphics Editor window, you can then use the **Clipboard (bitmap)** option to print this icon.

To print the Clipboard as a bitmap, first copy the appropriate image to the Clipboard. Now click on **File** in the SAS System main menu, then click on **Print** (or press CTRL-P), and click on the **Print as Bitmap** option. Now click on the down arrow by the **Contents of** field. Click on **Clipboard (bitmap)**, then click on **OK**. You see a message that your printer is now printing the bitmap.

Previewing a Print Job

FasTip: Click on the Preview icon on the SAS AWS tool bar.

HelpPath: Help→SAS companion→SAS Companion for Microsoft Windows→What's New in Release 6.12 for Windows→Print Preview Support

Help→SAS companion→SAS Companion for Microsoft Windows→Running the SAS System under Windows→Managing SAS Output→Printing→Previewing Your Output Before You Print

Before you print the contents of a window, such as the OUTPUT window, it may be helpful to see how it will appear when printed.

To preview a print job, follow these steps:

1. Make the window you want to print active by clicking in it.

2. Click on **File** in the SAS System main menu, then on **Print**, to open the Print dialog box. Use the **Setup** button to set your print job parameters. If you need help, refer to "Configuring Your Printer" earlier in this chapter.

3. Once your print job parameters are set, click on **Preview** in the Print dialog box. The Print Preview window appears, showing you your output.

For example, Figure 5.9 shows the Print Preview window for a page of output ready to print in landscape mode.

Figure 5.9
Using the Print Preview
Window

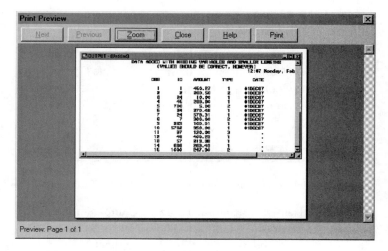

Use the PageUp and PageDown keys to scroll through multiple pages. To see the output in detail, click on **Zoom**.

4. To print your job, click on **Print** in the Print Preview window. If you decide you do not want to print, click on **Close** in the Print Preview window.

It is possible to go directly to the Print Preview window before you set your print job parameters. To do this, click on **File** in the SAS System main menu, then click on **Print preview**. Use the **Print** button to set the print job parameters. When you click on **OK** in the Print dialog box, the output is sent to the printer.

Printing Files without Starting the SAS System

HelpPath: Help→SAS companion→SAS Companion for
Microsoft Windows→Running the SAS
System under Windows→Managing SAS
Output→Printing→ Dragging and Dropping
SAS Files to the Printer

You may want to print a SAS program, a program's output, or a
SAS log. If so, you do not have to start the SAS System. Instead,
drag and drop the file's icon onto your printer's icon. This technique works with files with the following extensions:

• .SAS

• .LST

• .LOG

• .SD2

Note: Printing SAS data sets (.SD2) in this manner does not create
formatted output like you get with the PRINT procedure. However,
it is a quick way to print a data set.

Here are the steps involved in printing these files without starting
the SAS System:

1. Open the Windows Explorer by right-clicking on the **Start** button, then clicking on **Explore**.

2. Display the folder that contains the file you want to print.

3. Open the Printers window by clicking on the **Start** button, then
   clicking on **Settings**, then clicking on **Printers**.

4. Resize the Printers and Windows Explorer windows until you
   can see both.

5. Click once on the file you want to print, to highlight it.

6. Use the mouse to drag the file's icon over to the Printers window, and drop the file's icon on the printer you want to use.

After you drop the icon, you will see a message box that tells you the file is printing on the printer you selected.

Note: You may want to create a shortcut to your most commonly used printer and place that shortcut on the desktop. For instructions, follow this help path from any Windows **Help** menu:

> **Help→Help Topics→Tips and Tricks→For Setting Up the Desktop Efficiently →Putting shortcuts on the desktop**

Printing from the SAS System Viewer: Another way of printing files without starting the SAS System is to use the SAS System Viewer. To start the SAS System Viewer from the Windows Explorer, follow these steps:

1. Right-click on the file you want to view.

2. Click on **SASView**.

This opens the SAS System Viewer as well as the file on which you right-clicked.

To print the file, click on **File** in the SAS System Viewer menu, then click on **Print**.

You can also use the Print Preview, Print Setup, and Page Setup dialog boxes (available from the **File** menu) to format your file before you print it:

• The Print Preview dialog box works the same as it does in the SAS System (see "Previewing a Print Job" earlier in this chapter).

• For more instruction on the Print Setup dialog box, open the dialog box, click on the question-mark icon in the upper-right corner of the box, then click in the dialog box. This opens the help information for the dialog box.

• For more information on using the Page Setup dialog box, follow this help path from the SAS System Viewer menu:

> **Help→Help Topics→Formatting Your View of SAS Files→Changing the Page Setup for Printing a SAS File**

Delaying Printing

FasTip: Click on the **Start** button→**Settings**→**Printers**.
Click on the icon for the printer you want to pause,
then click on **File**→**Pause Printing**.

You may want to postpone printing all your SAS jobs and print
them all at once—perhaps you want to be sure the printer contains
a special type of paper, or you want to delay printing long jobs until
a more convenient time. Use the Windows print queue to delay
your print jobs.

To delay the printing of a print job, follow these steps:

1. Click on the **Start** button, then click on **Settings**→**Printers**.

2. When the Printers window appears, click on the name of the
   printer that handles your SAS print jobs. This highlights the
   printer name.

3. Now click on **File** in the Printers window menu, then click on
   Pause Printing.

If you need to pause more than one printer, repeat these steps. Each
printer that you have paused has a check mark next to **Pause
Printing** in the **File** menu in the Printers window.

Note: Be sure to pause the printer before you submit your print jobs.

When you have paused the appropriate printers, close the Printers
window by clicking on its Close button. All print jobs you submit
to the paused printers (from your SAS session or any other
Windows application) queue up in the Windows print queue, but
they do not print until you "resume" the printer. Resuming a printer
is discussed in the next section.

Resuming Printing

To release your paused print jobs, click on the **Start** button, then
click on **Settings**→**Printers**. When the Printers window appears,
click on the printer name. Now click on **File** in the Printers window
menu, then click on **Pause Printing**. This toggles the printer back
on and erases the check mark next the **Pause Printing** menu choice.

Changing the Order of Print Jobs

If you want to print the jobs in a different order, use the Windows print queue to change the job order by following these steps:

1. Click on the **Start** button, then on **Settings→Printers**.

2. Double-click on the icon for the printer you want to affect.

3. When the specific printer window appears, highlight the job you want to move up or down by clicking on it.

4. Use the mouse to drag the job icon up or down in the list, and drop it in the appropriate spot.

Note: You may find it helpful to pause the printer before rearranging print jobs.

Canceling a Print Job

Use the Windows print queue to delete print jobs you no longer want to print. You can delete a single print job, or you can delete all print jobs from a printer.

Canceling a Specific Print Job: To cancel a particular print job, follow these steps:

1. Click on the **Start** button, then click on **Settings→Printers**.

2. Double-click on the icon for the printer you want to affect.

3. When the specific printer window appears, highlight the job you want to delete by clicking on it.

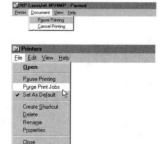

4. Click on **Document** in the printer's window, then click on **Cancel Printing**.

Canceling All Print Jobs: To delete all print jobs in the Windows print queue for a particular printer, follow these steps:

1. Click on the **Start** button, then click on **Settings→Printers**.

2. When the Printers window appears, click on the name of the printer you want to delete print jobs from. This highlights the printer name.

3. Now click on **File** in the Printers window menu, then click on **Purge Print Jobs**.

If you need to purge more than one printer, repeat these steps.

Using SAS Print Forms

FasTip: Click on **File→Print setup→Use Forms**.

Issue the FSFORM command to create a form.

Issue the FORMNAME command to set the current form.

HelpPath: Help→**SAS companion**→**SAS Companion for Microsoft Windows**→**Running the SAS System under Windows**→**Managing SAS Output**→ **Printing**→**Using SAS System Print Forms**, then choose a topic

With some previous versions of the SAS System under other operating systems, you were required to create SAS print forms to control the margins, typeface, and other aspects of printed output. Usually, these forms are no longer necessary with the SAS System for Windows because you can now set all these aspects using the Print Setup dialog box. However, there are times when print forms are useful, even under Windows.

For example, you may have inherited some SAS print forms from a previous SAS user. Also, SAS print forms are a good way to send strings of control characters to your printer, which you cannot do with the Print Setup dialog box.

This section provides some background information on creating and editing SAS print forms. Then, it presents two examples to give you practice creating and using a SAS print form.

Telling the SAS System to Use Forms: The SAS System does not by default use SAS print forms, so you must specify that you want to use them. Open the Print Setup dialog box by clicking on **File** in the SAS System main menu, then on **Print setup**. Now click on **Use Forms**, as shown in Figure 5.10, and click on **OK**.

Figure 5.10
Print Setup Dialog Box
when Using SAS Print
Forms

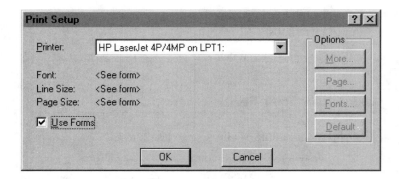

Creating a SAS Print Form: To create a SAS print form, issue the FSFORM command from the Command bar. The syntax of the FSFORM command is as follows:

FSFORM l*ibref.catalog.form-name*

If you omit the *libref* and *catalog* names, the SAS System uses the default values of SASUSER and PROFILE, respectively.

For example, to create an entry named LANDSCAP.FORM in your SASUSER.PROFILE catalog, type

```
FSFORM LANDSCAP
```

When you press Enter, the FORM window opens, as shown in Figure 5.11.

Figure 5.11
FORM Window - Printer
Selection Screen

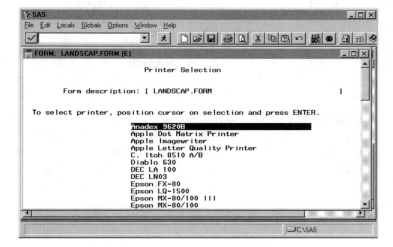

The FORM window consists of six screens:

* Printer Selection – sets the printer for the form

* Text Body and Margin Information – sets the margin information

* Carriage Control Information – controls page skips

* WINDOWS Print File Parameters – controls the character set

* Font Control Information – sets special text characters and text colors

* Printer Control Language – specifies PCL codes.

This chapter focuses primarily on using the last screen, the Printer Control Language screen. The other screens are described in the SAS online help.

Selecting a Printer for Your Form: Use the Printer Selection screen to select a printer. Scroll to find the printer you want, then click on the printer name. You automatically move to the Text Body and Margin Information screen.

Note: The Printer Selection screen appears only when you create a new SAS print form. You do not see this screen when editing existing forms.

Navigating the FORM Window: To navigate through the various screens of the FORM window, click on **Locals** in the SAS System main menu. Then, depending on what you want to do, click on one of the menu choices:

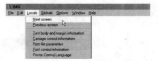

* To move sequentially to the next screen, click on **Next screen**.

* To move sequentially to the previous screen, click on **Previous screen**.

* To move to a specific screen, such as the Printer Control Language screen, click on the screen name.

Using the Printer Control Language Screen: Creating a form requires a good understanding not only of how the SAS System prints but also of your printer. You especially need to know what Printer Control Language (PCL) commands your printer supports— every printer is slightly different. The manual that accompanies your printer should contain a chapter or appendix detailing the printer's PCL details.

The Printer Control Language screen is the last screen of the FORM window. This is where you enter the printer control characters. This screen has line numbers, like the old PROGRAM EDITOR window. To add and delete lines, use line commands. Type the command in the line number area and press Enter. Table 5.1 gives you the basic line commands.

Table 5.1
Using Line Commands

TO	USE THE FOLLOWING COMMAND
insert a new line after an existing one	I
insert a line above an existing line	IB
insert several lines (where # is the number of lines you want to insert)	I# or IB#
delete a line	D
move a line	M on the line to move, A or B (after or before) on the target line
copy a line	C on the line to copy, A or B (after or before) on the target line

Exiting from the FORM Window: To save your form, click on **File** in the SAS System main menu, then click on **End**.

To exit the FORM window without saving your work, click on **File** in the SAS System main menu, then click on **Cancel**.

Setting the Current Form: The SAS print form that is used for print jobs is determined by the current form. To set the current form, issue the FORMNAME command from the Command bar. The syntax of the FORMNAME command is as follows:

FORMNAME *libref.catalog.member.type*

For example, the following command sets the current form to
SASUSER.PROFILE. LANDSCAP.FORM:

```
FORMNAME SASUSER.PROFILE.LANDSCAP
```

Displaying the Current Form: If you cannot remember which
form is the current one, issue the FORMNAME command from the
Command bar with no parameters. The current form name is displayed in the message area of the SAS AWS.

For example, if you set the SASUSER.PROFILE.LANDSCAP
form as the current form, then issue the FORMNAME command
without any parameters, the message area contains the following text:

```
NOTE: Current print form setting is
SASUSER.PROFILE.LANDSCAP.FORM.
```

Editing an Existing Form: As with creating a new form, use the
FSFORM command to specify which form you want to edit. The
FORM window appears, but the Printer Selection screen is inacces-
sible when you edit a form. (If you want to change a form's printer,
you must create a new form.)

When the FORM window appears, click on **Locals** in the SAS
System main menu, then click on the name of the screen to which
you want to move. When you have finished making changes, click
on **File** in the SAS System main menu, then click on **End** to save
your work.

Example 1 - Printing Envelopes: In this example, you create a
form that prints a #10 envelope address. The address is printed in
bold 12-point Antique Olive typeface (no one will have trouble
reading the address!). The printer used for this example is an HP
LaserJet 4P; these commands should work with most HP LaserJet
printers. If you have another type of printer, such as an Epson or
Apple, you need to modify the printer control commands accordingly—use your printer's manual to help you. If you want to print
addresses on different-sized envelopes, you need to adjust the top
and left margins to fit the envelope you're using.

Here are the steps for Example 1:

1. Create the form by issuing the following command from the Command bar:

```
FSFORM SASUSER.PROFILE.ENVELOPE
```

2. When the Printer Selection screen appears, click on **HP LaserJet(+)**. You have to press the PageDown key once to see this entry.

3. The screen that appears next is the Text Body and Margin Information screen. Do not change anything here.

4. Click on **Locals** in the SAS System main menu, then click on **Next Screen** to move to the Carriage Control Information screen.

5. On the Carriage Control Information screen, be sure **YES** is highlighted for **Generate Carriage Control Information**. Also, click on any selected options under **Signal Page Skips before**— when you finish, none of these options should have an asterisk in front of it.

6. Click on **Locals** in the SAS System main menu, then click on **Next Screen** to move to the WINDOWS Print File Parameters screen.

7. Do not change anything on this screen. Go to the next screen, the Font Control Information screen (**Locals→Next Screen**).

8. On the Font Control Information screen, be sure that the tilde (~) is listed in the **Character** column, that its **Number** column value is 27, and that the **Description** column reads `Escape`. You need the ESC character on the next screen, where you enter printer control commands. If the ~ is listed, go to the next screen. Otherwise, enter the correct information before continuing to the next screen (**Locals→Next Screen**).

9. This screen, the Printer Control Language screen, is the heart of printer forms. It is here that you send codes to the printer to set the page orientation, the font, the margins, and so on.

For the #10 envelope form, use Table 5.2 to enter the printer control codes. Type what is in the "Code" column for the given line. The "Explanation" column tells you what each code means.

The codes are case sensitive. The table uses a cursive lowercase ℓ to avoid confusion with the number 1. If there is room for doubt, the "Explanation" column offers further information (such as "use an uppercase O (the letter)" or " use the number 0 (zero)."

LINE	CODE	EXPLANATION
00001	PRINT INIT	Begins the section of controls that are sent to the printer before any text is sent to the printer.
00002	~&ℓ1O	Sets landscape mode. Use a number **1** (one), followed by an uppercase O (the letter).
00003	~&ℓ8E	Sets the top margin to 8 lines.
00004	~&a60L	Sets the left margin to 60 columns.
00005	~&ℓ3H	Sets the paper source to "manual envelope feed".
00006	~(8U	Sets the primary symbol set to Roman 8.
00007	~(s1P	Sets proportional spacing.
00008	~(s12V	Sets the point size to 12 points.
00009	~(s0S	Sets the type style to upright (as opposed to oblique, condensed, or shadowed). Use a zero between the s and S.
00010	~(s3B	Sets the type weight to bold.
00011	~(s4168T	Sets the typeface to Antique Olive.
00012	PRINT TERM	Begins the section of controls that are sent to the printer after all text has been sent.
00013	~9	Clears horizontal margins.
00014	~E	Resets the printer.

Table 5.2
Printer Control Codes for the Envelope Print Form

Here is an example of the typeface that this example uses:

123 XYZ Drive
Some Town, USA 00000

Note: If you do not have access to the Antique Olive typeface, check your printer manual for the PCL code for a typeface you do have and change line 00011 accordingly.

Example 2 - Controlling Output Page by Page: If all you want to do is adjust the font and margins for your output, you might as well use the Print Setup dialog box. But forms allow you to do far more than that. With forms, you can control the output page by page. In this example, the first page has a large top margin, to accommodate a letterhead sheet. The next two pages have regular one inch margins. The last page is printed in landscape mode.

As in Example 1, the printer used for this example is an HP LaserJet 4P; the commands should work with most HP LaserJet printers. If you have another type of printer, such as an Epson or Apple, you need to modify the printer control commands accordingly—use your printer's manual to help you.

Here are the steps for Example 2:

1. Create the new form by issuing the following command from the Command bar:

```
FSFORM SASUSER.PROFILE.COMPLEX
```

2. Choose your printer from the Printer Selection screen as you did in Example 1.

3. Click on **Locals** in the SAS System main menu, then click on **Next Screen**. Do not change anything on this screen. Go to the next screen.

4. On the Carriage Control Information screen, be sure **YES** is highlighted for **Generate Carriage Control Information**. Also, turn off all the options (by clicking on the ones with asterisks by them) under **Signal Page Skips before**.

5. Go directly to the Printer Control Language screen. Click on **Locals** in the SAS System main menu, then click on **Printer Control Language**.

6. Use Table 5.3 to enter the printer control codes on the Printer Control Language screen. Type what is in the "Code" column for the given line. The "Explanation" column tells you what each code means.

The codes are case sensitive. The table uses a cursive lowercase ℓ to avoid confusion with the number 1. If there is room for doubt, the "Explanation" column offers further information (such as "use an uppercase O (the letter)" or " use the number 0 (zero)."

Table 5.3
PCL Codes for Controlling the Output Page-by-Page

LINE	CODE	EXPLANATION
00001	PRINT INIT	Begins the section of controls that are sent to the printer before any text is sent to the printer.
00002	~&ℓ20E	Sets the top margin to 20 lines to leave space for the letterhead.
00003	PAGE 2	Begins the section of controls that are sent before any text is sent for page 2.
00004	~E	Resets the printer (and thus returns to default printer margins).
00005	PAGE 4	Begins the section of controls that are sent before any text is sent for page 4 (the landscape page).
00006	~&ℓ1O	Sets landscape mode. Use a number **1** (one), followed by an uppercase O (the letter).
00007	PRINT TERM	Begins the section of controls that are sent to the printer after all text has been sent.
00008	~E	Resets the printer.

Adjusting Your Windows Environment
6

Introduction

When you install the SAS System, it uses default settings that define how your windowing environment looks. For example, these settings affect the menu bar across the top of the AWS, the message area at the bottom of the AWS, the scroll bars, colors, and so on. However, you can adjust your SAS windowing environment—such as define new tools for the tool bar, replace the menus with command lines, or change the default colors of windows.

You make these changes in several ways. Some changes you make using a dialog box called Preferences. To define new tools, you use the TOOL EDITOR dialog box. Some options are set using the menus; others are set via commands issued from the Command bar.

Besides the changes discussed in this chapter, you can also make many other changes. Because this is a beginner's guide, not all possible options are discussed. For example, if you are developing a SAS/AF application, you can use SAS system options to control how the SAS AWS looks and works. Refer to your SAS reference documentation for more information.

Setting Session Preferences

FasTip: Click on **Options**→**Preferences**.

HelpPath: Help→SAS companion→**SAS Companion for Microsoft Windows**→**Running the SAS System under Windows**→**Using Graphical Interface Features of the SAS System**→**Customizing Your SAS Session**→**Setting Session Preferences**

Help→**How to**→**How to...with the SAS System**→**Customize Your SAS Session**→**Customizing the SAS Application Work Space**, then choose a topic

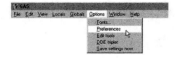

The Preferences dialog box controls many aspects of your windowing environment. To open this dialog box, click on **Options** in the SAS System main menu, then on **Preferences**. Figure 6.1 shows the Preferences dialog box with its default settings.

Figure 6.1
Preferences Dialog Box

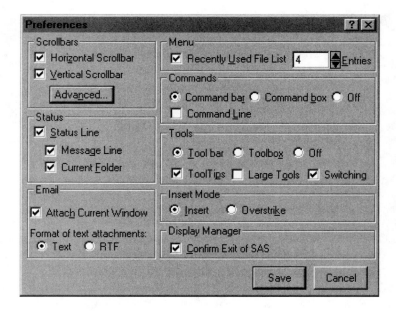

To change a setting, click on the option you want to change. For example, by default, the **Confirm Exit of SAS** field is checked. If you do not want the SAS System to ask you if you really want to end your SAS session, click on this option to deselect it.

Remember that options with round (radio) buttons by them are mutually exclusive—select only one; you can select one or more options that have square (check) boxes by them.

When you are finished making changes in the Preferences dialog box, click on **Save**. Your changes are saved to your SASUSER profile catalog. These changes last until you change your preferences again.

The following paragraphs explain several of the Preferences dialog box's choices.

Scroll bars: Use this section to turn off either the vertical or horizontal scroll bars or both. Clicking on **Advanced** brings up another dialog box that enables you to control how the LOG and OUTPUT windows scroll. Adjusting these advanced settings can help tune the performance of your SAS session so your programs run faster. However, the default values are sufficient for most users.

Status: Use this section to control how the status line (at the bottom of the SAS AWS) appears. Turn the whole thing off, or turn off portions, such as the message area or the working folder icon.

Menu: By default, the **File** menu of the SAS System main menu displays the four most recently used files. Use the **Menu** section to adjust this number up or down. You can display up to nine files or choose to display none.

Commands: Use this section to control how you issue commands to the SAS System. Your three choices are

- Command bar (the default)

- Command box

- command lines.

Although each of these features enables you to issue display manager commands, they differ in the following ways:

- A Command bar is a static element of the SAS AWS—you cannot move it. It appears in the upper-left corner of the SAS AWS, under the menu bar.

- A Command box can be moved around within the SAS AWS and even moved outside the SAS AWS.

- Command lines appear in every window and are static—you cannot move them.

You can mix and match these features. For example, you can have both command lines and a Command bar. Or, you can have only command lines. You can even turn off all these features, so that there is no way to issue display manager commands except through the menus and function keys.

When deciding how to set your **Commands** preferences, consider how you prefer to issue display manager commands and if you have any special needs. For example, choosing **Command box** may be useful if you are designing a SAS/AF application where you need as much of the SAS AWS as possible for data presentation. By having a Command box, it can be moved outside the SAS AWS so that it does not clutter the SAS windows, but you can still issue display manager commands.

In Figure 6.2, the SAS AWS takes up the right side of the display, while the SAS Command box lies in the left half of the display. The pointer indicates the Command box.

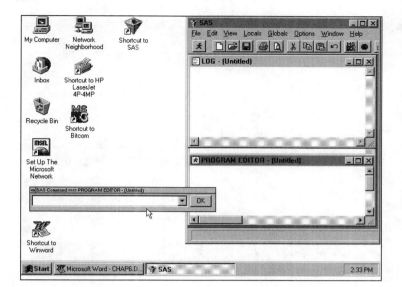

Figure 6.2
SAS Session with a
Command Box

Tools: Use this section to control how your tools appear on the display. Similar to the Command bar/box choice, you can choose to have a tool bar (the default) or a tool box. If you choose a tool box, the box can be moved around inside and outside the SAS AWS. You can also choose to have no tools at all.

By default, the **ToolTips** option is on. Tool tips are helpful hints that appear when you position the mouse pointer over a tool and leave it there for a few seconds. For example, if you place your mouse pointer over the Run tool, the tool tip for that tool says **Submit**, as shown in Figure 6.3.

Figure 6.3
Tool Tips Explain What
Tools Do

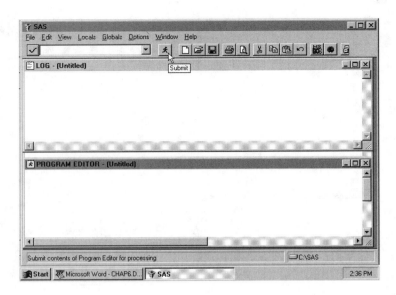

Clicking on the **Large Tools** option increases the size of the tool icons in the tool bar (this option does not affect the tool box). Large tools are most helpful with high-resolution displays because on these displays the tool bitmaps are small. If you have trouble distinguishing the tools, see if using the larger tools helps. If, when you choose this option, all the tools are no longer visible but extend off the right side of the screen, you do not have a high-resolution display, and you should not use the large tools.

The **Switching** option controls whether a new tool bar loads when you open another SAS window. For example, you can create a tool bar specifically for the NOTEPAD window. If **Switching** is on, the NOTEPAD-specific tool bar loads automatically when you open the NOTEPAD window. If you do not want the tool bars to change with the windows, deselect this option. "Associating a Tool Bar with a Specific SAS Window" later in this chapter shows you how to define window-specific tool bars.

Adding and Editing Tools on the Tool Bar

FasTip: Click on **Options→Edit tools**.

Use the TOOLLOAD command to load alternative tool bars.

HelpPath: Help→SAS companion→SAS Companion for
Microsoft Windows→Running the SAS System
under Windows→Using Graphical Interface
Features of the SAS System→Changing the Tools
on the Tool Bar, then choose a topic

Help→How to→How to... with the SAS
System→Customize Your SAS Session→
Customizing the SAS Application Work
Space→Adding a New Tool to the Tool Bar

The tool bar across the top of the SAS AWS is a handy way to execute commands. While the default tools may be sufficient for many users, you may want to add a tool, change the icon for a tool, or otherwise edit the look and feel of the tool bar.

To begin editing the tool bar, click on **Options** in the SAS System main menu, then click on **Edit tools**. The TOOL EDITOR dialog box opens, as shown in Figure 6.4.

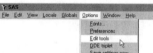

Figure 6.4
TOOL EDITOR Dialog Box

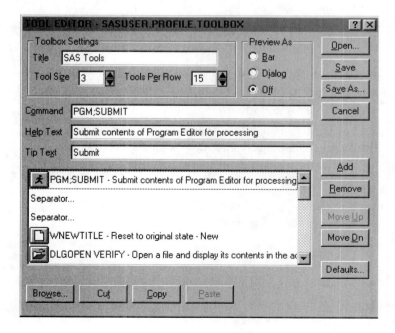

This section shows you how to

- add a tool to the tool bar

- edit an existing tool

- create an alternate tool bar

- associate a tool bar with a specific SAS window.

For information on other tasks, such as changing the order of tools, deleting tools, previewing changes, and so on, click on the **Help** button in the TOOL EDITOR dialog box, then click on the particular area of the dialog box you want help about. This displays an explanation of that dialog box field or button.

Returning to the Default Tools: Before you begin to make changes, remember you can always return to the default tools by clicking on **Defaults** in the TOOL EDITOR dialog box. When you do so, you are asked if you really want to return the definitions to their default values. Click on **Yes**, then click on **Save** to close the TOOL EDITOR dialog box.

Adding a Tool: The following example illustrates adding a new tool to the default SAS tool bar. Open the TOOL EDITOR dialog box and follow along:

1. Click on **Add**. Tools are added before the tool that is highlighted in the list of tools.

2. When you click on **Add**, you can choose to add a tool or a separator. For this example, click on **Tool**. A blank line and blank icon appear in the list of tools.

3. Click in the **Command** field once to move your cursor, and type the SAS windowing command you want the tool to execute. If you want the tool to execute a string of commands, separate the commands with semicolons.

For example, type the following to create a tool for submitting code stored on the Clipboard:

```
GSUBMIT
```

4. Click in the **Help Text** field, and type the help string that appears in the SAS AWS message area when you hold your mouse pointer over the tool. For example, type:

        Submit code from the Clipboard

5. Click in the **Tip Text** field, and type the help string that appears in the tool tip (the short description that appears under the tool when you place your mouse pointer over a tool). For example, type:

        Submit Clipboard

As you type in the **Command**, **Help Text**, and **Tip Text** field, your characters are copied to the tool definition in the list of tools.

Figure 6.5 shows how the TOOL EDITOR dialog box looks after you have typed all this text in.

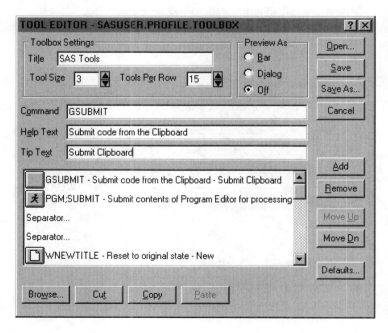

Figure 6.5
Adding a Tool

6. To pick an icon for the new tool, click on **Browse**. The Bitmap Browser dialog box opens, as shown in Figure 6.6.

Figure 6.6
Bitmap Browser Dialog Box

7. Click on the icon you want, then click on **OK**. The icon appears by the new tool.

For example, because you already have a submit tool that uses the jogger icon, you may want to choose a different icon for the new tool. Use the scroll bar at the bottom of the Bitmap Browser dialog box to scroll to the right, until your display matches that in Figure 6.7.

Figure 6.7
Choosing an Icon for Your
New Tool

Click on the jogger-on-a-page icon (first one in the bottom row, indicated by the mouse pointer), then on **OK**.

8. To save your changes, click on **Save** in the TOOL EDITOR dialog box. This closes the dialog box, and your new tool appears on the tool bar. Figure 6.8 shows the SAS AWS, with the mouse pointer pointing to the new tool.

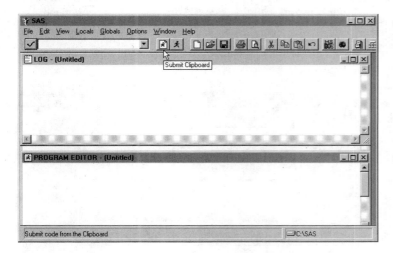

Figure 6.8
Tool Bar with the New Tool Added

Note: The number of tools visible on the tool bar depends on the resolution of your screen. Screen resolution is expressed in vertical X horizontal "pixels" or dots. On many screens, the resolution is 640 X 480. In this case, only 15 tools are visible at once; when you add the GSUBMIT tool, the right-most tool disappears off the right side of the screen. If you are using a low resolution such as 640 X 480, limit each set of tools to 15 tools, and create additional tool sets as described in "Creating an Alternative Tool Bar" later in this chapter. You can also use the EDIT TOOLS dialog box to delete the separators between tools. If you delete all separators, you can fit 16 tools on a 640 X 480 display.

Editing an Existing Tool: You do not have to accept how the tool icons look—you can choose a different icon for a tool. For example, you may not think that the icon for the tool that opens the Libraries dialog box is intuitive:

Change the icon for a tool by following steps similar to those in this example:

1. Open the TOOLS EDITOR dialog box by clicking on **Options** in the SAS System main menu, then click on **Edit tools**.

2. Use the scroll bar in the list of tools to scroll down until the tool you want to change is visible. In this example, we're going to change the tool with the open file drawers and the command DLGLIB.

3. Click on that line in the list of tools. It is highlighted, as shown in Figure 6.9.

Figure 6.9
TOOL EDITOR Dialog Box
with the Libraries Tool
Highlighted

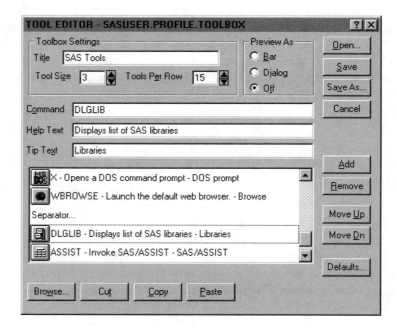

4. Click on **Browse** to display the Bitmap Browser dialog box. Be sure you are scrolled all the way to the left in the dialog box. Click on the second icon over in the bottom row–it looks like this:

5. Click on **OK**. The icon changes in the tool list. Click on **Save** to save your changes (this also closes the TOOL EDITOR dialog box).

Similarly, edit other parts of a tool by clicking on its line in the tool list, then clicking in the **Command**, **Help Text**, or **Tip Text** fields and editing the contents of these fields.

Creating an Alternative Tool Bar: One of the most powerful aspects of the SAS System's tool bar is that you can create several tool bars and load whichever set of tools you need for a specific SAS session. For example, you can create a tool bar for each SAS/AF application you write.

This section walks you through creating a small tool bar. One tool prints and clears the OUTPUT window; the other tool provides a shortcut to the How to... Help window. The following two sections show you how to load a specific tool bar and how to return to the original tool bar.

To create a new tool bar, follow steps similar to those in this example:

1. Click on **Options** in the SAS System main menu, then click on **Edit tools**. The TOOL EDITOR dialog box opens.

   Each tool bar you create is stored as a catalog entry. The title bar of the TOOL EDITOR dialog box shows the catalog entry name for the tool bar you are editing. The SASUSER.PROFILE. TOOLBOX.TOOLBOX entry is the default tool bar.

2. In the **Toolbox Settings** portion of the dialog box, give your new tool bar a title. This title serves as a descriptive label for the tool bar.

   Highlight the contents of the **Title** field by marking it with the mouse. Now type your new title. For example, type:

   ```
   My Personal Tool Bar
   ```

3. To delete tools you do not want, click on the tool in the tool list, then click on **Remove**. Continue clicking on **Remove** until all the tools and separators are gone.

4. Now add your own tools. In this example, we add two tools. Click on **Add**, then click on **Tool**. In the **Command** field, type:

```
OUTPUT; DLGPRT; CLEAR
```

In the **Help Text** field type:

```
Print the OUTPUT window and clear it
```

In the **Tip Text** field type:

```
Print/clear OUTPUT
```

5. Click on **Browse** to open the Bitmap Browser dialog box and choose an appropriate icon. For example, choose the printer icon that is approximately in the middle of the collection of icons (use the scroll bar to move to the right):

6. For the second tool, click on **Add**, then click on **Tool**. The **Command**, **Help Text**, and **Tip Text** fields should look like this:

```
%sysfunc(winhelp(help_index,
    c:\sas\core\winhelp\sashowto.hlp))
Open the How to... Help window
How to...
```

(The %SYSFUNC command should be all on one line.)

7. Click on **Browse** again and choose another icon. For example, choose the third icon in the first row:

8. Now you are ready to save your new catalog entry. Click on **Save As** (not on **Save**). The Save Tools dialog box appears, as shown in Figure 6.10.

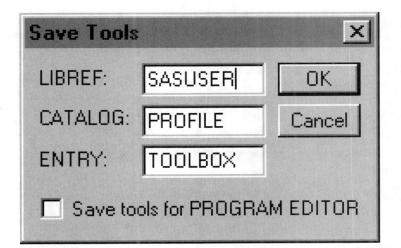

Figure 6.10
Save Tools Dialog Box

You can save the entry in any catalog. For this example, we'll store it in the SASUSER.PROFILE catalog and give it a name of MYTOOLS. Double-click in the **ENTRY** field to highlight the entry name and type MYTOOLS. Now click on **OK**. This writes the new catalog entry to the SASUSER.PROFILE catalog.

9. Notice that the title bar of the TOOL EDITOR dialog box now says **SASUSER.PROFILE.MYTOOLS**. Click on **Save** to close the dialog box.

Loading a Specific Tool Bar: To load your new tools, use the TOOLLOAD command. The basic syntax is as follows:

TOOLLOAD *tool-set*

For example, to load the tools you created in the previous section, issue the following command from the Command bar:

```
TOOLLOAD SASUSER.PROFILE.MYTOOLS
```

Figure 6.11 shows the SAS AWS with the new tools loaded.

Figure 6.11
Using the New Tool Bar

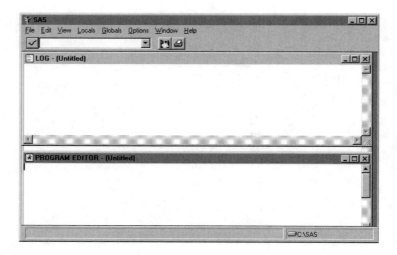

Instead of loading a tool bar manually with the TOOLLOAD command, you can associate a tool bar with a particular window and have that tool bar load automatically every time you open the window. See "Associating a Tool Bar with a Specific SAS Window" later in this chapter for more information.

You can also create a tool that invokes another tool bar—simply create a tool with the appropriate TOOLLOAD command in the **Command** field of the TOOL EDITOR dialog box.

Returning to the Default Tool Bar: To return to the default tool bar, issue the following command from the Command bar:

```
TOOLLOAD SASUSER.PROFILE.TOOLBOX
```

Associating a Tool Bar with a Specific SAS Window: Because you perform different tasks from different windows, it may be helpful to have a tool bar for each window. Follow these steps to set the window for a tool bar:

1. Click in the window with which you want the tool bar associated (this makes the window active).

2. Open the TOOL EDITOR dialog box by clicking on **Options** in the SAS System main menu, then click on **Edit tools**.

3. Create a new tool bar, as described earlier in this chapter.

4. Click on **Save As** in the TOOL EDITOR dialog box.

5. When the Save Tools dialog box appears, enter the catalog entry information, and also click in the check box by the line that reads

```
Save tools for active-window
```

The new tool bar is saved, and when you switch to the tool bar's window, the tool bar is automatically loaded.

Note: If tool bars do not load with windows, look at the **Switching** option in the **Tools** section of the Preferences dialog box. **Switching** must be checked in order for tool bars to load automatically with windows.

Changing Colors

FasTip: Use the SASCOLOR window (affects all SAS windows). Issue the COLOR command (affects individual SAS windows).

Click on the **Start** button, then click on **Settings**→**Control Panel**, then double-click on the **Display** icon. Now click on the **Appearance** tab (affects all Windows applications).

HelpPath: Help→**SAS companion**→**SAS Companion for Microsoft Windows**→**Running the SAS System under Windows**→**Using Graphical Interface Features of the SAS System**→**Customizing Your SAS Session**→**Customizing Your Windowing Environment**→**Changing the Window Colors**

Help→**SAS System**→**SAS System Help: Main Menu**→**SAS Windows**→**SASCOLOR**

Help→**SAS System**→**SAS System Help: Main Menu**→**SAS Global Commands**→**COLOR** (from any Windows Help menu) **Help→Help Topics→How to→Change Windows Settings→Change How Windows Looks→ Changing how items on the desktop look**

You can customize your SAS session by changing the color of windows and window elements. For example, you may not like the default stark white background of the PROGRAM EDITOR, LOG, and OUTPUT windows. Also, you may want titles in the OUTPUT window to appear in a certain color (default is blue) but footnotes in a different color. And you may want to adjust the color of title bars, scroll bars, and other window "decorations." Decide what you want to change, and whether you want to change the attribute

- for all windows in your SAS session

- for only a particular SAS window

- for all windows in all applications.

Deciding Which Method to Use: The three methods of changing colors and their effects in the SAS System are

- SASCOLOR window—affects all SAS windows

- COLOR command (issued from any SAS window)—affects only the SAS window from which the command is issued

- Display Properties window, from the Control Panel—affects all windows in all Windows applications, including the SAS System.

Each method lets you change the colors of a variety of window attributes; sometimes there is overlap, where an attribute can be changed by more than one method. In the latter case, one method has precedence over another.

Understanding the Precedence of Color Specifications: The Windows Control Panel overrides all other methods of color specification. For example, even though the COLOR command supports the SCROLLBAR option, it has no effect because scroll bars are controlled by the Control Panel.

Any specifications you make with the COLOR command override options set by the SASCOLOR window.

Using the SASCOLOR Window: Use the SASCOLOR window to set colors for all SAS windows. Table 6.1 shows the window elements supported by the SASCOLOR window.

Background	Secondary Background
Border	Secondary Border
Banner	Command
Message	Error
Warning	Note
Foreground	Label
Row Label	Informational Text
Column Label	Help Main Topic
Help Link	Help Subtopic & Syntax
Selected Area	Source
Data	Footnote
Header	Title
Byline	

Table 6.1
Window Elements Supported by the SASCOLOR Window

Open the SASCOLOR window by clicking on **Globals** in the SAS System main menu, then click on **Options**, then click on **Color setup**. Figure 6.12 shows the SASCOLOR window.

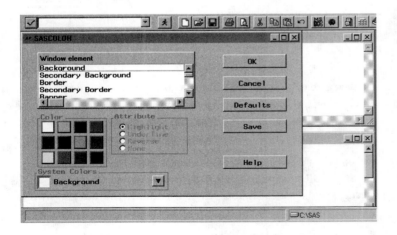

Figure 6.12
SASCOLOR Window

Note: You can also issue the SASCOLOR command from the Command bar to open the SASCOLOR window.

First, choose a window element by selecting one from the **Window element** list. Use the scroll bar to view the whole list. Select the element by clicking on it.

If the window element you have chosen supports attributes such as highlighting, reverse video, or underlining, these attributes are listed in the **Attribute** area. Unavailable attributes are light gray. Click on any attribute you want the window element to have. Now choose a color from the **Color** area. To change more window elements, chose a different element, then set its attributes and color.

The **System Colors** area of the SASCOLOR window allows you to link the color of SAS window elements to colors set by the Windows Control Panel. The three choices for system colors are **Foreground**, **Background**, and **Secondary Background**. Table 6.2 shows how these choices correspond to the choices in the Display Properties window of the Control Panel (on the **Appearance** tab):

Table 6.2
Correlation between SASCOLOR Window System Colors and Control Panel Choices

CHOICE IN SASCOLOR WINDOW	CONTROL PANEL WINDOW ELEMENT	CONTROL PANEL WINDOW ELEMENT ATTRIBUTE
Foreground	Window	Font Color
Background	Window	Item Color
Secondary Background	3D Objects	Item Color

For example, if you want selected text in SAS windows to always be the same color as the **3D Objects** color set in the Control Panel, select **Selected Area** in the SASCOLOR window **Window element** list. Then, click on the down arrow to the right of the **System Colors** area and click on **Secondary Background**.

When you are finished setting colors and attributes in the SASCOLOR window, click on **OK** if you want to save your changes and close the SASCOLOR window. If you want to save your changes but leave the SASCOLOR window open, click on **Save**.

When you click on **OK** or **Save**, a catalog entry named SAS.CPARMS is created in your SASUSER.PROFILE catalog.

If you change several window elements but decide you do not like your changes, return to the default configuration by clicking on **Defaults**.

To get information on what the various window elements are, click on the **Help** button in the SASCOLOR window, then click on **Window Element**. Now click on the name of the window element you want to know more about.

Two things to remember:

* Although the SASCOLOR window affects all SAS windows, if you have changed a window element's color with the COLOR command and then issued a WSAVE command to save your changes, that window's element is not affected by the changes you make via the SASCOLOR window.

* Currently open SAS windows do not reflect the new colors you have chosen from the SASCOLOR window until you close the windows and reopen them.

Using the COLOR Command: Use the COLOR command to set colors for a specific SAS window. You can issue the COLOR command from almost any SAS window. The basic syntax is

COLOR *window-element color*

where *window-element* is the name of a part of a window (like banner, note, or message) and *color* is an abbreviation for a supported color. Table 6.3 shows the window elements supported by the COLOR command, and Table 6.4 shows the supported colors and their abbreviations.

Background	Border	Banner
Command	Message	Scroll Bar
Byline	Data	Error
Footnote	Header	Mtext
Note	Numbers	Source
Text	Title	Warning

Table 6.3
Window Elements Supported by the COLOR Command

B	blue	R	Red	G	green
C	cyan	P	pink	Y	yellow
W	white	K	black	M	magenta
A	gray	N	brown	O	orange

Table 6.4
Colors Supported by the
COLOR Command

Note: Not all window elements listed in Table 6.3 are valid for all SAS windows. For example, the **Header** element is not valid in the LOG window.

If you issue the COLOR command, then end your SAS session, the default colors return the next time you invoke the SAS System. To make the changes permanent for a window, issue the WSAVE command from the Command bar after the COLOR command. This saves the window's attributes to a .WSAVE entry in your SASUSER.PROFILE catalog.

If you've saved changes but then decide to return to the default configuration, delete the appropriate .WSAVE entries from your SASUSER.PROFILE catalog. These entries include the DMS-DEF.WSAVE entry and .WSAVE entries that begin with a window name, like PROGRAM.WSAVE. The **Description** field in the CATALOG window can help you determine which .WSAVE entries to delete.

Caution: Deleting .WSAVE entries that begin with a window name can also delete attributes other than color, such as customized key definitions.

Using the Control Panel's Display Properties Window: Use the Control Panel's Display Properties window to set colors for all windows in all Windows applications. Table 6.5 shows the window elements supported by the Display Properties window.

Table 6.5
Window Elements
Supported by the Control
Panel's Display Properties
Window

3D Objects	Active Title Bar
Active Window Border	Application Background
Desktop	Inactive Title Bar
Inactive Window Border	Menu
Message Box	Selected Items
Tooltip	Window

To open the Control Panel's Display Properties window, click on the **Start** button, then click on **Settings→Control Panel**. Now double-click on the **Display** icon. The Display Properties window opens, as shown in Figure 6.13.

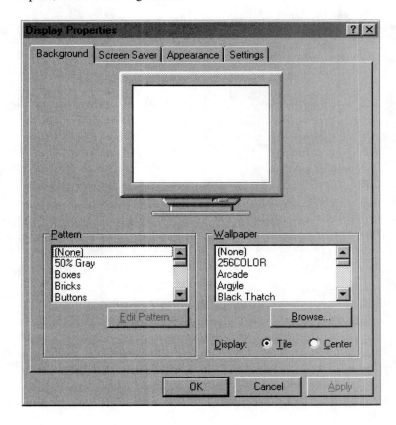

Figure 6.13
Control Panel's Display
Properties Window

Now click on the **Appearance** tab. Now the window looks like Figure 6.14.

Figure 6.14
Appearance Tab in the
Display Properties Window

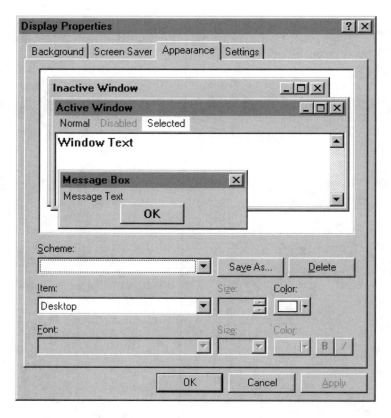

The window attributes you set on the **Appearance** tab of the Display Properties window affect all applications installed on your system. For example, if you set active title bars to be orange, the SAS System title bar is orange, and so is the title bar for Microsoft Word, Paint, and even the Control Panel.

To set the color of a particular window attribute, follow these steps:

1. Click on the down arrow by the **Item** field, and use the scroll bar to scroll to the element you want to set. For example, about halfway down the list you see **Scrollbar**.

2. To select an element, click on it. The name of the element appears in the **Item** field.

3. Click on the **Color** button next to the **Item** field, then on the colored square that represents the color you want for the window element. For window elements that also contain text, you can click on the **Color** button next to the **Font** field to change the text color.

   For example, tool tips are normally light yellow with black text. If you prefer light green with magenta text, click on the light green rectangle displayed by the **Color** button next to the **Item** field. Then click on the **Color** button next to the **Font** field, and click on the magenta rectangle.

   When you click on a color, the sample window on the left side of the **Appearance** tab reflects your changes, showing the effect.

4. If you want to change other window elements, use the **Item** list to select another element, then select its color. When you are finished, click on **OK** to close the Display Properties window and save your changes.

Warning: Be careful when you are selecting elements and colors. For example, it is possible to set both the window text and the window background to white, so that you cannot see anything. While you can fix this by going back to the Display Properties window, it is disconcerting to say the least.

Resizing and Organizing Windows

FasTip: Click on **Window→Tile, Cascade**, or **Resize**.

In Chapter 1, you learned how to move and resize windows using the mouse. You can also affect how windows are arranged within the SAS AWS by using the menus and commands.

Minimizing Windows: To minimize a window (that is, reduce it to an icon), click on the minimize button. If you want all your SAS windows minimized, click on **Window** in the SAS System main menu, then on **Minimize all windows**.

Tiling Windows: A quick way to make all open windows visible at once is to tile them. This arranges them in a mosaic pattern within the SAS AWS. To tile your windows, click on **Window** in the SAS System main menu, then on **Tile**. Figure 6.15 shows a SAS session with six tiled windows.

Figure 6.15
Tiled SAS Windows

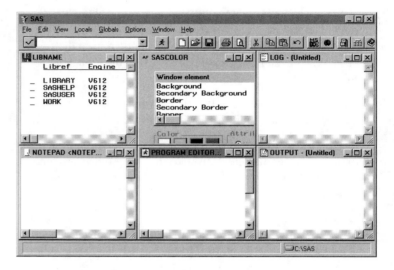

If you prefer issuing commands, issue the TILE command from the Command bar.

Cascading Windows: An alternative to tiling windows is to arrange them in layers, so that each window's title bar is visible. To cascade your windows, click on **Window** in the SAS System main menu, then on **Cascade**. Figure 6.16 shows a SAS session with six cascaded windows.

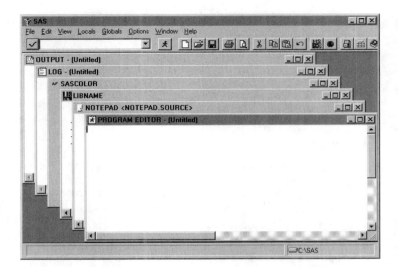

Figure 6.16
Cascaded SAS Windows

If you prefer issuing commands, issue the CASCADE command from the Command bar.

Note: If you want a different window on top but still want the windows cascaded, first switch to the window you want, then reissue the CASCADE command. The windows are cascaded with the active window on top.

Undoing Your Changes: If you decide you do not want your windows tiled or cascaded, return to the default arrangement by clicking on **Window** in the SAS System main menu, then on **Resize**. If you prefer issuing commands, issue the RESIZE command from the Command bar.

Note: Resize also resets other window attributes, such as size and position.

Defining Function Keys

FasTip: Open the KEYS window and redefine the key definitions.

HelpPath: Help→SAS System→SAS System Help: Main
Menu→SAS Windows→KEYS

While the point-and-click features of Windows applications are a boon to many users, you may not like this approach to issuing commands. You can issue commands to the SAS System in other ways, bypassing the menus.

Three common alternatives to using the menus are

- function keys

- keyboard shortcuts

- command-line commands.

Earlier in this chapter, you learned how to use the Preferences dialog box to turn off the Command bar and replace it with command lines in each window. And in Chapter 1, you learned about keyboard shortcuts (such as CTRL-C for Cut) and hotkeys (the underlined letters in the menus). This section shows you how to define function keys (such as F1 or Shift-F10) and other keys (such as CTRL-H and the mouse buttons) for use with the SAS System.

Many function keys come defined with the SAS System, and you can add and change the default definitions. To see what keys have been defined, open the KEYS window by clicking on **Help** in the SAS System main menu, then clicking on **Keys**. Figure 6.17 shows the default KEYS window.

Figure 6.17
KEYS Window

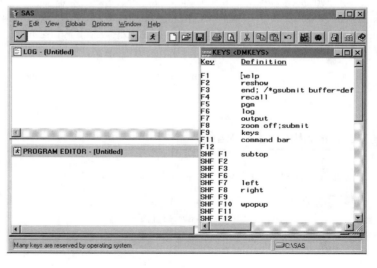

Use the scroll bars or PageUp and PageDown keys to see what keys are defined. Use Table 6.6 to understand the key name abbreviations.

ABBREVIATION	KEY
SHF	Shift key
CTRL	Control key
ALT	Alt key
RMB	right mouse button
MMB	middle mouse button

Table 6.6
Abbreviations Used in the KEYS Window

(If you have a two-button mouse, MMB is not listed in the KEYS window.)

To define a key, type the display manager command you want associated with that key in the **Definition** column. To assign a string of commands to a single key, separate the commands with a semicolon (;).

Returning to the Default Key Definitions: When you close the KEYS window, the changes you've made are saved to your SASUSER.PROFILE catalog in an entry named DMKEYS.KEYS. If you should ever want to go back to the default key definitions, delete the DMKEYS entry from your SASUSER.PROFILE catalog and close your SAS session. The next time you invoke the SAS System, the KEYS window lists the default function key definitions.

An alternative to deleting the DMKEYS entry is to rename it. (This prevents the SAS System from loading the definitions stored in the file). Because the SAS System cannot find the DMKEYS entry, it uses the default key definitions. When you want to use your customized definitions again, rename the entry back to DMKEYS.

Note: Windows also defines some useful keys. Refer to Table 1.1 for a list of keys you may find helpful while working with the SAS System for Windows.

Changing the Display Font

FasTip: Click on **Options**→**Fonts**.

HelpPath: Help→**SAS companion**→**SAS Companion for Microsoft Windows**→**Running the SAS System under Windows**→**Using Graphical Interface Features of the SAS System**→**Customizing Your SAS Session**→**Selecting Fonts**

Help→**How to**→**How to... with the**→**SAS System**→**Customize Your SAS Session**→ **Customizing the SAS Application Work Space**→**Selecting the Font to Use**

You may not like the default font used in SAS System windows. To change the SAS System display font, click on **Options** in the SAS System main menu, then on **Fonts**. This opens the Font dialog box. Now choose the font and typesize you want to use. Figure 6.18 shows the Font dialog box.

Figure 6.18
Font Dialog Box for
Changing the Display Font

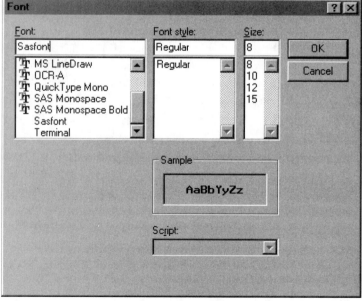

Only monospace fonts work well with the SAS System—proportional fonts do not produce satisfactory results. By default, the SAS System uses the Sasfont font in windows. Other monospace fonts that are common include Courier and IBMPCDOS.

Note: The font you choose in the Font dialog box accessed through the **Options** menu affects only the font used in SAS windows. To affect the font used for printer output, use the **Fonts** button in the Print Setup dialog box.

Using the SAS Desktop

FasTip: Click on **Globals**→**Desktop**.

HelpPath: **Help**→**What's New**→**SAS Desktop**

Help→**SAS System**→**Base SAS Documentation**→ **SAS Desktop**→**SAS Desktop**, then select a topic

Starting with Release 6.12, the SAS System offers an alternative way to deal with windows, files, SAS data libraries, and other "objects" used with the SAS System. This new interface is called the SAS Desktop. While this chapter does not provide full details on using the SAS Desktop, it does show you how to access this feature. Refer to the online documentation for more information.

Opening the SAS Desktop: To open the SAS Desktop, click on **Globals** in the main SAS System menu, then click on **Desktop**. The SAS Desktop window opens, as shown in Figure 6.19.

Figure 6.19
SAS Desktop

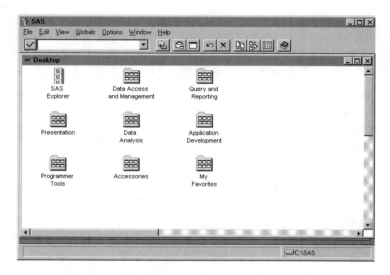

The SAS Desktop uses the folder analogy to store items such as files and SAS windows. For example, if you double-click on the **Programmer Tools** icon, a new window opens, which includes objects such as the LOG, PROGRAM EDITOR, OUTPUT, GRAPH, LIBNAME, and FILENAME windows. The **Accessories** folder contains windows such as the NOTEPAD, TITLES, FOOT-NOTES, SASCOLOR, and OPTIONS windows.

You can create new folders for the SAS Desktop and move objects around from folder to folder. If you like the icon-oriented folder approach, you may prefer to use the SAS Desktop in lieu of the menus and tool bars.

Using SAS Explorer: Part of the SAS Desktop includes SAS Explorer, which is similar to the Windows Explorer—it helps you find and manage SAS files and external files that are defined to the SAS System. To open SAS Explorer, double-click on the **SAS Explorer** icon in the SAS Desktop window. Again, refer to the online documentation for full details on using SAS Explorer.

Making the PROGRAM EDITOR Window Look Like Previous Releases

FasTip: Click on **Edit**→**Options**→**Numbers**.

Click on **Options**→**Preferences**. Turn the tool bar and Command bar off and click on **Command Line**; turn off **Horizontal Scrollbar**, **Vertical Scrollbar**, and **Status Line**.

HelpPath: Help→**SAS companion**→**SAS Companion for Microsoft Windows**→**Running the SAS System under Windows**→**Using Graphical Interface Features of the SAS System**→**Working within Your SAS Session**→**Using the Text Editor Windows**→**Using Line Numbers**

Help→**SAS companion**→**SAS Companion for Microsoft Windows**→**Running the SAS System under Windows**→**Using Graphical Interface Features of the SAS System**→**Customizing Your SAS Session**→**Setting Session Preferences**

You may have liked how the PROGRAM EDITOR and other windows looked in previous versions of the SAS System in mainframe environments—line numbers, a command line, no tools, status areas, or scroll bars. You can adjust the settings of various options in the SAS System to emulate the "old" look.

Activating Line Numbers: To activate line numbers in the PROGRAM EDITOR, click on **Edit** in the SAS System main menu, then click on **Options**, then click on **Numbers**. You must issue the WSAVE command from the PROGRAM EDITOR window (use the Command bar or command line) to save the line numbers attribute for future SAS sessions. If you do not issue the WSAVE command, the next time you invoke the SAS System, line numbers are not activated.

Turning Off the Menus, Command Bar, and Tool Bar: To turn off menus and tools and turn on command lines, click on **Options** in the SAS System main menu, then click on **Preferences**. In the **Commands** area, click on **Off** and also on **Command Line**. In the **Tools** area, click on **Off**. Note that even though the menu bar is not visible, popup menus, accessed by the right mouse button, are still available.

Suppressing the Status Area and Scroll Bars: To get rid of the status area and scroll bars, open the Preferences dialog box by clicking on **Options** in the SAS System main menu, then click on **Preferences**. In the **Status** area, deselect **Status Line**; in the **Scrollbars** area, deselect **Horizontal Scrollbar** and **Vertical Scrollbar**.

Returning to the Default Environment

If you want to undo only one change from among many, you may want to redo the command. For example, if you have used the COLOR command to change many aspects of several windows and want to save the majority of the changes, your best approach is to reissue the COLOR command for the few window aspects you want to change. Or, if you are happy with most of the settings in the Preferences dialog box but want to change one of them, open the dialog box, make your change, and click on **Save**.

If, however, you want to completely undo a set of changes, such as all color settings or all tool bar changes, use the techniques in Table 6.7. Where several actions are listed, try each of them in order—you may have to take several steps to completely return to the default settings.

WINDOW ELEMENT	TO RETURN TO DEFAULT SETTINGS
Keys	Delete or rename the DMKEYS entry in your SASUSER.PROFILE catalog
Tools	Open the TOOL EDITOR dialog box, click on **Defaults**
	Delete all .TOOLBOX entries in your SASUSER.PROFILE catalog
Colors	Open the SASCOLOR window and click on **Defaults**
	Delete all .WSAVE entries in your SASUSER.PROFILE catalog
	Delete the SAS.CPARMS entry in your SASUSER.PROFILE catalog
Preferences	Delete the PREFWSAV.WSAVE entry from your SASUSER.PROFILE catalog
Window size and position	Click on **Window** in the SAS System main menu, then click on **Resize**
	Delete .WSAVE entries that begin with a window name from your SASUSER.PROFILE catalog
	Delete or rename the DMSDEF.WSAVE entry in your SASUSER.PROFILE catalog
	Restart your SAS session

Table 6.7
Techniques for Returning to the Default Windowing Environment

7 | Managing SAS® Files

Introduction

It is often best to manage SAS files such as SAS data sets and catalogs using the SAS System's file management capabilities. However, the Windows Explorer does come in handy for copying and moving SAS files.

This chapter first discusses some data protection issues you should consider before deciding how to manage your SAS files. Then, it shows you how to perform the following file management tasks:

- rename and delete SAS files using the SAS System DIR window

- use the Windows Explorer to move and copy SAS files

- manage your SAS librefs and filerefs

- use the CATALOG window.

Understanding Data Protection

HelpPath: Help→SAS System →Base SAS Documentation→
Language Reference→SAS Data Set Options,
then choose **ALTER, READ,** or **WRITE**

The Windows environment and the SAS System both provide data protection services—which one you choose (or you may choose to use both) depends on how you plan to access and manage your files.

Setting SAS System Passwords: The SAS System lets you assign passwords to data sets. These passwords control file access and are assigned using the READ=, WRITE=, and ALTER= data set options:

- READ= allows read-only access to the file.

- WRITE= allows read and write access to the file (including the ability to modify, delete, and add observations).

- ALTER= allows read and write access to the file, plus the ability to delete the file, rename variables, and create indexes.

If you do not specify the correct password with the correct option, you cannot access the file. See the SAS online help for the syntax of these data set options.

Warning: If you forget the password, you will not be able to access your protected SAS files. Therefore, you may want to record the password in a safe place.

Using File Attributes: You can also use the Windows Explorer to set file attributes, which are different than SAS System passwords. Here are the steps to display a file's attributes in the Windows Explorer:

1. Open the Windows Explorer by right-clicking on the **Start** button, then clicking on **Explore**.

2. Display the folder containing the file for which you want to display attributes.

3. Right-click on the file for which you want to see attributes.

4. Click on **Properties** in the popup menu. The Properties dialog box for the file appears.

For example, Figure 7.1 shows the properties for APPEND.SAS.

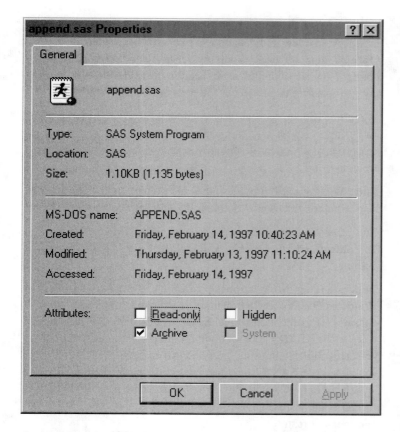

Figure 7.1
Using the Properties Dialog
Box to Set File Attributes

In the Properties dialog box, choose one or more of the following attributes:

• **Read-only** means users cannot write to the file, rename it, or delete it. All they can do is read it.

• **Archive** means the file is marked when it has changed since it was last backed up.

• **Hidden** means the file is not listed by default in the Windows Explorer's folder listings.

• **System** means the file is a Windows system file. You probably will not use this option with your SAS files.

Turn file attributes on and off by clicking in their respective check boxes.

If you want to see hidden files in the Windows Explorer folder listing, click on **View** in the Windows Explorer menu, then click on **Options**. In the Options dialog box, click by the **Show all files** option. Now all hidden files are listed in the folder listings, allowing you to select them and change their attributes if you want.

Warning: Hidden files are usually hidden for a purpose—they are rarely files that you need to manage in any way. Do not change the properties of a hidden file unless you know exactly what you are doing.

Note: Windows also provides other file-protection devices, such as lists of authorized users. Use the following help path to learn more:

(from any Windows **Help** menu): **Help**→**Help Topics**→**How To**→**Safeguard Your Work**→**Controlling access to a folder or printer**

Understanding the Relationship between SAS System and Windows File Protection: Setting passwords in the SAS System does not affect file access outside the SAS System. For example, if you use the READ= data set option to mark a data set read only, you can still delete it using the Windows Explorer. Therefore, if you depend on SAS System data protection, perform all your file management from within the SAS System using the DIR and CATALOG windows, the COPY procedure, and other SAS System file management features.

On the other hand, file attributes set with the Properties dialog box do affect the SAS System. For example, if you mark the program APPEND.SAS as read-only using the Properties dialog box and then try to save it from the PROGRAM EDITOR window, you receive the following error in your SAS log: `Insufficient authorization`.

Similarly, if you have marked a file as hidden, it is not listed in the SAS System dialog boxes, such as Open and Save As.

Renaming SAS Files

FasTip: Right-click on the SAS filename in the Libraries dialog
box, and click on **Rename**.

SAS files such as data files, data views, and catalogs are stored
in SAS data libraries. Use the Libraries dialog box to rename
SAS files.

To open the Libraries dialog box, click on the Libraries icon in the
SAS System tool bar:

Figure 7.2 shows the Libraries dialog box, listing the contents of
the SASUSER library.

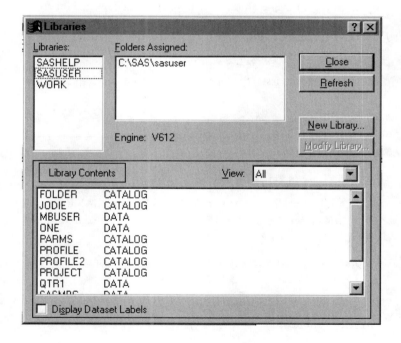

Figure 7.2
Libraries Dialog Box
Listing the Contents
of the SASUSER Data
Library

To rename a file from the Libraries dialog box, right-click on the
file you want to rename, then click on **Rename**. Another dialog box
appears, as shown in Figure 7.3.

Figure 7.3
Rename Member Dialog
Box

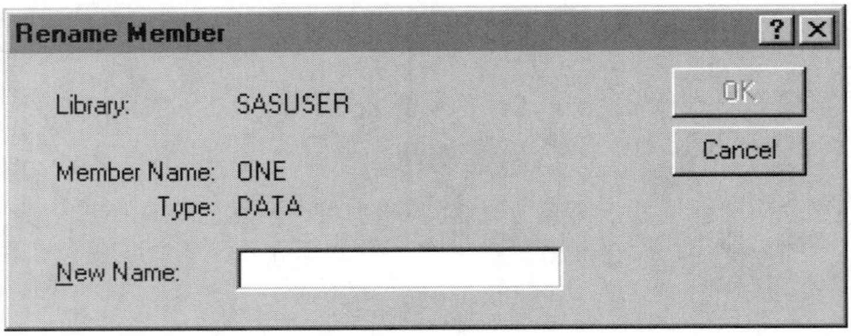

Type the new name in the **New Name** field, then click on **OK**.

Warning: Be careful when you rename files—some files, such as the SASUSER.PROFILE catalog, must have a particular name in order to work. In general, it is safe to rename catalogs and other files you have created; do not rename files created automatically by the SAS System.

Note: You can also rename SAS files from the DIR window. To open this window, issue the DIR command from the Command bar.

Deleting SAS Files

FasTip: Right-click on the SAS filename in the Libraries dialog box, and click on **Delete**.

Use the Libraries dialog box to delete SAS files in a SAS data library. (You can also use the Windows Explorer to delete files, as described in Chapter 1.)

To open the Libraries dialog box, click on the Libraries icon in the SAS System tool bar:

Figure 7.4 shows the Libraries dialog box listing the contents of the SASUSER library.

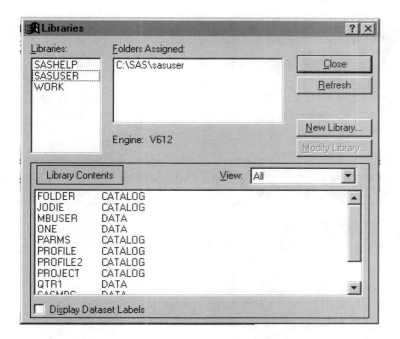

Figure 7.4
Libraries Dialog Box Listing the Contents of the SASUSER Data Library

To delete a file, right-click on the SAS file you want to delete, then click on **Delete**. Another dialog box appears, as shown in Figure 7.5.

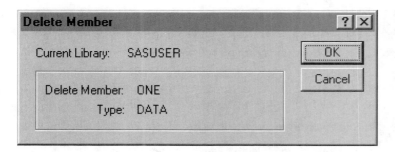

Figure 7.5
Delete Member Dialog Box

Note: You can also delete SAS files from the DIR window. To open this window, issue the DIR command from the Command bar.

Warning: Be careful when you delete files—some files, such as the SASUSER.PROFILE catalog, are necessary for the SAS System to work properly. In general, it is safe to delete catalogs and other files you have created; do not delete files created automatically by the SAS System.

Warning: SAS password-protection does not prevent you from deleting files using the Windows Explorer.

Warning: Files deleted via the DIR window or other methods within the SAS System are not sent to the Windows Recycle Bin, and therefore cannot be easily recovered. To recover such files, you must have a third-party file restoration utility, such as Norton Utilities.

Moving and Copying SAS Files Using the Windows Explorer

HelpPath: (from any Windows Help menu)→**Help**→**Help Topics**→**How To**→**Work with Files and Folders**, then select a topic

The SAS System provides the COPY procedure, and it works the same under Windows as it does under any other operating system. But if you prefer the pictorial method of moving and copying files, use the Windows Explorer to move and copy files from one folder to another.

Moving Files: To move a file using the Windows Explorer, follow these steps:

1. Open the Windows Explorer by right-clicking on the **Start** button, then clicking on **Explore**.

2. Display the folder you want to move the file from.

3. Select the file you want to move by clicking on it.

4. Click on **Edit** in the Windows Explorer menu, then click on **Cut**.

5. Now display the folder to which you want to move the file.

6. Click on **Edit** in the Windows Explorer menu, then on **Paste**. The file is moved to the new folder.

Warning: Moving files from one folder to another involves deleting a file from the original folder. If you have protected your SAS data sets with the ALTER= data set option (which prevents you from deleting the file without providing the password), you should

use only PROC COPY to move these data sets. If you use the
Windows Explorer to move these SAS protected files, it does not
recognize the SAS System's passwords and bypasses the SAS data
set protection.

Copying Files: Copying files is identical to moving files, except
you use the **Copy** menu choice instead of the **Cut** menu choice. To
copy a file using the Windows Explorer, follow these steps:

1. Open the Windows Explorer by right-clicking on the **Start** button, then clicking on **Explore**.

2. Display the folder you want to copy the file from.

3. Select the file you want to copy by clicking on it.

4. Click on **Edit** in the Windows Explorer menu, then on **Copy**.

5. Now display the folder to which you want to copy the file.

6. Click on **Edit** in the Windows Explorer menu, then on **Paste**.
   The file is copied to the new folder.

Selecting More than One File: You can move or copy more than
one file from the original folder to the target folder. To do so, use
your Shift and Control keys in combination with your left mouse
button to select multiple files, as described here:

- To select several contiguous files, click on the first filename, hold
  the Shift key down, and click on the last filename.

- To select several files that are separated by files you do not want
  to select, click on the first filename, hold down the Control key,
  and click on the subsequent filenames.

Listing Librefs in the LIBNAME Window

FasTip: Issue the LIBNAME command.

HelpPath: **Help→SAS System→SAS System Help: Main
Menu→SAS Windows→LIBNAME**

If you have assigned many librefs during a SAS session, it is often
difficult to remember which libref points to which folder. Use the
LIBNAME window to display a list of currently assigned librefs.

To open the LIBNAME window, issue the LIBNAME command from the Command bar. The LIBNAME window appears.

To see the members of a particular library, double-click on the libref. This opens the DIR window for that data library.

Figure 7.6 shows a sample LIBNAME window, displaying the three automatically defined librefs (SASHELP, SASUSER, and WORK). Notice that the LIBNAME window shows you which SAS engine is associated with each library and the library's physical pathname.

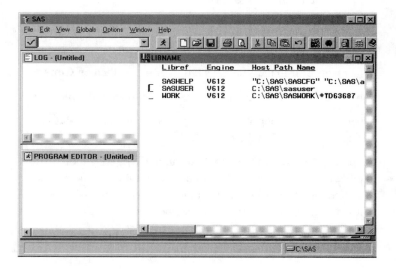

Managing SAS Data Libraries with the Libraries Dialog Box

FasTip: Click on the Libraries icon on the SAS AWS tool bar.

HelpPath: Help→**SAS companion**→**SAS Companion for Microsoft Windows**→**Running the SAS System under Windows**→**Using SAS Files**→**Using Data Libraries**→**Assigning SAS Libraries with the SAS Libraries Dialog Box**

Help→**How to**→**How to... with the SAS System**→ **Access Data with the SAS System**→**Working with SAS Data Libraries**, then choose a topic

The Libraries dialog box is like the LIBNAME window combined with a point-and-click LIBNAME statement. It shows the contents and physical pathname for each SAS data library, but unlike the LIBNAME window, the Libraries dialog box also enables you to create and modify librefs.

To open the Libraries dialog box, click on the Libraries icon on the tool bar, which looks like a file cabinet with an open drawer.

Figure 7.7 shows a sample Libraries dialog box.

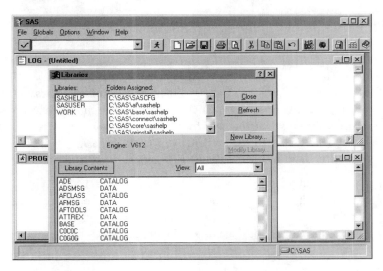

Figure 7.7
Libraries Dialog Box

Viewing the Contents of a SAS Data Library: To view the contents of a particular data library, click on its name in the **Libraries** list. The contents are displayed in the **Library Contents** area. The **Folders Assigned** area shows you which physical folder is assigned to the libref you selected. The library engine is also displayed. If the library contains many files and you want to see only one type, click on the down arrow by the **View** field, and click on the file type you want to see listed.

Creating a New Libref: To create a new libref, click on **New Library** in the Libraries dialog box. The New Library dialog box appears, as shown in Figure 7.8.

Figure 7.8
New Library Dialog Box

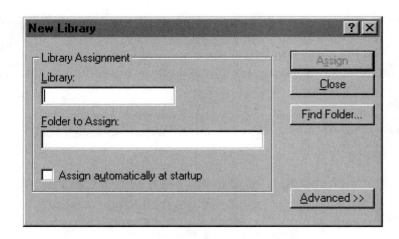

Type the new libref in the **Library** field. Use the **Folders**, **Files**, **Drives**, and **List Files of Type** fields to orient yourself and choose the right folder. When you have found the folder you want, type its name in the **Folder to Assign** field. Now click on **Assign**. This creates a new libref with the default V612 engine.

To create a libref using another engine besides V612, before you click on **Assign** in the New Library dialog box, click on **Advanced**. Click on the down arrow by the **Engine** field, and click on the name of the engine you want to use. Figure 7.9 shows the New Library dialog box with the advanced options.

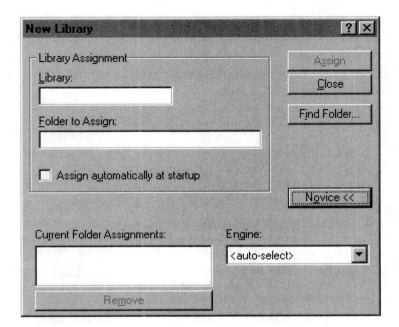

Figure 7.9
Advanced Options in the
New Library Dialog Box

Using another engine (such as V606 or V604) enables you to access SAS files created with earlier versions of the SAS System under Windows 3.1, DOS, or OS/2. To suppress the advanced options again, click on **Novice**.

Assigning Librefs Automatically: If you select the **Assign automatically at startup** check box in the New Library dialog box, a library definition is stored in your SASUSER.PROFILE catalog. The libref is available as soon as you start your SAS session—no LIBNAME statement or other action is necessary.

Creating a Concatenated Data Library: To create a libref that points to several folders, click on **Advanced** in the New Library dialog box (before you click on **Assign**). Type the first folder in the **Folder to Assign** field and click on **Assign**. This does not close the dialog box but causes the **Current Folder Assignments** field to list the folder. Now type the second folder in the **Folder to Assign** field and click on **Assign**. The **Current Folder Assignments** field now lists two folders. Keep this up until you have entered all the folders. Now click on **Close**.

Modifying an Existing Libref: To modify an existing libref, click on it in the Libraries field in the **Libraries** dialog box. Now click on **Modify Library.** (You cannot modify the SASUSER, SASHELP, or WORK librefs.) The Modify Library dialog box appears, as shown in Figure 7.10.

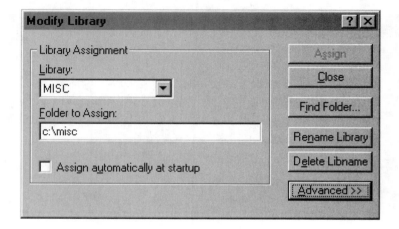

If you clicked on the wrong library, click on the down arrow by the **Library** field and select the libref you want to modify. Add folders by typing their names in the **Folder to Assign** field and clicking on **Assign**.

If the library is a concatenated library and you want to remove a folder, first click on **Advanced** in the Modify Library dialog box. Then click on the folder name in the **Current Folder Assignments** list, then click on **Remove**. When the Remove Folder dialog box appears, click on **OK**.

Renaming a Libref: To rename a libref, click on **Rename Library** in the Modify Library dialog box. This opens the Rename Library dialog box, as shown in Figure 7.11. Type the new libref in the **New Name** field, then click on **OK**.

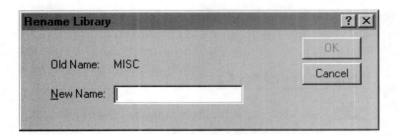

Figure 7.11
Rename Library Dialog Box

Deleting a Libref: To delete a libref, click on **Delete Libname** in the Modify Library dialog box. When prompted if you really want to delete the libref, click on **OK**. (Remember, this deletes the libref, which is a pointer to the folder, but this does not delete the actual folder.)

Managing Your SAS Filerefs

FasTip: Issue the FILENAME command.

HelpPath: **Help→SAS System→SAS System Help: Main Menu→SAS Windows→FILENAME**

Filerefs can be as hard to remember as librefs. Use the FILENAME window to keep track of your filerefs during a SAS session.

To open the FILENAME window, issue the FILENAME command from the Command bar. Figure 7.12 shows a sample FILENAME window.

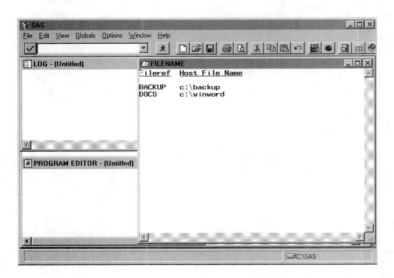

Figure 7.12
FILENAME Window

The FILENAME window lists each fileref and the physical file the fileref points to.

Managing Your SAS Catalogs

FasTip: Right-click on the catalog name in the Libraries dialog box, then click on **CATALOG window.**

HelpPath: Help→SAS System→SAS System Help: Main Menu→SAS Windows→CATALOG

While you can manage your catalogs programmatically with the CATALOG procedure, you may find it easier to use the CATALOG window to rename and delete SAS catalog entries. (If you need to move or copy SAS catalogs, use the CATALOG procedure.)

One way to access the CATALOG window is from the Libraries dialog box. To open this dialog box, click on the Libraries icon in the SAS System tool bar:

Click on the SAS data library name that contains the catalog you want to access, then right-click on the catalog name in the **Library Contents** area. When the popup menu appears, click on **CATA-LOG window.**

Note: You can also open the CATALOG window by issuing the CAT command from the Command bar.

Figure 7.13 shows a sample CATALOG window.

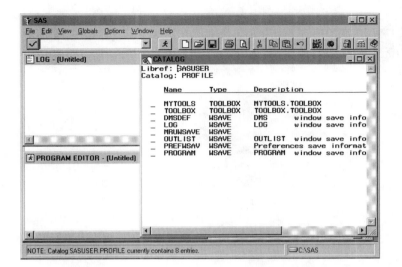

Figure 7.13
CATALOG Window
Showing the Contents of
the SASUSER.PROFILE
Catalog

If the entry is an executable entry, such as NOTEPAD.SOURCE or
a BUILD entry, double-clicking on an entry opens that entry. This
is the same as pointing at the entry name, right-clicking to activate
the popup menu, and clicking on **Select**. Other possible actions,
depending on the type of entry you are pointing at, include **Edit**,
Browse, **Rename**, **Delete**, **Verify**, and **Print**. Printing is valid only
for entries of type GRSEG (created with SAS/GRAPH software).

You must have the mouse pointer over an entry name or selection
field for the correct popup menu to appear. If the mouse pointer is
somewhere else, the right mouse button opens the generic
popup menu.

Warning: Be careful renaming catalog entries—some entries have
required names (such as SAS.CPARMS). In general, it is safe to
rename entries you have created but not entries created automatically by the SAS System. Also, exercise care when deleting entries.
For example, if you delete the entry PREFWSAV.WSAVE, you lose
all the preferences you have set via the Preferences dialog box.

8 Customizing Your Start-up Files

Introduction

HelpPath: Help→SAS companion→SAS Companion for Microsoft Windows→Running the SAS System under Windows→Getting Started→Files Used by the SAS System→SAS Configuration File or SAS Autoexec File

Under every operating system, the SAS System uses two start-up files: the CONFIG.SAS and AUTOEXEC.SAS files. This chapter explains how these two files work under Windows and how to modify them. Much of the information is similar to other operating systems, so you should quickly become adept at using these files under Windows.

As a reminder, here are the differences between the CONFIG.SAS and AUTOEXEC.SAS files:

- The CONFIG.SAS file sets SAS system options. These options control various aspects of the SAS System, such as SAS AWS size, printer options, and more. When you install the SAS System, a default CONFIG.SAS file is created in the SAS folder.

- The AUTOEXEC.SAS file executes SAS programming statements immediately after the SAS System starts. No AUTOEXEC.SAS file is created at SAS System installation—if you want one, you must create it yourself.

Under Windows, you can also specify SAS system options in the **Target** field of the Properties dialog box for the **SAS System** icon. The system options you specify in the **Target** field are used in addition to the system options in the CONFIG.SAS file. Later in this chapter, "Altering the Properties of the SAS System Icon" presents more information on this technique.

Note: This and subsequent chapters cover complex tasks with many steps and considerations. Therefore, these chapters do not contain FasTips like the earlier chapters.

Editing Your Start-up Files—An Overview

To edit your CONFIG.SAS or AUTOEXEC.SAS file, you need to use a text editor that saves the file as plain text. (If you use a word processing application, be sure to save the file as a plain ASCII text file without formatting codes.) Here are two text editors to choose from:

• Windows WordPad editor

• SAS Text Editor window such as the PROGRAM EDITOR or NOTEPAD window.

Note: If you use a SAS window to edit your CONFIG.SAS or AUTOEXEC.SAS files, you must restart the SAS System to see the effects of your changes.

This section shows you the basics of using the Windows WordPad editor. If you use the SAS System to edit the SAS start-up files, refer to Chapter 3 for information on using the SAS Text Editor.

Warning: When editing your start-up files, it is important to use an editor that creates plain ASCII files, so no special formatting codes get inserted into the files. If you decide to use an editor other than the ones listed here, be sure to save the file as ASCII text.

Using the Windows WordPad Editor: To open a file in the Windows WordPad editor, click on the **Start** button, then click on **Programs**, then click on **Accessories**. Finally, click on **WordPad**.

Click on **File** in the WordPad menu, then click on **Open**. Type either C:\SAS\CONFIG.SAS or C:\SAS\AUTOEXEC.SAS in the

File name field, and click on **Open**. The file is copied to the WordPad window.

Use your cursor arrow keys and the PageUp and PageDown keys to move to where you want to make your changes. When you have finished editing the file, click on **File** in the WordPad menu, then click on **Save**. Now click on WordPad's Close button to close WordPad.

Making Changes to the CONFIG.SAS File

While the default CONFIG.SAS file that is created when the SAS System is installed may be sufficient for some users, you may need to add or modify option specifications.

There are many required system options in the default CONFIG.SAS file. Unless you are certain of your changes, do not edit the existing option specifications. When you add options, you should not add them in the portion of the file that the SAS System INSTALL utility controls. Figure 8.1 shows the CONFIG.SAS file open in the WordPad editor; add your options above the boxed comment.

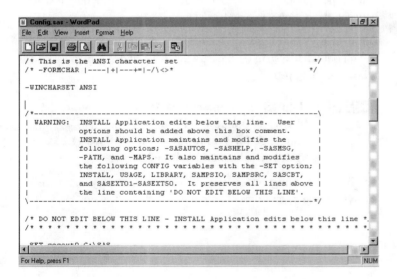

Figure 8.1
CONFIG.SAS File Open in the Windows WordPad Editor

When you have opened the CONFIG.SAS file in the editor of your choice, use the scroll bars or the PageDown key to scroll to the boxed comment shown in Figure 8.1. Click your cursor in the blank line right above the box and press Enter twice. Now type your new option specifications. Precede each option with a hyphen (dash).

System options come in two types—the on/off kind and the kind that take some value. For example, the SPLASH option is an on/off option. It controls whether the SAS System logo and copyright information appears when the SAS System initializes. To suppress the logo (also called the splash screen), specify NOSPLASH.

The FONT option is an example of a system option that takes a value. It controls the screen font used by the SAS System. Here is how these two options might look if you add them to your CON-FIG.SAS file:

```
-NOSPLASH
-FONT 'Sasfont' 12
```

Some options can take both the on/off and value forms. The PRINT option is an example of this kind of option. Notice that for the value-type options, you do not use an equal sign—use only a space between the option name and its value.

Discovering What System Options Are Available: An easy way to find out what system options are available under Windows is to follow this help path:

HelpPath: Help→**SAS companion**→**SAS Companion for Microsoft Windows**→**Features of the SAS Language for Windows System Options**→**List of System Options under Windows**

The list of operating-system-specific options is displayed. To see the syntax and description of an option, click on its name.

For example, Figure 8.2 shows the help available for the SPLASH option.

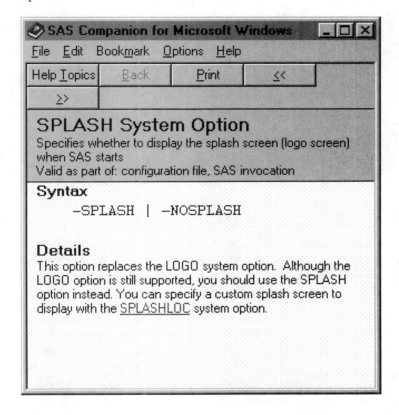

Figure 8.2
Example Help
Window for SAS
System Options

Creating and Editing the AUTOEXEC.SAS File

The AUTOEXEC.SAS file contains SAS programming statements that are executed before your SAS session begins. Use the AUTOEXEC.SAS file to customize and automate your SAS session. Here are some ways to use your AUTOEXEC.SAS file:

- set SAS system options with the OPTIONS statement

- issue windowing commands with the DM statement

- define SAS librefs and filerefs with the LIBNAME and FILE-NAME statements

- perform data processing with DATA and PROC statements

- invoke SAS/AF applications with the AF statement.

For example, suppose your reports need a special line size, and you find yourself creating the same libref every time you invoke the SAS System. You also need to see all your open windows at once. Your AUTOEXEC.SAS file might look like this:

```
options linesize=50;
libname currdata 'c:\saledata\current';
dm 'tile';
```

When your SAS session initializes, the line size is set to 50, the CURRDATA libref is created, and the LOG, PROGRAM EDITOR, and OUTPUT windows are tiled.

No AUTOEXEC.SAS file is created when the SAS System is installed, so you must create it yourself. If you use the Windows WordPad editor, open the editor, then click on **File** in the WordPad menu, then click on **New**. A new document window opens. Type your SAS programming statements in this window.

To save the file, click on **File** in the WordPad menu, then click on **Save As**. When the **Save As** dialog box opens, click on the down arrow next to the **Save as type** field, and click on **Text Document**. Now type C:\SAS\AUTOEXEC.SAS in the **File name** field, and click on **Save**. To close the editor, click on its Close button.

If you or someone else has already created an AUTOEXEC.SAS file, edit it using the same techniques as described for the CON-FIG.SAS file.

Remember to end each statement with a semicolon. There is no size limitation on the AUTOEXEC.SAS file—it can contain as many SAS programming statements as you want.

Some system options are not valid in the OPTIONS statement, and therefore you cannot specify them in the AUTOEXEC.SAS file. The AUTOEXEC.SAS file cannot contain system options that affect the SAS System initialization (such as ALTLOG or SPLASH). If you look up an option in the SAS online help and the

Syntax section lists only the format preceded by a hyphen, that option is not valid in the AUTOEXEC.SAS file. If the syntax lists both the hyphen form and the OPTIONS statement form, you can use that option in the AUTOEXEC.SAS file.

Altering the Properties of the SAS System Icon

When you click on an icon to start an application, Windows uses properties to control how that application behaves. For example, for the SAS System, properties can include what folder to use as the working folder, what system options are used at invocation, and whether the application begins as a normal-sized, maximized, or minimized window.

To change the system options used in the SAS command that starts the SAS System, use the Properties dialog box. To access this dialog box, follow these steps:

1. Right-click on the **Start** button, then click on **Explore**.

2. By default, Windows shows you the contents of the **Start Menu** folder. Double-click on the **Programs** folder in the right half of the window.

3. Double-click on **The SAS System** folder.

4. Right-click on the **SAS System** icon, then click on **Properties**.

5. Click on the **Shortcut** tab.

6. Click in the **Target** field, and use the Backspace and Delete keys to delete any system options you do not want to use; type any new system options after the SAS.EXE. Remember that each system option begins with a hyphen.

7. When you have finished editing the **Target** field, click on **OK**. The next time you click on the **SAS System** icon to start the SAS System, the new system options will be in effect.

Note: This change applies only to the shortcut to the SAS System accessed from the **SAS System** program group. If you have created additional shortcuts to the SAS System (such as on the desktop), you must change each shortcut's properties individually.

Using the Run Dialog Box to Specify SAS System Options

You can use the Run dialog box to specify SAS System options, instead of editing your CONFIG.SAS file or the properties of the **SAS System** icon. This technique is useful when you need the options only occasionally.

To open the Run dialog box, click on the **Start** button, then click on **Run**. Type C:\SAS\SAS.EXE in the **Open** field, followed by whatever system options you want to use for that session. For example, if you do not want to see the SAS logo as the SAS System starts up, type the following in the **Open** field:

```
c:\sas\sas.exe -nosplash
```

Click on **OK** to start the SAS System.

The system options you add to the **Open** field in the Run dialog box are used in conjunction with the options in the CONFIG.SAS file (that is, they do not replace the CONFIG.SAS file).

The **Open** field can contain up to 255 characters, which allows you to specify a fair number of system options. If you need more space than this, put the options in your CONFIG.SAS file instead.

Understanding the Precedence of System Options

Because system options can appear in several places, it is important to know which specifications take precedence:

- An OPTIONS statement in the AUTOEXEC file has the last word and overrides options specified in either the CONFIG.SAS file or the Run dialog box.

- The Run dialog box overrides options set in the CONFIG.SAS file.

For example, if the same option is specified in the CONFIG.SAS file and in the **Open** field of the Run dialog box, the value in the dialog box takes precedence. Or, if the same option is specified in

the CONFIG.SAS file and in an ÒPTIONS statement in the
AUTOEXEC.SAS file, the AUTOEXEC.SAS value is the one used.

Accommodating Multiple Users

HelpPath: Help→SAS companion→SAS Companion for
Microsoft Windows→**Running the SAS System
under Windows**→Getting Started→**Starting the
SAS System**→**Starting from Custom Shortcuts**
or **Program Items**

Sometimes several people use the same PC, and each person may
have a different concept of what the SAS session should look like,
what it should do, and so on. The same problem arises when people
on a network use a single copy of the SAS System.

The answer to this problem lies in setting up CONFIG.SAS and
AUTOEXEC.SAS files for each user. Alternatively, create SAS
System shortcuts for each user. The following sections discuss how
to use each approach.

Creating Start-up Files for Each User: Suppose three people use
the same PC—Nancy, Kurt, and Paulo. Nancy does the sales data
reporting with PROC REPORT, while Kurt uses SAS/GRAPH to
produce monthly sales charts. Paulo, a summer intern, does not
know much about the SAS System, but he is responsible for using a
SAS/AF application to enter weekly sales data into the data sets
that Nancy and Kurt use. These three users have distinct needs, yet
must share the same software. Separate SAS System start-up files
help them use the SAS System efficiently.

Up to this point, the system option file has been called
CONFIG.SAS, and the SAS programming statements file has been
called AUTOEXEC.SAS. While these are the default names, these
files can have any name, as long as you tell the SAS System where
to find them. Here are the steps to creating start-up files for each
user:

1. Use the Windows Explorer to copy the original CONFIG.SAS
   file, located in the SAS folder, to three new files in the same
   folder.

To do this, highlight the original CONFIG.SAS, then click on **Edit→Copy** in the Windows Explorer menu. Now click on **Edit→Paste**. A file named "Copy of CONFIG.SAS" appears in the folder listing. Rename this file to NANFIG.SAS. Now repeat this step to create KURTFIG.SAS and PAULFIG.SAS.

2. Have each user edit their personal configuration files and save them.

3. Have each user create a file with the SAS programming statements they want to have executed each time the SAS System initializes, and save these files with names like AUTONAN.SAS, AUTOKURT.SAS, and AUTOPAUL.SAS.

Continuing with the above example, here is what each file might contain:

AUTONAN.SAS
```
libname sales 'c:\products\saleinfo\qtr4';
libname expense 'c:\products\expinfo\qtr4';
     proc report;
... report-generating statements
```

AUTOKURT.SAS
```
libname sales 'c:\products\saleinfo\qtr4';
proc gplot;
... chart-generating statements
```

AUTOPAUL.SAS
```
libname apps 'c:\products\sasapps';
af apps.product.entry.menu;
```

Now each user has his or her own version of the CONFIG.SAS and AUTOEXEC.SAS files. All that remains is to tell the SAS System which files to use. When Nancy, Kurt, or Paulo invoke the SAS System, they must open the Run dialog box and type the following in the **Open** field:

```
c:\sas\sas.exe -CONFIG C:\SAS\xyzFIG.SAS -AUTOEXEC
C:\SAS\AUTOxyz.SAS
```

where *xyz* is the user's name (NAN, KURT, or PAUL). If the
options are already typed, use the cursor arrow keys to position the
cursor where the changes need to be made, and type the new name
(use the Backspace key, if necessary, to erase extra characters).
Click on **OK** to start the SAS System. The appropriate start-up files
are used.

Creating Copies of the SAS System Icon: Using the Run dialog
box to change the options for an application every time you want to
use it can be cumbersome. Another approach is to create copies of
the SAS System icon, each having its own properties. Each user
can double-click on the SAS System icon he or she needs.

A drawback to this approach is that displaying several icons uses
system resources. If your Windows desktop is pretty cluttered, you
may run out of system resources if you add too many more icons.

When you create a copy of a program icon, it is called a *shortcut*.
To create customized SAS System shortcuts, follow these steps:

1. Right-click on the **Start** button, then click on **Explore**.

2. By default, the Windows Explorer shows you the contents of the
   Start Menu folder—double-click on the **Programs** folder in the
   right half of the window.

3. Double-click on **The SAS System** folder.

4. Right-click on the **SAS System for Windows v6.12** icon, then
   click on **Create Shortcut**. An icon appears named **SAS System
   for Windows v6.12 (2)**. Rename this icon to something descriptive, such as **Nancy's SAS System**.

5. Right-click on the new icon, and click on **Properties**. The
   Properties dialog box appears, as shown in Figure 8.3.

Figure 8.3
Properties Dialog Box for
the New SAS System
Shortcut

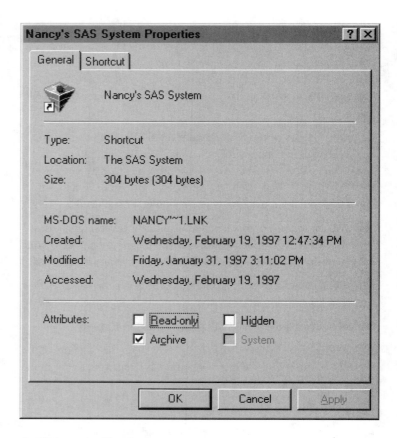

6. Click on the **Shortcut tab**.

7. In the **Target** field, edit the SAS system options to suit the individual user, then click on **OK**.

Create as many shortcuts as you need. Figure 8.4 shows how the SAS System program group might look after you have added Nancy's copy of the SAS System icon.

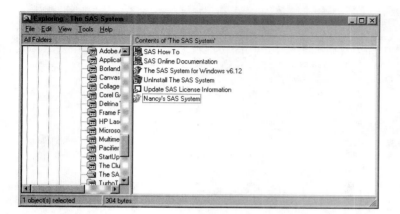

Figure 8.4
SAS System Program
Group with the New SAS
System Shortcut

Relocating Shortcuts: Shortcuts can be moved from their folders to more convenient places. For example, you may want to have the shortcut icons on the desktop so you can start the SAS System without having to click on the **Start** button.

To move a shortcut to the desktop, open the Windows Explorer, double-click on **Programs**, then double-click on **The SAS System**. Click once on the shortcut you want to move, to highlight it. Now use the mouse to drag the shortcut out of the Windows Explorer and onto the desktop. (Resize other applications if necessary, so you can see the desktop.) Release the mouse button when the shortcut is where you want it. Figure 8.5 shows how the Windows desktop might look after dragging the **Nancy's SAS System** shortcut onto the desktop. Double-clicking on the shortcut starts the SAS System.

Figure 8.5
Windows Desktop with the
New SAS System Shortcut

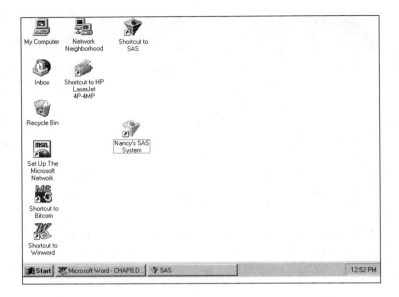

9 | Using Batch Mode

Introduction

While Windows is considered a point-and-click operating system, it does support batch execution of the SAS System. If you are more familiar with a mainframe operating system such as MVS or CMS, the Windows definition of batch is not quite the same as the mainframe definition, at least at the technical level. But for practical purposes, think of them as the same: batch execution under Windows means that you do not see any display manager windows, and the SAS programs you submit run without input from you.

The methods for starting a batch job are numerous. Here are some of the more common methods:

- right-clicking on a SAS program file icon in the Windows Explorer

- dropping a SAS program file icon onto the SAS.EXE file icon

- clicking on the **SAS System** icon

- using the Run dialog box from the **Start** button

- double-clicking on a SAS program file icon in the Windows Explorer

- starting the SAS job from a DOS prompt.

This chapter first helps you decide when to use batch mode and which method of submitting batch jobs is best for you. Then it shows you how to use each of the methods.

At the end of the chapter, you learn how to print from a batch job, control where the logs and output are stored, combine using batch and display manager in one job, and submit more than one batch job at a time. Finally, you learn how to interrupt a batch job.

Note: The "DOS prompt" referred to in this chapter is called the "command prompt" under Windows NT. Other than this difference in terminology, all the examples and explanations are the same for both Windows 95 and Windows NT users.

Understanding How Batch Mode Works

Unlike using display manager, when you submit a batch job you do not interact with the SAS System. When you submit the job, by default you see the SAS System logo appear, followed by the SAS BATCH window, which tells you what program is running and where the log and output files are being stored.

Several system options affect SAS batch processing, including the following:

- NOSPLASH suppresses the SAS logo and copyright screen when the job starts

- ICON minimizes the BATCH window when the job starts.

You can add these and other system options to your CONFIG.SAS file, as described in Chapter 8.

Deciding When to Use Batch Mode

Batch mode helps save system resources by not using windows, tool icons, scroll bars, and so on. If your programs can run without user input, they may run faster and use fewer system resources in batch mode. Another approach to using batch mode is to split your job in two—run the intensive data creation, analysis, sorting, etc. part in batch mode, then run a display manager session, using the SAS files created by the first job, after all the crunch work is finished. Either way, you use the "expensive" (in terms of system resources) windows only when needed.

Deciding How to Start Your Batch Job

Which method you use to submit your SAS batch jobs depends on several factors, including how often you submit batch jobs, whether you submit the same program over and over or run lots of different jobs, and, of course, on personal preferences. Use the decision-making chart in Figure 9.1 to decide which method to use, then read the appropriate section.

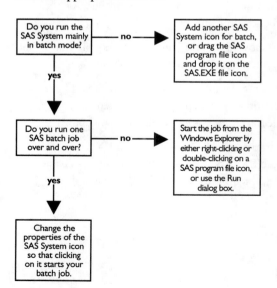

Figure 9.1

Deciding Which Method to Use for Batch Submission

Right-Clicking on a File in the Windows Explorer

Perhaps the easiest way to submit a SAS file in batch mode is to use the Windows Explorer. To submit a batch job in this manner, follow these steps:

1. Open the Windows Explorer by right-clicking on the **Start** button, then clicking on **Explore**.

2. Display the folder that contains the SAS program you want to submit.

3. Right-click on this file, then click on **Batch Submit**.

Dropping a File on the SAS.EXE Icon in the Windows Explorer

Another easy way to submit batch SAS jobs is to drag and drop SAS program icons onto the SAS.EXE file icon in the Windows Explorer. To use this method, follow these steps:

1. Open the Windows Explorer by right-clicking on the **Start** button, then clicking on **Explore**.

2. Display the C:\SAS folder so the SAS.EXE file icon is visible.

3. Open another Windows Explorer window (right-click on the **Start** button and click on **Explore**).

4. In this second Windows Explorer window, display the folder that contains the SAS program file you want to submit.

5. Use the mouse to drag the file icon you want to submit, and drop it on the SAS.EXE icon. For step-by-step instructions, refer to "Dropping File Icons on the SAS.EXE Icon" in Chapter 4.

Note: You cannot drop multiple files on the SAS.EXE icon. See "Submitting Multiple Batch SAS Programs" later in this chapter for information on submitting more than one batch file at a time.

Clicking on the SAS System Icon in the Start Menu

By default, clicking on the **SAS System** icon in the **SAS System** program group begins a display manager SAS session. However, you can add the filename for the SAS program you want to run to the **Target** field of the SAS System's Properties dialog box. Then when you click on the **SAS System** icon, the SAS System runs in batch mode. Because you have to edit the Properties dialog box to run a different program, this method is good for SAS users who run the same batch job over and over.

To use this method, follow these steps:

1. Open the Windows Explorer by right-clicking on the **Start** button, then clicking on **Explore**.

2. By default, the Windows Explorer shows you the contents of the **Start Menu** folder. Double-click on the **Programs** folder in the right half of the window, then double-click on **The SAS System** folder.

3. Right-click on the **SAS System** icon, then click on **Properties**.

4. When the Properties dialog box appears, click on the **Shortcut** tab.

5. Click in the **Target** field, right after the SAS.EXE. Add a space, then type the name of the SAS program you want to submit. For example, Figure 9.2 shows the Properties dialog box with a program named C:\SAS\APPEND.SAS added to the **Target** field.

Figure 9.2
Adding the Program Name
to the Target Field

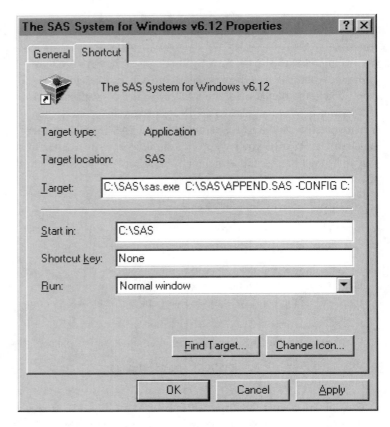

Be sure that the program name is right after the SAS.EXE and before any system options (these start with hyphens).

6. Click on **OK** to close the Properties dialog box. Now when you click on the **SAS System** icon, the APPEND.SAS program is submitted in batch mode.

Note: The program name is not a system option, so it does not need a hyphen, as long as it immediately follows the SAS.EXE portion of the **Target** field contents. If you want to place the program name elsewhere, after some system options, use the SYSIN system option to specify the program name.

Note: These changes apply only to the shortcut to the SAS System accessed from the **SAS System** program group. If you have created other shortcuts (like a shortcut to SAS on the desktop), you must change each shortcut's properties individually.

Creating Additional SAS System Shortcuts: Suppose you want to run both display manager and batch jobs. Or, you run three or four different batch jobs, but you still want to start the SAS System in batch mode by clicking on the **SAS System** icon. If this is the case, add additional **SAS System** shortcuts to the **SAS System** program group.

To add another **SAS System** shortcut to the **SAS System** program group, follow these steps:

1. Open the Windows Explorer by right-clicking on the **Start** button, then clicking on **Explore**.

2. By default, the Windows Explorer shows you the contents of the **Start Menu** folder—double-click on the **Programs** folder in the right half of the window, then double-click on **The SAS System**.

3. Right-click on the **SAS System for Windows v6.12** icon, then click on **Create Shortcut**. An icon appears named **SAS System for Windows v6.12 (2)**. Rename this icon to something descriptive, like **Run the APPEND Procedure in Batch Mode**. (See "Becoming Familiar with the Windows Explorer" in Chapter 1 for information on how to rename a file in the Windows Explorer.)

4. Right-click on the new icon, and click on **Properties**.

5. Click on the **Shortcut** tab.

6. In the **Target** field, add the program name after the SAS.EXE portion of the field.

7. Click on **OK**.

Repeat these steps to create additional shortcuts, giving each a descriptive name and adding the appropriate filename to the **Target** field contents.

A drawback of this approach is that each icon takes up system resources. Adding several SAS System shortcuts to your program group can cause system resource problems in the following situations:

- You are running a PC with minimal RAM (Random Access Memory). For best results, your PC should have at least 16M of RAM.

- You run a lot of applications simultaneously.

- You have a lot of icons on your screen.

If you try this method but get error messages about system memory, shut down all other open applications and try again. If the error messages persist, you should probably try a different approach to running your batch jobs.

Starting Your Batch Job from the Run Dialog Box

The Run dialog box enables you to run any program, without having to click on an icon. Follow these steps to use this method:

1. Click on the **Start** button, then click on **Run**. The Run dialog box appears, as shown in Figure 9.3.

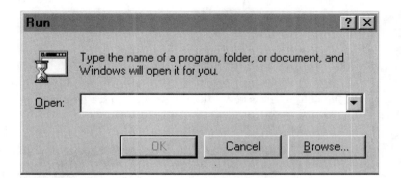

Figure 9.3
Run Dialog Box

2. Type the following in the **Open** field:

>   C:*SAS-folder*\SAS.EXE *your-SAS-program*

For example, if your SAS.EXE file is stored in the C:\SAS folder, and the SAS program you want to submit is C:\SAS\APPEND.SAS, type the following:

>   C:\SAS\SAS.EXE C:\SAS\APPEND.SAS

Add any necessary system options after the program name.

3. Click on **OK**. The program is submitted in batch mode.

Double-Clicking on a File Icon in the Windows Explorer

By default, when you double-click on a SAS program file with an extension of .SAS or .SS2, the SAS System starts in display manager mode. However, you can change the default action so that double-clicking on a SAS program file submits the program in batch mode.

To change the default double-click action for .SAS and .SS2 files, follow these steps:

1. Open the Windows Explorer by right-clicking on the **Start** button, then clicking on **Explore**.

2. Click on **View** in the Windows Explorer menu, then click on **Options**.

3. When the Options dialog box appears, click on the **File Types** tab.

4. Scroll the list of **Registered file types** until you see the entry **SAS System Program**, as shown in Figure 9.4.

Figure 9.4
Finding the SAS System
Program Entry in the
Registered File Types Field

5. Click once on **SAS System Program**, then click on **Edit**.

6. The Edit File Type dialog box appears. In the **Actions** area, click on **Batch Submit**, then click on **Set Default**.

7. If you want to add system options to your batch job, click on **Edit** in the Edit File Type dialog box. If you do not want to change the system options, skip to Step 9.

8. When you click on **Edit** in the Edit File Type dialog box, another dialog box opens, titled "Editing action for type: SAS System Program". In the field labeled **Application used to perform action**, click at the end of the text and add the system options you want (e.g., LINESIZE, MACRO, etc.). When you've finished adding system options, click on **OK**. This returns you to the Edit File Type dialog box.

9. Click on **Close** in the Edit File Type dialog box. This returns you to the Options dialog box.

10. Click on **Close** in the Options dialog box.

The next time you double-click on a SAS program file icon in the Windows Explorer, the program is submitted in batch mode.

Note: Follow similar steps to change the default action for SAS System stored programs (files with an extension of .SS2).

Should you ever want to return to the original default action (which is to start a display manager session and include the file into the PROGRAM EDITOR window), follow the same steps, except choose the **Open** action instead of **Batch Submit** in Step 6.

Starting Your Batch Job from the DOS Prompt

Although Windows 95 and Windows NT do not require the DOS operating system like previous versions of Windows, they do support the DOS prompt for compatibility reasons. If you want to invoke SAS from a DOS prompt, you can.

First, open a DOS window from Windows by clicking on the **Start** button, then on **Programs**, then on **MS-DOS Prompt**. Now type the following command at the DOS prompt:

```
C:\SAS\SAS.EXE batch-program.SAS -CONFIG
C:\SAS\CONFIG.SAS
```

This command must be all on one line when you type it in.

Here is an explanation of the various parts of this command:

- The C:\SAS\SAS.EXE part starts the SAS System.

- *batch-program*.SAS is the name of the SAS program you want to submit.

- Specifying the CONFIG system option enables the SAS System to find your CONFIG.SAS file. Add any other system options after the CONFIG option.

Note: If you do not specify the batch program name immediately after the SAS.EXE portion of the command, you must use the SYSIN system option.

The DOS window you started the SAS System from is "frozen"; that is, you cannot issue any other DOS commands from this DOS window until you close your SAS session. However, you can start other DOS windows (using the **Start** button).

Printing in Batch Mode

When you print in batch mode, you do not have access to the Print and Print Setup dialog boxes. However, you can accomplish many of the same things using system options and the PRINTTO procedure. The following list explains some of the most useful techniques for printing in batch mode:

- Use the LOG and PRINT system options to send the log and procedure output to a printer.

- Use the FILENAME statement and PRINTER keyword to define a fileref that points to a printer. Then, use a FILE statement and that fileref to send DATA step output to a printer.

- Use the PRINTTO procedure to route the log and procedure output to a printer.

- Use the SYSPRINT and SYSPRINTFONT system options to define the default printer and printer font.

Depending on which techniques you use and how you use them, Windows spools your print jobs, or your jobs bypass the Windows printer spooling and go directly to the printer. This section gives three examples of printing in batch mode. Mix and match the techniques used in these examples to fit your own circumstances. If you need more information on one of the system options or on the PRINTTO procedure, refer to the SAS online help.

Understanding Port and Printer Names: Before you begin to print in batch mode, you must understand how Windows printers work.

Printers are connected to "ports" on your computer's CPU. Each port has a name, such as LPT1:, LPT2:, COM1:, or COM2:. Usually, desktop printers are connected to the LPT1: and LPT2: ports.

Along with a port address, a printer has a name. For example, an HP LaserJet 4P printer has the following name:

```
HP LaserJet 4P/4MP
```

To find your printers' names, look in the SAS Print dialog box or in the Control Panel's Printers window. Familiarize yourself with the name of each printer you use, as you need this information when printing in batch mode.

Controlling Whether You Use Windows Print Spooling: In general, the value of the SYSPRINT system option in your CONFIG.SAS file decides whether Windows spools your print jobs.

The SYSPRINT option has the following form:

SYSPRINT *port <printer-name>*

The *port* parameter is required. The *printer-name* parameter is optional, and controls whether Windows spools your print jobs, as follows:

• If you specify only the *port* parameter, print jobs are not spooled—they go directly to the printer.

• If you specify both the *port* and *printer-name* parameters, print jobs are spooled.

• If you do not specify the SYSPRINT option at all, print jobs are spooled.

Here is an example SYSPRINT specification, assuming your printer is an HP LaserJet 4P and is connected to LPT1:

```
-sysprint lpt1: 'HP LaserJet 4P/4MP'
```

Note: The SYSPRINT option is also valid in the OPTIONS statement. In this case, surround both parameters with single quotes and omit the hyphen.

When you bypass print spooling, you do not always get automatic page feeds. If your output is only one page, you may have to press the Off-line key on your printer, then the FormFeed key, then the Off-line key again to cause the page to eject. You may also have to follow this procedure to get the last page of a multipage print job. Usually, if Windows is spooling your print jobs, page feeds are automatic.

Sending the Log and Procedure Output Directly to the Printer Using the LOG and PRINT System Options: Suppose the printer you want to use to print your log and procedure output is connected to the LPT1: port. In addition, you decide you want to send your output directly to the printer (bypassing print spooling). Follow these steps to accomplish this:

1. Add the following options to your CONFIG.SAS file:
```
-log lpt1:
-print lpt1:
```

2. Submit your job.

Note: The log and procedure output are interleaved when you use this technique. If you want the log separate from the procedure output, send them to separate files, then print the files.

Sending DATA Step Output Directly to the Printer: If you want to send DATA step output directly to the printer (bypassing print spooling), follow these steps:

1. Add the SYSPRINT option to your CONFIG.SAS file, specifying only the port parameter for the printer you want to use.

2. Define a fileref using the FILENAME statement and PRINTER keyword, as in the following example:

```
filename myfile printer;
```

3. Submit your DATA step, including a FILE statement that uses the fileref you have defined. For example, the following DATA step prints "This is a test":

```
data _null_;
      file myfile;
      put 'This is a test';
run;
```

4. Submit your program.

Routing Procedure Output to the Printer Using Print Manager:
If you want to use print spooling when you send your procedure output to the printer, follow these steps:

1. Add the SYSPRINT option to your CONFIG.SAS file, specifying both the *port* and *printer-name* parameters for the printer you want to use.

2. Define a fileref using the FILENAME statement and PRINTER keyword, as in the following example:

```
filename myfile printer;
```

3. Add a PROC PRINTTO step before the rest of your code. This step routes the output to the fileref you have defined. Here is an example:

```
proc printto print=myfile new;
run;
```

4. Submit your program.

Controlling the Printer Font in Batch Jobs: If you do not want to use the default typeface in your batch output, use the SYSPRINT-FONT system option.

The simplest form of the SYSPRINTFONT option is as follows:

SYSPRINTFONT *'font-name' <point-size>*

Note: The SYSPRINTFONT option is also valid in the OPTIONS statement.

For example, if you want to use the Courier New font in 14 point, add the following option to your CONFIG.SAS file:

```
-sysprintfont 'Courier New' 14
```

Typeface names are case sensitive; type the font name exactly as it appears in the list of fonts. (Use the SAS Font dialog box to list available fonts.) Remember that only monospace fonts work well with the SAS System—proportional fonts result in misaligned output.

Caution: Once you set the SYSPRINTFONT option in your CONFIG.SAS file, that font and typesize is used, even if you then comment out the SYSPRINTFONT option. If you set the SYSPRINTFONT options with an OPTIONS statement and then end your SAS session, the next time you submit a job, the same font is used.

To return to the default font and point size, specify the following in your CONFIG.SAS file:

```
-sysprintfont 'SAS Monospace' 10
```

Alternatively, submit an OPTIONS statement to reset the SYSPRINTFONT option.

One other method to return to the default font and point size is to delete the WNSPRINT.WINPRINT entry in the SASUSER.PROFILE2 catalog (which is where the font information is stored).

Submitting Multiple Batch SAS Programs

HelpPath: Help→How to→How to... with the SAS System→
Get Started with the SAS System→Submitting
SAS Code→As Multiple Programs in Batch Mode

With display manager mode, you submit several programs at once
by dragging and dropping the file icons onto the LOG window.
There is no correspondingly easy way to submit multiple batch
files—but it is possible.

The basic approach is to create a "dummy" SAS program that contains %INCLUDE statements for each program you want to submit.
Then submit the dummy file as a batch job.

If your dummy program contains only %INCLUDE statements,
however, the logs and output from all the files are written to big
concatenated log and output files. In addition, the logs do not show
the included statements. Therefore, it is usually best to add some
other options and statements to control how the logs and output are
created and stored. These options and statements can be defined in
either the dummy file or in the individual SAS programs that you
include.

Here is an example dummy file that includes two programs and
controls the logs and output. The SOURCE2 system option, specified in the OPTIONS statement, causes the included lines to be listed in the log. The PRINTTO procedure lets you control where the
logs and output are stored.

```
    /* Lists the included program */
    /* code in the log. */
options source2;
    /* Sends log & output to */
    /* PROG1.LOG and PROG1.LST. */
proc printto log='prog1.log'
      print='prog1.lst' new;
    /* Includes the PROG1.SAS */
    /* program. */
```

```
%include 'prog1.sas';
   /* Resets the page number */
   /* for the output file. */
options pageno=1;
   /* Sends log and output */
   /* to PROG2.LOG and PROG2.LST. */
proc printto log='prog2.log'
   print='prog2.lst' new;
   /* Includes the PROG2.SAS */
   /* program. */
%include 'prog2.sas';
```

The SAS BATCH window does not reflect the PROC PRINTTO information. For example, if your dummy file is named BATCH.SAS, the SAS BATCH window indicates that the log and output files are being written to BATCH.LOG and BATCH.LST. However, the BATCH.LST file is never created, and the BATCH.LOG file contains only an abbreviated log. The real logs are in the PROG1.LOG and PROG2.LOG files, as specified in your program.

Understanding Where Batch Logs and Output Go

When you submit a batch SAS job, by default the log and output files are stored in the SAS working folder. Normally, this is the folder that contains the SAS.EXE file. The log and output files have the same filename as the SAS program, with different extensions. The log file has an extension of .LOG, and the output file has an extension of .LST.

For example, if the SAS program you submit is C:\SAS\APPEND.SAS, the log file is C:\SAS\APPEND.LOG and the output file is C:\SAS\APPEND.LST.

Accept these default filenames and locations, or add system options to either the **Target** field in the Properties dialog box or to the CONFIG.SAS file to control where the log and output files are stored. The PRINTTO procedure is also useful when routing the log and output files elsewhere.

Exceptions to the Rule: When you drop a program file icon onto the SAS.EXE icon in the Windows Explorer, the log and output files are created on the desktop for Windows 95. The full pathname for these files is C:\WINDOWS\DESKTOP*filename*.LOG and C:\WINDOWS\DESKTOP*filename*.LST.

Note: The **Desktop** folder is not displayed as a folder in the Windows Explorer. To open this folder in the Windows Explorer, display the contents of the **Windows** folder, then double-click on the **Desktop.grp** icon.

For Windows NT, the log and output files are created in the WINNT folder.

Creating Two Copies of the Log and Output: To create copies of the log and output files, use the ALTLOG and ALTPRINT system options. This technique creates two copies of the log and output files—one in the default place and one in the place you specify. For example, add the following options to your CONFIG.SAS file:

```
-ALTLOG  C:\SASLOGS
-ALTPRINT C:\SASOUT
```

These options tell the SAS System to place one copy of the log and output files in the SAS working folder and one copy in the folders C:\SASLOGS and C:\SASOUT, respectively. The filenames are the same as the SAS program filename, with extensions of .LOG and .LST.

Creating Only One Copy of the Log and Output: If you want only one copy of your log and output files, use the LOG and PRINT system options. For example, adding the following options to your CONFIG.SAS file causes the batch logs and output to be stored in the specified folders:

```
-LOG  C:\SASLOGS
-PRINT C:\SASOUT
```

In this case, no copies of the log and output are stored in the SAS working folder.

Combining Display Manager and Batch Mode

There may be times when the choice between batch mode and a display manager session is a hard one to call—you like to edit your code using display manager, but you like submitting your code in batch. Or, the majority of your program is noninteractive, but you'd really like to view the data with the FSVIEW procedure.

One of the nice features of using the SAS System under Windows is that it allows you this flexibility. The next two sections describe two methods you can use to mix and match display manager and batch sessions at will.

Submitting Batch Jobs from Display Manager: Because Windows 95 and Windows NT support multiple SAS sessions, you can edit your programs using display manager and then submit the finalized code in a separate batch job. Here the basic steps for this approach:

1. Start a display manager SAS session. Open your file into the PROGRAM EDITOR window, and edit it.

2. When the code is finalized, save it.

3. Submit an X statement from your display manager session:

```
x 'c:\sas\sas.exe saved-code';
```

In the X statement, *saved-code* is the full pathname of the file that contains the program you saved. This X statement starts a separate SAS session, running in batch mode. When the batch job is finished, you can examine the log and output from the batch job using your display manager session.

Calling Display Manager from a Batch Job: Sometimes, you want to do the opposite of the previous scenario—that is, start a display manager session from a batch job. This is possible in certain situations. For example, suppose your program first does a lot of number crunching and statistics generating—no windows needed for that. So you save system resources by starting your program in batch mode. But you want to see your data in tabular form, using PROC FSVIEW. When your program calls PROC FSVIEW, it switches to windowing mode.

While you can look at your data and scroll through it, you cannot issue any display manager commands. When you close the FSVIEW window, your program returns to batch mode.

Interrupting a Batch Job

To stop a batch SAS job, make the SAS BATCH window active and click on **Cancel**.

Alternatively, press CTRL-Break. Make sure the SAS BATCH window or the SAS icon (representing the minimized batch job) is active. It may take a few seconds for the BREAK dialog box to appear; do not press CTRL-Break more than once.

Of course, if something goes terribly wrong and your display is frozen, try pressing CTRL-ALT-DEL to end the SAS task or to reboot, as described in "Canceling the Entire SAS Session" in Chapter 4. If the worst has happened, turn off your computer. However, this technique can result in lost or corrupted data, so use it only when absolutely necessary.

Executing DOS Commands and Windows Applications from Your SAS® Session

10

Introduction

Sometimes you may want to issue DOS commands or start another Windows application without leaving your SAS session. To do so, use the X statement from the PROGRAM EDITOR window or the X command from the Command bar. Alternatively, click on the DOS session icon on the tool bar, which starts a full-screen DOS session.

The following sections describe the details of using each technique, as well as two SAS system options that affect DOS commands you issue from your SAS session. This chapter also discusses how to add an application name to the SAS System **File** menu.

Note: The "MS-DOS prompt" referred to in this chapter is called the "command prompt" under Windows NT. Other than this difference in terminology, all the examples and explanations are the same for both Windows 95 and Windows NT users.

Understanding How DOS Commands Are Executed by the SAS System

Unless you specify a folder with your DOS command, the command is executed in the SAS working folder. This is usually the folder in which the SAS.EXE file is stored, unless you have changed the working folder with the Change Folder dialog box.

For example, if you submit the DOS command, DIR, which lists all the files in a folder, you see the contents of the SAS working folder. If you want to see the contents of the root folder, C:, you must specify that folder in the command: DIR C:\. Remember, to change the working folder, click on the working folder icon in the lower-right corner of the SAS AWS. For more details, see "Changing the SAS Working Folder" in Chapter 3.

Using the X Statement and X Command

HelpPath: Help→**SAS companion**→**SAS Companion for Microsoft Windows**→**Running the SAS System under Windows**→**Getting Started**→**Running DOS or Windows Commands from within SAS**, then choose a topic

Help→**How to**→**How to... with the SAS System**→**Use the SAS System with Other Applications**→**Running Other Programs from within SAS**→**Invoking a DOS or Windows Command from within a SAS Program** or **Exiting Your SAS Session Temporarily**

The X statement is a SAS programming statement and can be submitted in any SAS program under Windows. The X command is a display manager command that serves the same purpose as the X statement.

You can use the X statement and X command to issue DOS commands and to start other Windows applications. The following discussion uses the X statement in the examples; however, the syntax and examples are identical for the X command (except that display manager commands are not followed by a semicolon).

The syntax of the X statement to issue a DOS command is as follows:

X '*DOS-command*';

If the DOS command contains no spaces, you can omit the single quotes. Here is an example that tells DOS to display the contents of the C:\SAS\SASUSER folder:

```
x 'dir c:\sas\sasuser';
```

Sometimes, you may want to start a Windows application (such as Microsoft Word) without leaving your SAS session. (An example of when this is useful is in the discussion of Dynamic Data Exchange in Chapter 11.)

To start a Windows application, use the following syntax:

X '*Windows-executable*';

Here is an example that starts Microsoft Word:

```
x 'c:\winword\winword.exe';
```

When you submit the X statement, the screen displays the results of the DOS command (such as a folder listing), and you are prompted to press any key to return to your SAS session. If the X statement invokes another Windows application, that application appears on top of your SAS session, ready for input.

Using the X Statement and X Command with No Parameters:
You can execute the X statement or X command without any parameters. That is, submit

```
X;
```

When you submit this statement, a full-screen DOS session is started. You can work as long as you like in the DOS session, issuing DOS commands. To return to your SAS session, type EXIT at the DOS prompt and press Enter.

While the default behavior is to start a full-screen DOS session, you can change the DOS session to a windowed session (one that does not take up the whole display) by pressing ALT-Enter. Pressing ALT-Enter again toggles the session back to full-screen.

The default folder for the DOS session is the SAS working folder. Use the DOS CD (change folder) command to switch to another folder.

Note: You cannot use your SAS session until you close the DOS session. However, you can use ALT-ESC, ALT-TAB, or CTRL-ESC to return to Windows to work in other applications while the DOS session started from your SAS session is still active. To return to the DOS session, click on the **MS-DOS Prompt** button in the Task Bar.

Clicking on the DOS session icon on the tool bar is equivalent to issuing the X statement or X command with no parameters. That is, it starts a full-screen DOS session, with a default folder of the SAS working folder. Type EXIT at the DOS prompt and press Enter to return to your SAS session.

Controlling How the X Statement and X Command Work

HelpPath: Help→SAS companion→SAS Companion for Microsoft Windows→Features of the SAS Language for Windows→System Options→List of System Options under Windows→XWAIT or XSYNC

Two SAS system options affect how the X statement and X command work. These two system options are XWAIT and XSYNC.

Making a DOS Session Automatically Return to Your SAS Session: The XWAIT option controls whether you have to press a key to return to your SAS session when you issue a DOS command from your SAS session.

By default, if you execute a DOS command via the X statement or command, you have to press a key to return to your SAS session. If you do not want to press a key, that is, you want the command to execute and then immediately return you to your SAS session, set this option to NOXWAIT.

To set the XWAIT option, issue an OPTIONS statement from the PROGRAM EDITOR window. Here is a sample OPTIONS statement:

```
options noxwait;
```

After you submit this statement, any time you execute a DOS command using the X statement or command, you do not have to press a key to return to your SAS session. The DOS screen still appears but flashes by fairly quickly. If you want to read the results of your DOS command, do not specify NOXWAIT.

Note: Setting the XWAIT system option with the OPTIONS statement affects only the current SAS session. If you want to permanently set the XWAIT system option, edit your CONFIG.SAS file, as described in Chapter 8.

Starting an Autonomous DOS Session or Application: The XSYNC option controls whether you can use your SAS session while the DOS session or other Windows application is active. By default, you cannot do anything in your SAS session until you type EXIT at the DOS prompt or close the Windows application that you started with the X statement or command. If you want to be able to use your SAS session while the DOS session or Windows application is still active, set this option to NOXSYNC.

Note: If your SAS program needs the results of an X statement or command before continuing, do not use NOXSYNC; if you do, your program continues to run before the results of the X statement or command are available. This may generate error messages or incorrect results.

To set the XSYNC option, issue an OPTIONS statement from the PROGRAM EDITOR window. Here is a sample OPTIONS statement:

```
options noxsync;
```

After you submit this statement, any time you execute a DOS command or start another Windows application using the X statement or command, your SAS session is still active.

Note: Setting the XSYNC system option with the OPTIONS statement affects only the current SAS session. If you want to permanently set the XSYNC system option, edit your CONFIG.SAS file, as described in Chapter 8.

Adding Applications to the File Menu

`HelpPath:` Help→**SAS companion**→**SAS Companion for Microsoft Windows**→**Running the SAS System under Windows**→**Using Graphical Interface Features of the SAS System**→**Customizing Your SAS Session**→**Customizing Your SAS Session with System Options**→**Adding Applications to the File Menu**

If you find yourself consistently needing to start another Windows application (such as Microsoft Word or Lotus 1-2-3) from your SAS session, you may want to add the application's name to the **File** menu in the SAS System, so that all you have to do is click on **File** and then on the application's name to start it.

To add an application to the **File** menu, use the REGISTER system option in your CONFIG.SAS file. The syntax of the REGISTER system option is as follows:

REGISTER '*menu-text*' '*command*' < '*working-folder*'>

- *menu-text* is the text you want displayed in the **File** menu.

- *command* is the DOS command that starts the application.

- *working-folder* is optional and specifies a working folder for the application. (Some applications require a working folder specification, others do not; read your application documentation for more information.)

For example, to start Microsoft Word, you might add the following to your CONFIG.SAS file:

```
-REGISTER 'Microsoft Word' 'C:\WINWORD\WINWORD.EXE'
```

Figure 10.1 shows the resulting **File** menu.

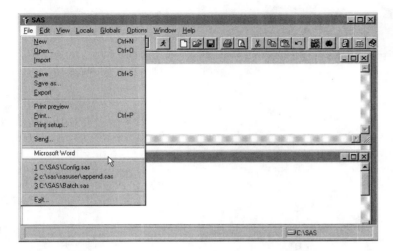

Figure 10.1
File Menu with the MS
Word Application Added

You can add up to eight applications to the SAS System **File** menu.

Sharing Data between Your SAS® Session and Other Windows Applications

11

Introduction

One of the biggest advantages of working under Windows is that many different applications can share data. For example, you can transfer PROC TABULATE output to a Microsoft Word file or bring spreadsheet data into a SAS data set.

There are many ways of sharing data between the SAS System and other Windows applications; this chapter demonstrates the fundamental aspects of data sharing using four methods:

- cut-and-paste

- SAS Import/Export Wizard

- Dynamic Data Exchange (DDE)

- Object Linking and Embedding (OLE).

More information is available in some of the books listed in the "Welcome to the SAS System for Windows" section at the beginning of this book. The discussions and examples in this chapter use the following software:

- Excel

- Microsoft Word for Windows (version 6)

- Microsoft Paint

- Corel Gallery 2.

Data sharing works with many software packages. So, if you do not have the software the examples use, you can still use the examples as a starting point; but you cannot use them exactly as written.

Deciding Which Method to Use

Each data sharing technique discussed in this chapter has its advantages and disadvantages, times when it is useful and times when it is not. To begin, here are some brief definitions of each technique:

- cut-and-paste lets you use the Windows Clipboard to transfer data between two applications. It preserves rich text formatting (RTF); you can use this method to transfer text and graphics. This is a manual method, in that you must mark and copy the object in the source application, then paste the object into the target application. Cut-and-paste is a static method—once the data is pasted in, any changes in the original file do not affect the pasted copy.

- The SAS Import/Export Wizard helps you import files (such as a spreadsheet) into the SAS System or export a SAS data set to another format (such as a database or comma-delimited file). Like cut-and-paste, the data transfer is not dynamic (if the original data change, the change is not reflected in the imported or exported copy).

- Dynamic Data Exchange (DDE) lets Windows applications programmatically share text-based data (e.g., between the SAS System and a spreadsheet). For the SAS System, this method usually uses the FILENAME statement and DATA steps. This method is fairly automatic, and you can create a dynamic link between the SAS System and the other application.

- Object Linking and Embedding (OLE) lets Windows applications share "objects," which are a combination of data (including graphics, sound files, videos, and so on) and the functionality needed to work with that data. The examples in this chapter use OLE with SAS/AF software FRAME entries. SAS/EIS software also supports OLE.

Consider the following when choosing a data-sharing method:

- All Windows applications support cut-and-paste.

- The SAS Import/Export Wizard supports many file types, including comma-delimited files, tab-delimited files, or user-formatted files.

- For you to use either DDE or OLE, both applications—the "sender" and "receiver" (or, in computer terms, the server and the client)—must support the data sharing method.

When designing your data sharing applications, check your other applications' documentation to see if they support the data-sharing technique you want to use. Also, use Table 11.1 to choose a method that meets your needs.

METHOD	SUPPORTS TEXTUAL DATA	SUPPORTS GRAPHICS	CAN BE DYNAMIC
cut-and-paste	X	X	
Import/Export	X		
DDE	X		X
OLE	X	X	X

Table 11.1
Choosing a Data-Sharing Method

Using Cut-and-Paste

HelpPath: Help→How to→How to... with the SAS System→Using the SAS System with Other Applications →Moving Information between the SAS System and Other Applications, then select a topic

Cut-and-paste is probably the simplest data sharing method.

To copy text or graphics, mark the text or graphic in the source application (such as Microsoft Word or Excel). Click on **Edit,** then click on **Copy** in the source application's menu (if you want to delete the text or graphic from the source application, use **Cut** instead of **Copy**). This transfers the data to the Windows Clipboard.

Now click in the SAS window into which you want to paste the text or graphic (such as the PROGRAM EDITOR, SOURCE, or the GRAPH window). Click on **Edit** in the SAS System main menu, then on **Paste** (or press CTRL-V).

Of course, you can also cut or copy text and graphics in the SAS System, and paste them into other applications.

Note: In order to paste graphics into the SAS System (such as into the GRAPH window or into a Graphic entry in a SAS/AF application), you must have access to SAS/GRAPH software.

When cutting and pasting text, RTF attributes (such as font, type size, and highlighting attributes such as underlining) are preserved when you copy from the SAS System to another application, provided the target application supports RTF. When you copy text from another application to the SAS System, such formatting is lost.

Note: You can paste text only into SAS windows that support text input, such as the PROGRAM EDITOR, NOTEPAD, and SOURCE windows.

For more information on cutting and pasting, as well as drag and drop (which is another method of cutting and pasting), see Chapter 3.

Using the SAS Import/Export Wizard

FasTip: File→Import or File→Export

HelpPath: Help→SAS System→What's New in Release 6.12→What's New in Base SAS→Import/Export Facility Wizard

Also, use the **Help** button in the Import/Export Wizard

The SAS Import/Export Wizard is a handy method of converting data from one format to another. For example, using the Import Wizard, you can bring a tab-delimited set of data from a Word document into the SAS System as a SAS data set. Or, using the Export Wizard, you can convert a SAS data set into an Excel spreadsheet or PC File Formats file (a database file).

To access the Import/Export Wizard, click on **File** in the SAS System main menu, then on **Import** or **Export**. The Import/Export Wizard is also available from other portions of the SAS System, such as the SQL Query window and SAS/ASSIST software.

Note: To use the Import/Export Wizard with database files, you must license SAS/ACCESS software.

Suppose you have a set of data about vegetables in a tab-delimited Excel file. The data is separated by tabs and looks like this:

```
Vegetable Germination    Zone
corn      1 week   all
eggplant  2 weeks  7 and above
beans   4 days   all
carrots  10 days   all
```

To convert this data into a SAS data set using the Import Wizard, follow these steps:

1. Click on **File** in the SAS System main menu, then on **Import.**
   The Import Wizard appears, as shown in Figure 11.1.

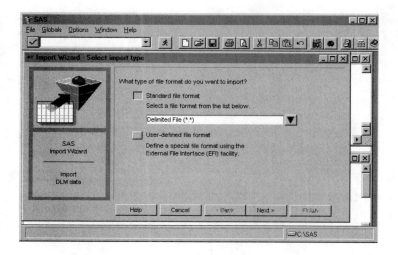

Figure 11.1
Import Wizard -
Import data Screen

2. Because your file is tab-delimited, click on the down arrow next to the **Standard file format** field, and click on **Tab Delimited File (*.txt)**. Now click on **Next**, to display Figure 11.2.

Figure 11.2
Import Wizard - Select file
Screen

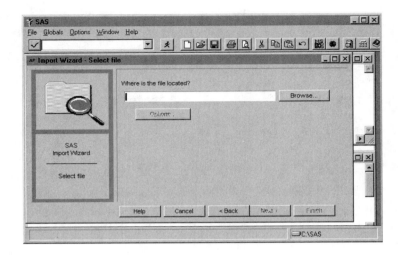

3. Type the name of the Excel file in the text-entry field. For example, the filename might be C:\VEG.TXT.

Once you type the filename into the text-entry field, you can click on the **Options** button to set the import options. Figure 11.3 shows a sample Delimited File Options dialog box.

Figure 11.3
Delimited File Options
Dialog Box for the Import
Wizard

Once you've set the options, click on **OK**, then click on **Next** in the **Select file** screen to progress to Figure 11.4.

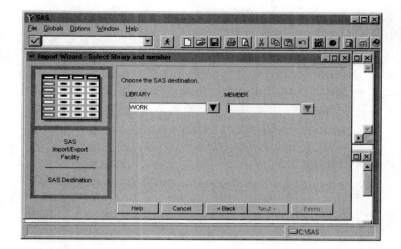

Figure 11.4
Import Wizard - SAS
Destination Screen

Click on the down arrow next to the **LIBRARY** field, and click on
the SAS data library you want to store the new SAS data set in.
Then, type the name of the new member in the **MEMBER** field.
For example, you might select SASUSER as the data library, and
give the data set a member name of VEGGIES.

Once you've selected the library and member name, click on
Finish. The new data set is created.

You might want to scan the SAS log after the Import Wizard is finished, to see if the data set creation went as you expected. Also, you
may want to print the data set to see if it was created properly. For
example, Figure 11.5 shows the PROC PRINT output for the data
set created in this example.

Figure 11.5
PROC PRINT Output for
the New Data Set

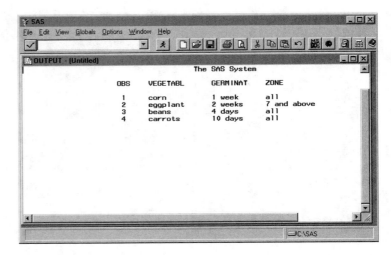

The SAS Export Wizard works very similarly to the Import Wizard—simply follow the instructions on the screen, and use the **Help** button if you need help on a particular screen.

Understanding Dynamic Data Exchange (DDE)

HelpPath: Help→SAS companion→SAS Companion for Microsoft Windows→Using SAS with Other Windows Applications→Using Dynamic Data Exchange, then choose a topic

Help→How to→How to... with the SAS System→Use the SAS System with Other Applications→Using Dynamic Data Exchange→ Reading Data from Another Application

Using DDE with the SAS System requires a FILENAME statement that sets up a fileref for the specific data you want to transfer (either from the SAS System to the other application or from the other application to the SAS System). For DDE, the syntax of the FILENAME statement is as follows:

FILENAME *fileref* DDE 'DDE-*triplet*|CLIPBOARD'
    <*DDE-options*>;

Here is an explanation of the components of this form of the FILE-NAME statement:

- *fileref* can be any valid fileref for the SAS System.

- DDE is a required keyword that tells the SAS System you are using DDE.

- *DDE-triplet* or CLIPBOARD tells the SAS System exactly what data you want to transfer. Think of the DDE triplet as the ID for the data. Each unique set of data has a unique ID.

- *DDE-options* are one or more options that control how the data exchange is handled. For example, the NOTAB option is useful when you want to transfer data that does not contain tabs between values.

Specifying the DDE Triplet: When you specify CLIPBOARD in the FILENAME statement, the SAS System looks at the data stored in the Clipboard and determines the DDE triplet for you. The only step you have to do is to copy the data you want to transfer to the Clipboard. To do this, highlight the data in the other Windows application, click on **Edit** in the application's menu, then click on **Copy**. Now return to your SAS session to submit the FILENAME statement.

But sometimes the SAS System cannot find the DDE triplet using the Clipboard; in these cases (e.g., with Microsoft Word), you must specify the DDE triplet directly.

To specify the DDE triplet directly, you must know three things about the application you are writing data to or reading data from:

- the name of the executable file for the application

- the name of the file you want to access (worksheet, document, etc.)

- how to refer to the access point in the file (rows/columns, book-marks, etc.).

This information is separated by special characters, as follows:

executable-file|data-file!access-point

The executable file is always followed by a vertical bar, while the name of the data file is always followed by an exclamation point.

Here are three examples of DDE triplets, and an explanation of each:

`123w|august.wk4!a:a1..a:f5`

> `123w` is the name of the Lotus 1-2-3 executable file.
>
> `august.wk4` is the name of the Lotus 1-2-3 file you want to access.
>
> `a:a1..a:f5` refers to worksheet A and the row/column range A1 through F5.

`winword|august.doc!bookmk1`

> `winword` is the name of the Microsoft Word executable file.
>
> `august.doc` is the name of the Word document you want to access.
>
> `bookmk1` is the name of the bookmark in the Word file that marks the place in the document you want to access.

`excel|sheet1!r5c1:r27c3`

> `excel` is the name of the Excel executable file.
>
> `sheet1` refers to the Excel file that contains the data you want to access.
>
> `r5c1:r27c3` refers to rows 5 to 27, columns 1 to 3.

If you want to use DDE with another application, you must figure out how files are named and how you reference the exact place in the file you want to access. But once you determine how one type of DDE triplet is formed (e.g., for spreadsheets or word processing documents), you can almost guess the triplet for another application of the same type.

If you do not want to use the CLIPBOARD keyword but are not sure of the format of the DDE triplet, use the Clipboard to help you determine the triplet. First, copy some data from the other application to the Clipboard. Now, click on **Options** in the SAS System main menu, then click on **DDE triplet**. The DDE Triplet in Clipboard dialog box shows you the triplet. Press CTRL-C to copy the DDE triplet to the Clipboard, then press CTRL-V to paste it into your FILENAME statement.

DDE Example 1—Reading Data from Microsoft Word: Here is an example of reading data from Microsoft Word using DDE. The online help and SAS Institute documentation contain many other examples. For DDE to work between the SAS System and Microsoft Word, you must define bookmarks in your Word document at each place you want to read or write data. Then, you submit a FILENAME statement for each bookmark. Also, Word must be running and the document must be open when you access it via DDE from your SAS session.

This example uses a Word document named AUGUST.DOC. It contains data about a company's billing for August. In the document, a bookmark named NUMBER marks the invoice number, and a bookmark named CLIENT marks the client's name. The SAS program reads the information at each of these bookmarks and prints them in the OUTPUT window.

Here is the code for this example:

```
    /* Define the filerefs for the two bookmarks. */
    /* The NOTAB option is necessary so the */
    /* SAS System does not expect tabs */
    /* between variables. */
filename number dde 'winword|august.doc!number'
         notab;
filename client dde 'winword|august.doc!client'
         notab;
    /* Associate the libref INVOICE with */
    /* the folder C:\SAS\INVOICES. */
libname invoice 'c:\sas\invoices';
    /* Create the data set INVOICE.AUGUST, */
    /* read the information at the two */
    /* bookmarks, and store the data in variables. */
data invoice.august;
    /* Set the variable length to an */
    /* arbitrary number. */
length invnum $45 invclnt $45;
    /* Get ready to read the first bookmark. */
```

```
        infile number;
           /* Read the invoice number as a */
           /* character variable. */
        input invnum $;
           /* Get ready to read the second bookmark. */
           /* Because the data include spaces, use some */
           /* other arbitrary character as the */
           /* delimiter. */
        infile client dlm='@';
           /* Read the client as a character variable. */
        input invclnt $;
run;

   /* Print the output. */
proc print;
run;
```

DDE Example 2—Opening and Closing a Word Document:
Because you must have all the documents open before submitting your DDE code, you may want to have your SAS program open the documents for you. You accomplish this using the special keyword SYSTEM in the DDE triplet, which enables you to send commands to another application.

In this example, the null DATA step sends the appropriate file-open command to Word. Word must be running before you submit this code.

```
filename cmds dde 'winword|system';
data _null_;
   file cmds;
   put
'[FileOpen.Name="c:\invoices\august.doc"]';
run;
```

(This example does not start Word itself—see the next example for how to do that.)

When your program is finished, you may want to close the document and close Word. The following code accomplishes this (assuming the fileref CMDS is still active):

```
data _null_;
   file cmds;
      /* Close the active Word document. */
   put '[FileClose]';
   put '[FileExit]'; /* Close Word. */
run;
```

If you have more than one file open, you can use a DO loop to close all the files, then close Word.

The syntax of the commands is totally application dependent. For example, Excel has different commands to open a file than Word does. A good way to determine the commands that your application accepts is to use the application's macro recorder. For example, to determine Word's file-open command, turn on the macro recorder and open a file. Then look at the text of the macro you generated. Usually, commands sent via DDE are enclosed in square brackets.

DDE Example 3—Starting Word from Your SAS Session: In Example 2, you had to start Word manually, before you submitted your SAS program. Your SAS program can start an application by using the X statement. The X statement is not part of DDE but is useful in DDE programs. For example, the following statement starts Word:

```
x 'c:\winword\winword.exe';
```

Before using the X statement to start another Windows application, submit an OPTIONS statement to specify NOXSYNC. Otherwise, your SAS session is unusable until you close the other Windows application. Also, because it takes awhile for the other Windows application to start up, you may want to submit a null DATA step and the SLEEP function after the X statement to pause your SAS program long enough for the application to get ready.

The following code sets the NOXSYNC option, starts Word, and pauses the SAS System for 15 seconds:

```
options noxsync;
x 'c:\winword\winword.exe';

data _null_;
   x=sleep(15);
run;
```

Refer to Chapter 10 for more information on using the X statement.

DDE Example 4—Putting it All Together: Here is the entire program to start Word, read some data from it, close the file, then close Word.

```
   /* Let Word and your SAS session run */
   /* independently of each other. */
options noxsync;

x 'c:\winword\winword.exe'; /* Start Word. */

data _null_;
   x=sleep(15); /* Pause for 15 seconds. */
run;

   /* Set up a DDE fileref to send commands to Word. */
filename cmds dde 'winword|system';

   /* Define the filerefs for the two bookmarks. */
   /* The NOTAB option is necessary so the */
   /* SAS System does not expect tabs between */
   /* variables. */
filename number dde 'winword|august.doc!number' notab;
filename client dde 'winword|august.doc!client' notab;

   /* Associate the libref INVOICE with */
   /* the folder C:\SAS\INVOICES. */
libname invoice 'c:\sas\invoices';

data _null_;
   file cmds;
      /* Open the Word doc. */
   put '[FileOpen.Name = "C:\INVOICES\AUGUST.DOC"]';
run;
```

```
/* Create the data set INVOICE.AUGUST, */
/* read the information at the two */
/* bookmarks, and store the data in variables. */
data invoice.august;
      /* Set the variable length to an */
      /* arbitrary number. */
   length invnum $45 invclnt $45;
      /* Get ready to read the first bookmark. */
   infile number;
      /* Read the invoice number as a character */
      /* variable. */
input invnum $;
      /* Get ready to read the second bookmark. */
      /* Because the data include spaces, use some */
      /* other arbitrary character as the */
      /* delimiter. */
   infile client dlm='@';
      /* Read the client as a character variable. */
   input invclnt $;
run;

proc print; /* Print the output. */
run;

data _null_;
   file cmds;
      /* Close the active Word document. */
   put '[FileClose]';
   put '[FileExit]'; /* Close Word. */
run;
```

Understanding Object Linking and Embedding (OLE)

HelpPath: Help→SAS companion→SAS Companion for
Microsoft Windows→Using SAS with Other
Windows Applications→Using OLE in SAS/AF
Software, then choose a topic

**Help→How to→How to... with the SAS
System→Use Special Features for SAS/AF
Programmers→Using Object Linking and
Embedding (OLE)**, then choose a topic

**Help→SAS companion→SAS Companion for
Microsoft Windows→Appendices→OLE Custom
Controls Provided with the SAS System and SCL
Methods for Automating OLE Objects**

Like DDE, Object Linking and Embedding (OLE) is a way of sharing data between Windows applications. But OLE is more flexible
and powerful than DDE. While this chapter does not explain or
illustrate all aspects of using OLE with the SAS System, it does
provide enough information to get you started.

Note: OLE is not simple to use. By the time you understand OLE
and have followed the examples, you will no longer be a "Windows
neophyte."

Using OLE with the SAS System requires SAS/AF or SAS/EIS
software. However, once you've created the application, it can be
run by users who do not have SAS/AF or SAS/EIS software
installed. This chapter illustrates creating a SAS/AF application; the
procedures are similar for creating SAS/EIS applications.

With OLE, you store "objects" in your SAS/AF application. Each
object represents not only data but also how to work with that data.
For example, if you place a Word document in your SAS/AF application, the SAS/AF application does not store the text—it stores
information about the Word document and about how to retrieve
that document. With OLE, you can share anything that is "data" in
its widest sense: graphics, sound files, text files, video clips, spreadsheets, and so on.

In OLE parlance, your SAS/AF application is the client (or "container") application—it stores the object. The application that created the object is called the OLE server.

Understanding Linked Objects: "Linking" refers to creating a dynamic connection between an object in your SAS/AF application and that object's OLE server.

An example helps demonstrate this. Suppose you want to display a Microsoft Word text file in your SAS/AF application. You could cut and paste the text into the application. But that is a one-way process—if you change the text in your SAS/AF application after you cut and paste the text, the changes are not reflected in the original Word document. Or, if you edit the original file, the changes are not visible in the SAS/AF application.

But if you use OLE to link the text file to your application, you can edit the file by clicking on its image in your SAS/AF application, or you can edit the file by bringing up Word and editing the file from there. In either case, the changes are visible on the other end of the link.

In technical terms, the Word file is a "linked object," and the location and size of the object is stored with your SAS/AF application. (This information is called metadata and is like a map.) The actual data (the text) is not stored in the SAS/AF application.

Understanding Embedded Objects: "Embedding" an object differs from linking, in that the connection between an embedded object and the object's OLE server is not dynamic. You can edit the object only from your SAS/AF application. If you change the original file, the changes are not visible in the SAS/AF application. With embedding, both the object and its data are stored with the SAS/AF application.

Embedded objects come in two types: static and nonstatic.

- Static objects appear in the SAS/AF application, but you cannot edit them. These objects are useful in applications where you are providing information that you do not want people to change (for example, a picture).

- Nonstatic objects can be edited by the SAS/AF application user, usually by double-clicking on the object's representation in the FRAME entry. This type of object is useful in applications where you want the user to either be able to edit the object or at least have access to the application that created the object.

Understanding OLE Verbs: Every OLE object (except static embedded objects, which are really pictures) supports one or more actions, called *OLE verbs*. For example, a Word OLE object supports the Edit verb, while a sound file supports two verbs: Play and Edit. These verbs are defined by the OLE server application. There is always a default verb for an object—to activate the object with the default verb, you double-click on the object's icon in your SAS/AF application.

Understanding Visual versus Open Editing: Another OLE concept you need to understand is "visual editing" versus "open editing." Visual editing is available only with applications that support OLE 2.0. Visual editing means that when you edit an OLE object in your SAS/AF application, you edit that object from the SAS window—another window does not need to open. All the tools from the application that created the OLE object are available to you in the SAS window (menus, tool bars, etc.) Only the **File** and **Window** menus are maintained by the client application (in this case, the SAS/AF application). Visual editing is the default action for embedded objects.

Open editing means that when you edit an OLE object, the object's server is launched in its own window instead of sharing the client's window. Open editing is the default action for linked objects.

Adding OLE Objects to Your SAS/AF Application—An Overview: The first step to using OLE in your SAS/AF applications is to use the BUILD procedure to create a catalog. Then, within this catalog, create entries—in particular, FRAME entries to hold OLE objects. Next, add OLE objects to the FRAME entry. Remember, to use the BUILD procedure, you must have SAS/AF software.

The following two examples walk you through creating two SAS/AF applications using OLE. The examples assume you know a little bit about SAS/AF software and the BUILD procedure, but you do not need to be an expert.

There are two levels of OLE—OLE 1.0 and OLE 2.0. The SAS System supports both levels—other applications you may be using may support only OLE 1.0 (check your application's documentation). If this is the case, you may be able to use only a subset of the

OLE capabilities of the SAS System. Both these examples use only features supported by OLE 1.0. More complicated examples illustrating OLE 2.0 features are included in SAS Institute documentation.

Note: OLE takes up a lot of system resources and RAM. It is possible to run out of RAM when loading large pictures and files. If you are using OLE extensively, you should probably have at least 16M of RAM, and 32M is even better.

Example 1—Using Embedded Objects: You teach driver's education, and you are creating an online study application for students. The application displays road signs and their meanings. The students look at each screen to learn the sign, then progress to the next screen. This example uses embedded objects.

1. To begin, use the BUILD procedure to create the catalog for your application. In this example, the catalog is stored in the SASUSER data library; you can use any existing data library. Submit the following statements from the PROGRAM EDITOR window:

```
proc build cat=sasuser.traffic;
run;
```

The BUILD: DIRECTORY window appears, as shown in Figure 11.6.

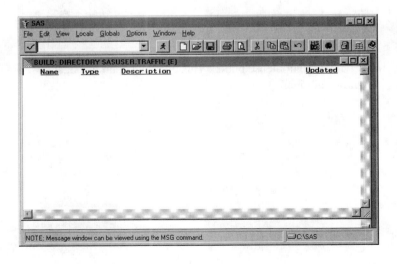

Figure 11.6
BUILD: DIRECTORY Window

2. Place the picture of the road sign in the Clipboard. Do this by opening your graphics package, opening the sign's file, then copying it to the Clipboard. (This is usually done by clicking on **Edit**, then clicking on **Copy** in the graphics package's main menu.)

3. Once the Clipboard contains the sign's image, you're ready to create the FRAME entry. Issue the following command from the Command bar:

```
EDIT SIGN1.FRAME
```

The BUILD: DISPLAY window appears, as shown in Figure 11.7.

Figure 11.7
BUILD: DISPLAY Window

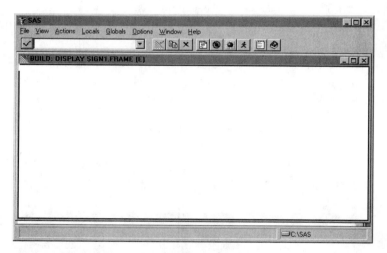

4. Click the right mouse button. This opens a popup menu, as shown in Figure 11.8.

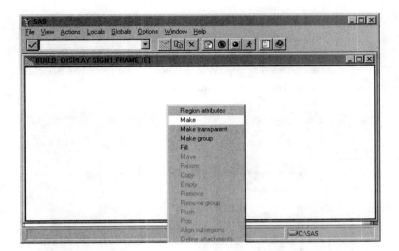

Figure 11.8
Popup Menu in the BUILD:
DISPLAY Window

5. Click on **Make**. This opens the Selection List. Repeatedly click on the down arrow in the vertical scroll bar until you see **OLE - Paste Special**. Click on this line, then click on **OK**. A dotted box (called a region) appears with a hand inside it, as shown in Figure 11.9.

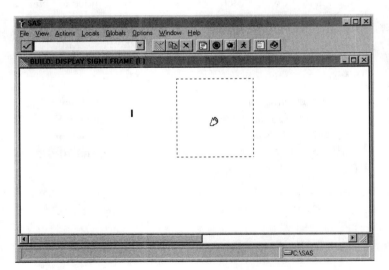

Figure 11.9
Region Ready for
Placement

6. Move the mouse around (do not click) until the box is centered horizontally and in the upper third of the screen. (This leaves enough space for the text that describes the sign.) Now click the left mouse button. The region is positioned and the Paste Special dialog box appears, as shown in Figure 11.10.

Figure 11.10
Paste Special Dialog Box

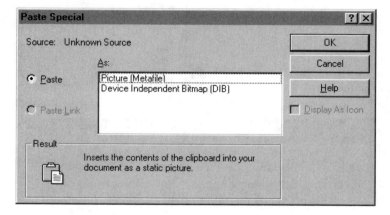

If you click at the wrong time and the region is not where you want it, don't worry. Step #9 shows you how to move regions.

7. To create an embedded object, make sure the **Paste** option is selected, not **Paste Link**. In Figure 11.10, the **Paste Link** option is grayed out because the source of the graphic (Corel Gallery 2, version 2.0 in this case) does not support OLE.

Choose the format of the graphic in the **As** field. In Figure 11.10, the **Metafile** format is chosen. If you plan to share your SAS/AF application across computer systems (such as Windows and OS/2), you may want to choose the **Device Independent Bitmap** format.

8. Once the options are set to your satisfaction, click on **OK**. Now the OLE - Paste Special Attributes dialog box appears, as shown in Figure 11.11.

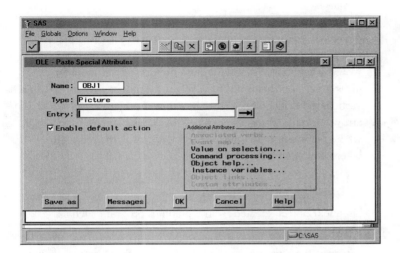

Figure 11.11
OLE - Paste Special
Attributes Dialog Box

Most of the information is filled in—all you have to provide is an entry name. For this example, type SIGN1 in the **Entry** field, then click on **OK**.

Depending on your graphic's source, you may see another dialog box before the graphic appears in the BUILD: DISPLAY window. For example, Corel Gallery displays a Paste Graphic dialog box that allows you to set the size of the graphic. Some graphics packages do not display this type of dialog box. Once you've filled in any additional dialog boxes and clicked on **OK**, the picture appears in the BUILD: DISPLAY window, as shown in Figure 11.12.

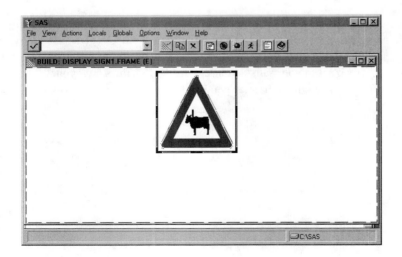

Figure 11.12
The SIGN1 Object in the
BUILD: DISPLAY Window

9. If the sign is not the right size or in the right place, resize and move it. Click once inside the region to select it. Now place the mouse pointer over the corners or sides and resize it as you would a window. When the mouse pointer is over a corner, it turns into a four-headed arrow. When the mouse pointer is over a vertical or horizontal resize area, it turns into a two-headed arrow. To move the graphic, place the mouse pointer over a side where the pointer turns into a hand. Now drag the region to where you want it.

10. To describe the sign, you need to create an object that displays text. There are several ways to do this, but one way is to paste in a text object, created from a graphics program such as Microsoft Paint.

To open the Paint application, click on the **Start** button, then click on **Programs**, then click on **Accessories**, then click on **Paint**.

Type the sign's description, and mark the text. Now copy it to the Clipboard. If you have never used Paint before, use the **Help** menu in the Paint window to learn how to type text.

Now return to the BUILD: DISPLAY window, and click the right mouse button to open the popup menu. Click on **Make**, then click on **OLE - Paste Special**. In the Paste Special dialog box, choose **Paste**, and click on the **Picture** object type. Now click on **OK**.

Give the object a name in the OLE - Paste Special Attributes dialog box, such as SIGN1TXT, and click on **OK**. The text appears in the object; if it is not positioned correctly, move and resize it to your satisfaction. Figure 11.13 shows how your screen should look after you have added the sign's description.

Figure 11.13
The First Sign and Its
Description

This method of inserting a text object ensures a static object—
that is, one that cannot be edited by users of your SAS/AF
application (you do not want people changing the sign's description).

11. You must save your work before the OLE objects become permanent parts of your FRAME entry. To save your work, click
on **File** in the SAS System main menu, then click on **Save**.

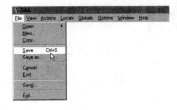

12. For some signs, you may need to provide more information
than the small description can hold. For these signs, add a "Text
Document" icon. First, create the text file that contains the
detailed information about the sign. Create this file with a word
processing program that supports OLE, such as Microsoft
Word, Windows Notepad, or the Windows WordPad editor.
Save the file.

Now return to the BUILD: DISPLAY window. Click the right
mouse button, and click on **Make**. Scroll down and double-
click on **OLE - Insert Object**. When the dotted region appears,
click the mouse button when the region is placed where you
want it. The Insert Object dialog box appears, as shown in
Figure 11.14.

Figure 11.14
Insert Object Dialog Box

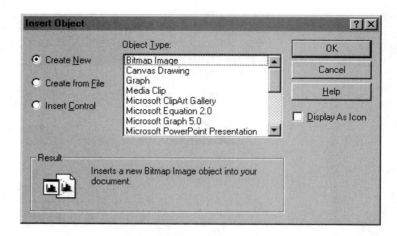

13. Click on **Create from File**, and type the full pathname of the text file in the **File** field. Also click on **Display As Icon**, so the entire text does not appear in the FRAME entry. When you click on this option, the default icon for the file you've selected appears, as does a **Change Icon** button. For this example, we'll use the default icon; it is possible to create your own icons and use them instead.

Note: When you use the Insert Object dialog box instead of the Paste Special dialog box, you do not need to have the object on the Clipboard.

Figure 11.15 shows the Insert Object dialog box as it should look when you are finished, assuming you used the Windows WordPad program to create the text file and saved it as a plain ASCII file. The dialog box may look slightly different if you used another word processing program or different file type.

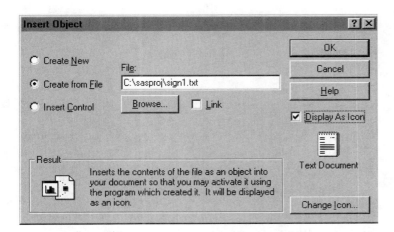

Figure 11.15
Insert Dialog Box after
Changes

14. Now click on **OK**, and when the OLE - Insert Object Attributes dialog box appears, give the entry a name, such as INFO1, and click on **OK**. The icon is added to your FRAME entry, as shown in Figure 11.16.

Figure 11.16
FRAME Entry with the Text
Document Icon Added

While the sign and the sign description are static embedded objects, the INFO1 object is a nonstatic embedded object.

15. Save the catalog entry by clicking on **File**, then clicking on **Save**.

16. Close the BUILD: DISPLAY window by clicking on **File**, then clicking on **End**.

17. Close the BUILD: DIRECTORY window by clicking on **File**, then clicking on **End**.

When the student runs the SAS/AF application and double-clicks on the **Text Document** icon, the additional information is displayed, as shown in Figure 11.17.

Figure 11.17
Viewing the Text
Represented by the Text
Document Icon

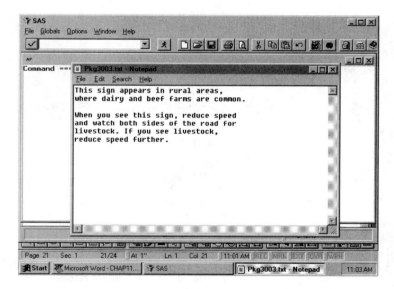

To close the editor application, click on its Close button.

Obviously this is a small piece of the entire application; you need to add SCL code and other objects to your FRAME entries to enable students to progress from one sign to the next, do error checking, and so on.

Example 2—Using Linked Objects: Example 1 used embedded objects, both static and nonstatic. Embedded objects were useful in that example because the information did not change—the signs would always look the same, and the descriptions were finalized. In this example, you use linked objects. Linked objects are useful in applications where the information changes often, and you want your SAS/AF application user to have access to the latest changes or to be able to make changes to the information.

In this example, the SAS/AF application provides information about a company's construction project overseas. The application lets the user view the latest cost figures for the project, shows up-to-date floor plans, and even provides photos (updated weekly) of various parts of the project. While only a portion of the application is shown here, you get a good idea of how to create the other portions using the illustrated techniques.

1. As with Example 1, the first step is to create a catalog and a FRAME entry. In Example 1, you used procedure statements to run the BUILD procedure. You can also use the BUILD command. For example, issue the following command from the Command bar:

```
BUILD SASUSER.PROJECT
```

This command creates a catalog in the SASUSER data library; you can use any existing data library. The BUILD: DIRECTORY window appears, as shown in Figure 11.18.

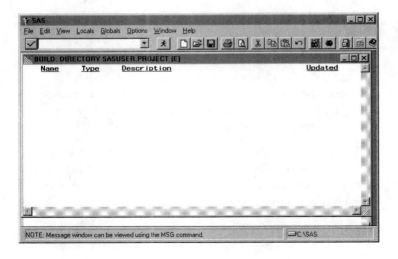

Figure 11.18
BUILD: DIRECTORY
Window

2. In Example 1, you used the EDIT command to create the entry. You can also use the menus. Click on **File** in the SAS System main menu, then click on **New**. The New dialog box opens, as shown in Figure 11.19.

Figure 11.19
Using the New Dialog Box
to Create a Catalog Entry

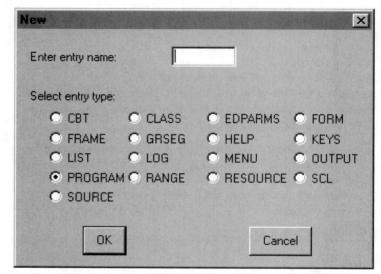

Type the FRAME entry's name in the field (for this example, use the name PROJINFO), and click on the word **FRAME** to create a FRAME entry. Now click on **OK**. The BUILD: DISPLAY window opens, ready for input.

3. The first piece of the application we'll create is the floor plan for the project. These plans are updated periodically to reflect changes the engineers make. Therefore, you need to create a linked object, so each time the SAS/AF application runs, it accesses the most recent data.

For this example, the floor plans are stored in graphics files created by Windows Paint. You can use any other graphics program that supports OLE, such as Visio. Be sure you've saved your graphics file before continuing.

4. After you've created and saved your floor plan graphics file, return to the BUILD: DISPLAY window. Click the right mouse button, then click on **Make**. Double-click on **OLE - Insert Object** from the Selection List. Anchor the region wherever you want by clicking the mouse button. The Insert Object dialog box appears.

5. Click on **Create from File**, and type the graphic's filename in the text field. Also click on **Link** and **Display As Icon**. If you do not want to use the default icon, you must create your own icon using a bitmap editor, and use the **Change Icon** button to specify this new icon.

6. When you've finished with the Insert Object dialog box, click on **OK**. The OLE - Insert Object Attributes dialog box opens next, where you specify a name for the object. For this example, use the name FLRPLAN, and click on **OK**. Now you see the object's icon, as shown in Figure 11.20.

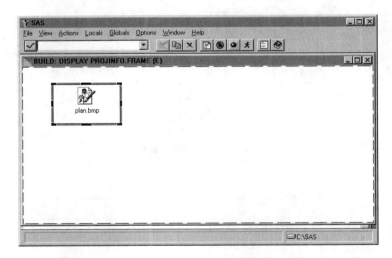

Figure 11.20
Floor Plan Icon Added to the FRAME Entry

Note: Some graphic file types do not support being used in this manner. You may need to experiment a bit with your graphics package to find a file type that works for you. Also, because the filename is displayed below the icon, it is best to have a meaningful filename.

By default, the link between your SAS/AF application and the data source (the graphics file) is automatic. That is, whenever the source is updated, the changes are reflected in the SAS/AF application. To view the object, the user of the SAS/AF application double-clicks on the object's icon. If the engineers have added a new wing to the existing plan, your SAS/AF application shows that wing.

7. To add a photo to your application, repeat the steps 1-6, except you may not want the photo shown as an icon—you may prefer to display the actual photo. It may be small, but the SAS/AF application user can double-click on the photo to open the graphics application, where the photo can be examined in detail.

Figure 11.21 shows the PROJINFO FRAME entry with both the floor plan icon and a photo.

Figure 11.21
FRAME Entry with Floor
Plan and Photo

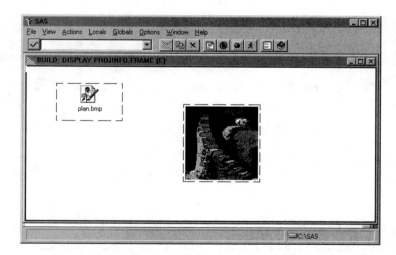

Note: As with other graphics, some photo file types work better than others. For example, while JPEG files are detailed, they are also large and may use up too much RAM. The BMP and TIFF file formats are good choices for OLE because they preserve detail well, are supported by many programs, and create smaller files than some other formats.

8. When you finish adding objects to the FRAME entry, click on **File** in the SAS System main menu, then click on **Save**.

9. Close the BUILD: DISPLAY window by clicking on **File→End**, then close the BUILD: DIRECTORY window by clicking on **File→End**.

You can use similar techniques to add a spreadsheet object to your FRAME entry (possibly using Excel or Lotus 1-2-3) that shows the current expenditures for the project. Another possible component of the application could be a timeline, created with a graphics package. You could also add more FRAME entries if necessary, and add SCL code to let the user move from one FRAME to the next. Using OLE and linked objects, your SAS/AF application users always have access to the latest data and information.

Running a SAS/AF Application: To run your SAS/AF application, issue the following command from the Command bar:

```
AF CAT=libref.catalog.entry.type
```

libref.catalog.entry.type is the first entry of the application (the starting point).

To close the SAS/AF application and return to the PROGRAM EDITOR window, click on **File** in the SAS System main menu, then click on **End**.

Using SAS/CONNECT®
Software to Connect Your PC
12 to Other Computer Systems

Introduction

Except for Chapter 11, which discussed using SAS/AF software, this book has confined itself to discussing features of base SAS software. However, this chapter also discusses a separate product, SAS/CONNECT software. SAS/CONNECT software enables you to connect your Windows SAS session to SAS sessions running on other computer systems—perhaps an MVS mainframe, a UNIX workstation, or even another PC on your network.

The beauty of SAS/CONNECT software is that it lets you access data stored on other machines and also to use more powerful machines to do "number-crunching" or other CPU-intensive programming tasks. This chapter shows, by example, the basics of using SAS/CONNECT software.

To use SAS/CONNECT software, you need some sort of connection between your computer and the other system and also some communications software (e.g., Trumpet Winsock, Novell's Netware Requestor, IBM's LAN Support Program, or DEC's PATHWORKS software).

This chapter does not teach you how to install your communications software because there many configurations and options available. Nor does this chapter discuss all features and considerations of SAS/CONNECT software; it is intended only to get you started. If you plan to use SAS/CONNECT software extensively, you definitely need to read the latest edition of SAS Institute's documentation for SAS/CONNECT software.

As with most computer topics, communications between computers has its own jargon. So, this chapter first acquaints you with the terms you encounter while using SAS/CONNECT software. Then, the chapter helps you conceptualize how SAS/CONNECT software works and how it can help you. Finally, five examples give you concrete experience using SAS/CONNECT software.

Learning Client/Server Terminology

SAS/CONNECT software is called "client/server" software. That is, it provides a bridge between your computer (the client), which requests data and services, and another computer (the server), which provides these data and services. Your computer is also referred to as the local computer, whereas the server computer is referred to as the remote computer. You need the SAS System installed on both the local and remote computer in order to use SAS/CONNECT software. Once you have SAS/CONNECT software installed, you can send data in both directions between the local and remote computer.

As an example, suppose you have data stored on MVS, but you want to analyze that data from your Windows SAS session. With SAS/CONNECT software, you connect your Windows SAS session to a SAS session on MVS. You then submit program statements (such as DATA and PROC steps) to the MVS session. The MVS SAS session does the data analysis and passes the results to the OUTPUT window on your PC. Or, the MVS SAS session can pass data from MVS to your PC for analysis there. When you move data from the remote computer to your PC, you "download" the data. When you move data in the opposite direction, from your PC to the remote computer, you "upload" the data.

To establish the link between your PC and the remote computer, you use a "communication method." A communication method is a protocol for how two computers talk to each other. Examples of communication methods include TCP/IP, TELNET, RASYNC, and EHLLAPI.

Under Windows, several communication methods are available, depending on what remote operating system you want to connect to. Follow this help path to see a table of available communication methods (assuming you have SAS/CONNECT software installed):

HelpPath: **Help→SAS System→SAS/CONNECT Software→ SAS/CONNECT Software: Changes and Enhancements for Release 6.12→SAS/CONNECT in the SAS Software: Changes and Enhancements for Release 6.11→Access Methods for SAS/CONNECT**

In the folder C:\SAS\CONNECT\SASMISC are several text files that give you some helpful hints about using several communication methods.

If you are connected to the Internet under Windows, you probably already have some TCP/IP software installed. TCP/IP supports numerous remote connections. If you do not have communications software installed already, choose a product that supports connections to the remote operating systems you want to connect to.

Understanding How SAS/CONNECT Software Works

HelpPath: **Help→Sample programs→SAS Sample Library→SAS/CONNECT**, then choose a program

Help→SAS System→SAS System Help: Main Menu→Data Management→SAS/CONNECT, then choose a topic

SAS/CONNECT software uses a "script file" that invokes the SAS System on the remote computer and defines the parameters of the connection between the local and remote SAS sessions. These script files are plain text files that are shipped with SAS/CONNECT software. You can use these files as-is, or you can modify them to meet your particular needs. There is a script file for every type of communication method supported by the SAS System under Windows, except for the APPC and DECnet communication methods, which do not require a script file.

When you set up a connection between the local and remote SAS sessions, you must specify the following information from the local SAS session:

- the script file

- the communication method to use

- an identification code for the remote SAS session (the remote session ID).

On the remote side, the SAS System must be configured properly for the connection. The configuration differs, depending on what operating system you are connecting to. For example, if you are connecting to MVS, several SAS system options need to be set in the remote SAS session.

It is possible to connect to several different remote SAS sessions at the same time, using different remote session IDs. And while beginning SAS/CONNECT software users may prefer to specify the connection information using dialog boxes, it is also possible to specify this information programmatically, using SAS statements and system options. This enables you to use SAS/CONNECT software in batch mode. The last example in this chapter is a batch mode example.

Initiating the Connection: To initiate the connection, make the PROGRAM EDITOR window active. Click on **Locals** in the SAS System main menu, then click on **Signon**. The Signon dialog box appears, as shown in Figure 12.1.

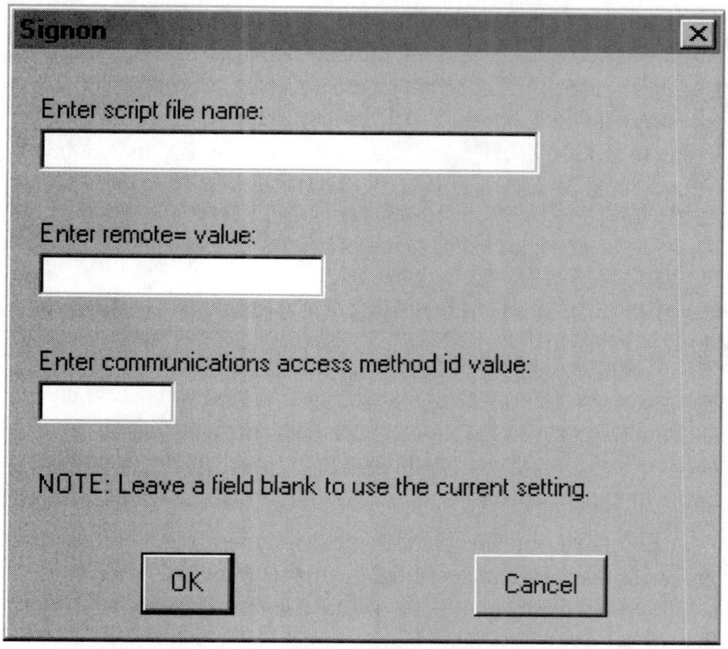

Figure 12.1
Signon Dialog Box

In the top field in the Signon dialog box, type the script file you want to use. By default, the SAS System looks for script files in C:\SAS\CONNECT\SASLINK. If your script file is located in another folder, be sure to type the full pathname.

In the middle field, type the remote session ID you want to use. The value of this field depends on what communication method you are using. It can be as simple a code as an "a" or a long Internet address. Your communications software documentation can help you determine this ID.

In the last field, enter the communication method. When you've typed the values, click on **OK**.

Note: Completing the connection may take a few minutes, depending on the speed of your networks and the response time of the computer you are connecting to.

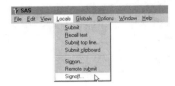

Terminating the Connection: To end the connection to a remote computer, make the PROGRAM EDITOR window active. Click on **Locals** in the SAS System main menu, then on **Signoff**. The Signoff dialog box appears, which looks exactly like the Signon dialog box. Specify the script file, remote session ID, and communication method for the connection you want to terminate, and click on **OK**.

Deciding How to Use SAS/CONNECT Software

When you submit SAS statements that execute on the remote system, you are using "compute services." When you access data stored on the remote system, you are using "data services." What services you should use depends on your particular needs and how your computers are set up.

For example, if you have a PC that has minimum RAM and a slow processor and your data is stored on a mainframe, you probably want to use a combination of compute services and data services so that all the processing and number crunching occurs on the mainframe, and only the results get passed back to your PC. On the other hand, if your PC is a fast machine, you need to do lengthy data analysis, and your network is overworked, you may want to use only data services to download a copy of the data to your PC and do the computing there.

When you take advantage of data services, you can choose to either transfer the data between the remote and local SAS sessions, or you can access the data directly on the remote system, using "remote library services" (RLS). This means you submit a LIBNAME statement that defines the SAS data library on the remote system. Then, you can use this libref in any of your programming statements—either statements submitted on the local system or on the remote system. Think of data transfer as a moving van—the physical data are moved from one system to the other. RLS, on the other hand, is like a periscope from your PC to the remote system—you can see and use the data, but the data are not physically moved.

Figure 12.2 shows how SAS/CONNECT services can work.

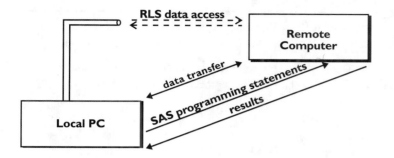

Understanding SAS/CONNECT Software's Compute Services

Submitting code that executes on a remote computer is as simple as submitting code on your own PC, once you have established the connection to the remote computer. Type the code into the PROGRAM EDITOR window. Then, click on **Locals** in the SAS System main menu, then click on **Remote submit**. Remember that any librefs, filerefs, and data sets that you reference in remote submitted code exist on the remote computer—not on your PC.

If you prefer to use SAS statements instead of menus, use the RSUBMIT and ENDRSUBMIT statements to remote submit your code. Example 1 later in this chapter gives an example of using compute services, and Example 5 illustrates how to use the RSUBMIT and ENDRSUBMIT statements.

Deciding When to Use Compute Services: In general, use compute services when the remote computer has better, faster hardware resources than your PC. Also, use compute services to take advantage of printers and plotters connected to the remote computer. When you use compute services, you can use SAS components on the remote computer that are not installed on your PC (such as SAS/STAT or SAS/INSIGHT software).

Understanding SAS/CONNECT Software's Data Transfer Services

To copy data from the remote computer to your PC and vice versa, use the DOWNLOAD and UPLOAD procedures.

The DOWNLOAD procedure copies data from the remote computer to your PC; the UPLOAD procedure sends data from your PC to the remote computer. Both these procedures can transfer SAS data sets, SAS catalogs, and external files (e.g., executable files, text files, and so on). By using subsetting features of the SAS System, such as the WHERE statement, you can move only the data you need.

Both the DOWNLOAD and UPLOAD procedures execute on the remote computer and must be submitted with the RSUBMIT statement or the **Remote submit** menu item. Any librefs or filerefs used with these procedures must have been previously defined to the remote computer with remote submitted LIBNAME and FILENAME statements.

Example 2 later in this chapter illustrates using the DOWNLOAD and UPLOAD procedures.

Deciding When to Use Data Transfer Services: In general, use data transfer services when you are developing an application that repeatedly accesses data. If you do not download the data, you tie up the network every time you access the data. By downloading it, you use the network only once. Also, use data transfer services to make a backup copy of data.

Understanding SAS/CONNECT Software's Remote Library Services

Instead of using PROC DOWNLOAD to move data from the remote computer to your PC, you can use SAS/CONNECT software's Remote Library Services (RLS) to directly access data on the remote computer. What makes RLS unique is that it enables you to execute your SAS program on your PC, but use data, without downloading it, that reside on the remote computer.

Note: Not all communication methods support RLS. You need a program-to-program communication method. Examples of program-to-program communication methods include APPC, DECnet, NetBIOS, and TCP/IP.

To use RLS, you submit a special LIBNAME statement on your PC, which defines a libref on the remote computer. This LIBNAME statement uses several keywords not used in a regular LIBNAME statement. Example 3 later in this chapter shows you how this LIBNAME statement and RLS work.

Using RLS with SAS Data Sets: RLS can access all types of SAS data sets (including data defined by SAS data views and SAS/ACCESS access descriptors).

Using RLS with SAS Catalogs: RLS can access SAS catalogs only if both the local and remote computers use the same internal representations of data. This means that the local and remote operating systems must store both character and numeric data in the same way.

For example, both Windows 95 and Windows NT use the ASCII character set and store numbers in byte order, so you can use RLS to access SAS catalogs on a Windows NT machine. But MVS uses the EBCDIC character set and stores numbers in byte-reversed order, so you cannot access MVS SAS catalogs using RLS from your Windows SAS session. And even though both Win32s (the 32-bit version of Windows, required for Release 6.11 and later of the SAS System) and OS/2 store numeric data the same way, OS/2 uses a different version of the ASCII character set—so you cannot use RLS to access SAS catalogs on an OS/2 machine. The following operating systems use the same internal data representation as Windows and therefore support RLS catalog access:

- Windows (Win32s)

- Windows NT

- Windows 95.

Using RLS with SAS Stored Programs: RLS cannot access SAS PROGRAM files from any remote computer.

Deciding When to Use Remote Library Services: In general, use RLS when you need to execute your SAS program on your local computer but you need access to data on the remote computer and do not want to download the data. Remember that RLS requires use of the network every time you access the data, so if your network is slow or crowded, you may not want to use RLS.

Example 1: Using Compute Services

Your PC is connected to OpenVMS via the DECnet communication method. You want to use the SAS System on OpenVMS to execute your code because it requires a large data set to be sorted. Because your PC is a slow 386 machine, the SAS System can sort the data faster on OpenVMS than on your PC. Here are the steps to work this example:

1. Determine your remote session ID. For DECnet access, the remote session ID usually takes the form of *node" username password"* . However, the remote session ID must be eight characters or fewer. So, you must use a SAS macro to define a nickname for the remote session ID.

   Suppose the node you need to access is WALKER, your username is SMITH01, and your password is MAGIC123. The remote session ID is WALKER"SMITH01 MAGIC123". The following SAS statement assigns the nickname SMITH to this ID:

   ```
   %let smith=walker"smith01 magic123";
   ```

   Submit this statement locally (e.g., press F3).

2. Now signon. Click on **Locals** in the SAS System main menu, then click on **Signon**.

   Leave the script file field blank because DECnet access does not require a script file. In the second field, type the nickname for the remote session ID (in this example, SMITH). In the last field, type DECNET. Now click on **OK** to initiate the connection.

3. Now you're ready to type the program you want to run under OpenVMS. Here is the program:

```
    /* Tell the OpenVMS SAS session to use */
    /* the HOST sort utility. /*
options sortpgm=host;
    /* Define a libref on OpenVMS. */
libname panthers 'species::[florida.cats]';
proc sort data=panthers.kittens
     out=females (where=(sex='f'));
     by age idnum;
run;
proc print data=females;
     title='Female Florida Panther Kittens';
     by age;
run;
```

4. When the program is ready to submit, click on **Locals** in the SAS System main menu, then click on **Remote submit**. The code is submitted to the SAS session on OpenVMS, and when it is finished, the OUTPUT window on your PC displays the results of the program.

5. When you are finished with the OpenVMS SAS session, signoff by clicking on **Locals** in the SAS System main menu, then clicking on **Signoff**. Type the same values you typed in the Signon dialog box, and click on **OK**.

Example 2: Using Data Transfer Services

Your PC is connected to MVS through the EHLLAPI communication method. You need to access some car emission data on MVS. The data set is not large, and you need only about half of it, but you do need to do repetitive analysis on it. So, you decide to download the data set to your PC using PROC DOWNLOAD. Then you use PROC UPLOAD to send the results back to MVS.

Here are the steps to work this example:

1. Determine your remote session ID. For EHLLAPI access, the remote session ID is the remote computer's session ID. You created this ID when you installed the communications software that enables your PC to connect to MVS.

2. Now signon. Click on **Locals** in the SAS System main menu, then click on **Signon**. Type TSO.SCR in the script file field. For the second field, type the remote session ID from your communications software package. In the last field, type EHLLAPI. Now click on **OK** to initiate the connection.

3. Now you're ready to type the DOWNLOAD procedure statements. Here is the program. The WHERE statement pulls out only the data for vehicles made from 1975 to 1977 whose weight is larger than 6000 pounds and whose hydrocarbon emissions are greater than 750 parts-per-million.

```
        /* Define a libref on MVS. */
     libname pollute 'vehicle.test.results';

     proc download data=pollute.large out=large;
        where year between 1975 and 1977
           and weight > 6000
           and hydcarb >= 750;
     run;
```

Note: It may be more efficient to use the WHERE= data set option in the previous example, instead of the WHERE statement.

4. When the program is ready to submit, click on **Locals** in the SAS System main menu, then click on **Remote submit**. The code is submitted to the SAS session on MVS. When it is finished, the temporary data set LARGE is created on your PC. You can now analyze this data repeatedly, without tying up the network with further traffic.

5. After you have finished analyzing the data, send the results back to MVS. Suppose the results of your analysis are in the temporary data set HYDCARB. Type the following program into the PROGRAM EDITOR window.

```
proc upload data=hydcarb
            out=pollute.hydcarb;
run;
```

Click on **Locals** in the SAS System main menu, then click on **Remote submit** to submit the PROC UPLOAD step to MVS.

6. When you are finished with the MVS SAS session, signoff by clicking on **Locals** in the SAS System main menu, then click on **Signoff**. Type the same values you typed in the Signon dialog box, and click on **OK**.

Example 3: Using Remote Library Services

Your PC is connected to a UNIX workstation via the TCP/IP communication method. A data set containing vehicle emissions data is stored on the UNIX machine. You need to access a small portion of this data set to plot which vehicles had high carbon monoxide emissions. Because you need only a small portion of the data and you do not plan to repeatedly analyze the data, RLS is an efficient method of accessing the data.

Here are the steps to work this example:

1. Determine your remote session ID. For TCP/IP access, the remote session ID is the remote computer's Internet address. However, the remote session ID must be eight characters or fewer. So, you must use a SAS macro to define a nickname for the remote session ID.

   Suppose the Internet address for the remote UNIX machine is 1.20.327.45. The following SAS statement assigns the nickname TOUNIX to this ID.

   ```
   %let tounix=1.20.327.45;
   ```

   Submit this statement locally (e.g., press F3).

2. Now signon by clicking on **Locals** in the SAS System main menu, then clicking on **Signon**. Type TCPUNIX.SCR in the script file field. For the second field, type the nickname for the remote session ID (in this example, TOUNIX). In the last field, type TCP. Click on **OK** to initiate the connection.

3. To use Remote Library Services, you submit a special LIBNAME statement to your PC that identifies the remote SAS session. For example, the LIBNAME statement in the following program defines the libref CO. The REMOTE option tells the local SAS session this is an RLS LIBNAME statement, and the SERVER option specifies the remote session ID for the UNIX SAS session, where the SAS data library resides. Submit this program locally (e.g., press F3).

```
libname co remote
     '/home/user/smith/vehicles/light/tests'
     server=tounix;

data co.high_co;
   set co.year81;
   where carbmono > 1.2;
run;

proc plot data=co.high_co nolegend;
   title1 '1981 Vehicles Weighing Less than
       6,000 Pounds';
   title2 'with High Carbon Monoxide
Emissions';
   title3 '(Measured in Percentage)';
   plot vin*carbmono='*';
run;
```

The OUTPUT window on your PC displays the plot, although no data have been physically moved to the PC.

4. When you are finished with the UNIX SAS session, signoff by clicking on **Locals** in the SAS System main menu, then click on **Signoff**. Type the same values you typed in the Signon dialog box, and click on **OK**.

Example 4: Combining Compute, Data Transfer, and Remote Library Services

Your PC is connected to CMS via the TELNET communication method. Your application uses a combination of compute, data transfer, and remote library services. This application uses RLS to merge two data sets (one on CMS, one on the PC) into a new one, then uses data transfer services to upload the new data set to CMS. Then, the program uses compute services to do some tabulation, using CMS. The output of the TABULATE procedure appears on the local PC. TELNET access requires the remote session to run in line mode, which is fine for your needs. Also, although the communication method for the local machine is TELNET, the CMS session should be set up to use the RASYNC communication method.

Here are the steps to work this example:

1. Determine the remote session ID for the CMS session. For TELNET access, the remote session ID is the remote computer's Internet address. However, the remote session ID must be eight characters or fewer. So, you must use a SAS macro to define a nickname for the remote session ID.

   Suppose the Internet address for the remote CMS machine is tiger@cms.company.com. The following SAS statement assigns the nickname TOCMS to this ID:

   ```
   %let tocms=tiger@cms.company.com;
   ```

   Submit this statement locally (e.g., press F3).

2. Now signon by clicking on **Locals** in the SAS System main menu, then click on **Signon**. To initiate the CMS session, type TELCMS.SCR in the script file field. For the second field, type the nickname for the CMS remote session ID (in this example, TOCMS). In the last field, type TELNET. Now click on **OK** to initiate the connection.

3. The next step is to submit an RLS-type LIBNAME statement that refers to a SAS data library on CMS and a regular LIBNAME statement to define a libref for a local SAS data library:

   ```
   libname cms remote 'data a' server=tocms;
   libname win 'c:\wildcat\info';
   ```

Submit these two statements locally (e.g., press F3).

4. Now you are ready to merge the two data sets (one remote, one local) together, to form a new, local data set that contains both vital statistics (like weight and age) and location information for the various species of wild cats in the US. Again, these statements are submitted locally and create a temporary data set, CATINFO, on the PC.

```
    /* First, sort each data set by ID, so */
    /* the match-merge works. */
proc sort data=cms.vital;
    by id;
run;

proc sort data=win.region;
    by id;
run;

    /* Now create the merged data set. */
data catinfo;
    merge cms.vital win.region;
    by id;
run;
```

5. Now you want to move the CATINFO data set to CMS, using the UPLOAD procedure. Note that a new LIBNAME statement is necessary because this portion of the program is not using RLS. Submit these statements remotely (**Locals→Remote submit**).

```
libname cat 'data a';
proc upload data=catinfo
      out=cat.catinfo;
run;
```

6. Because you want to do the tabulation on CMS, the PROC TABULATE step is also remote submitted (**Locals→Remote submit**):

```
proc tabulate data=cat.catinfo
              format=comma8.;
    title 'Tabulation of Wild Cat Information
          Organized by Species and Region';
    class species region;
    var weight age;
    table species*region,
    age*mean*f=8.2 weight*mean*f=8.2 age*n;
run;
```

This program tabulates the mean weight and age of each species of cat, organized by region. It also tells you how many cats are in each region. Even though the program was submitted remotely, the results of the TABULATE procedure appear in the OUTPUT window on your PC.

7. When you are finished with the CMS SAS session, signoff by clicking on **Locals** in the SAS System main menu, then click on **Signoff**. Type the same values you typed in the Signon dialog box, then click on **OK**.

Example 5: Using SAS/CONNECT Software in Batch Mode

Your PC is connected to OS/2 via the TCP/IP communication method. You have a batch program that uses SAS/CONNECT software to process some data on the OS/2 machine and download a resulting data set to your PC.

SAS/CONNECT software works equally well in display manager or batch mode, and you can use compute, data transfer, and remote library services in both modes. The only differences between using SAS/CONNECT software in batch mode and in display manager are the following:

- how you specify the script file, remote session ID, and communication method

- how you initiate and terminate the connection
- how you remote submit programs.

Specifying the Script File in Batch Mode: Instead of typing the script file in the Signon dialog box, in batch mode use the special fileref RLINK by submitting a FILENAME statement that associates RLINK with the script file. Here is an example for the TCP/IP communication method between Windows and OS/2:

```
filename rlink
     'c:\sas\connect\saslink\tcpos2.scr';
```

Submit this statement locally before you signon to the remote computer.

Specifying the Remote Session ID in Batch Mode: Instead of typing the remote session ID in the Signon dialog box, in batch mode use the REMOTE SAS system option. Put this option in your CONFIG.SAS file or in an OPTIONS statement. This example uses an OPTIONS statement.

Follow these steps to specify the remote session ID in batch mode:

1. Determine the remote session ID for the OS/2 session. For example, for TCP/IP access, the remote session ID is the remote computer's Internet address. However, the remote session ID must be eight characters or fewer. So, you must use a SAS macro to define a nickname for the remote session ID.

   Suppose the Internet address for the remote OS/2 machine is 1.45.735.26. The following SAS statement assigns the nickname TOOS2 to this ID:

   ```
   %let toos2=1.45.735.26;
   ```

   Submit this statement locally before you initiate the connection to the remote computer:

2. Now use this nickname in the REMOTE system option, as in the following example:

   ```
   options remote=toos2;
   ```

Put the OPTIONS statement in your AUTOEXEC.SAS file if you use SAS/CONNECT software regularly.

Specifying the Communication Method in Batch Mode: Instead of typing the communication method in the Signon dialog box, in batch mode use the COMAMID SAS system option. Put this option in your CONFIG.SAS file or in an OPTIONS statement. This example uses an OPTIONS statement.

For example, for the TCP/IP communication method, the value for the COMAMID option is TCP. Here is a sample COMAMID option specification:

```
options comamid=tcp;
```

Put the OPTIONS statement in your AUTOEXEC.SAS file if you use SAS/CONNECT software regularly.

Initiating the Connection in Batch Mode: Instead of clicking on **OK** in the Signon dialog box, in batch mode use the SIGNON statement. The SIGNON statement takes the remote session ID as an argument. Here is an example:

```
signon toos2;
```

Submit this statement locally.

Remote Submitting SAS Statements in Batch Mode: Instead of using the **Remote submit** menu item, in batch mode use the RSUBMIT and ENDRSUBMIT statements in your code. Place the RSUBMIT statement before the first statement in the remote program; place the ENDRSUBMIT statement after the last state-ment in the remote program, as in the following example:

```
rsubmit;
    libname os2data 'c:\temp\july';
    proc sort data=os2data.hightemps;
                    by date;
    run;
endrsubmit;
```

This example defines a libref for an OS/2 SAS data library and performs an in-place sort on a data set in that library.

Terminating the Connection in Batch Mode: Instead of clicking on **OK** in the Signoff dialog box, in batch mode use the SIGNOFF statement with the remote session ID as the argument, as in the following example:

```
signoff toos2;
```

Submit this statement locally.

Batch Example Code: Here is an entire sample batch program, with comments.

```
/* Define a nickname for the remote session */
/* ID. */
%let toos2=1.45.735.26;

/* Set the remote session ID and */
/* communication method. */
options remote=toos2 comamid=tcp;

/* Assign the RLINK fileref to the */
/* appropriate script file. */
filename rlink
    'c:\sas\connect\saslink\tcpos2.scr';

/* Define a libref on the local PC, where */
/* the downloaded data set is stored. */
libname windata 'c:\temp\july';

signon toos2; /* Initiate the connection. */

/* Begin the remote submitted block */
/* of code. */
rsubmit;

/* Define a libref for an OS/2 */
/* data library. */
libname os2data 'c:\temp\july';
```

```
    /* Create a temporary data set that */
    /* contains the high and low temperatures */
    /* for July. */
data hilo;
        merge os2data.hi (drop=date place
                    rename=(time=hitime))
              os2data.lo
                    (rename=(time=lotime));
run;

    /* Download the merged data set. */
proc download data=hilo out=windata.hilo;
run;

    /* End the remote submitted block of code. */
endrsubmit;

    /* Terminate the connection. */
signoff toos2;
```

Appendix 1   Troubleshooting

Introduction

This appendix provides some hints for solving commonly encountered problems. The problems are organized into groups that match the chapters, such as printing, batch programming, and using SAS/CONNECT software.

If your problem is not addressed in this appendix, you may want to visit the Knowledge Base on the SAS Institute Web site (www.sas.com), under the Technical Support topic.

Learning to Do Windows and Performing the Basic SAS Software Tasks under Windows

Problem: The SAS System has caused a General Protection Fault (GPF).
Solution: Press CTRL-ALT-DEL. Follow the instructions in the dialog box that appears to end applications that are not responding, or to reboot your computer. The latter causes you to lose any unsaved data sets and catalogs you created in your SAS session and in other applications as well.

Problem: Your keyboard has locked up and your cannot type or use the mouse.
Solution: First, press CTRL-ALT-DEL. If that does not work, turn off your computer, then turn it back on. This causes you to lose all unsaved data in all Windows applications.

Problem: Your mouse buttons do not work the way you expect.
Solution: Someone may have changed the mouse from a right-handed to a left-handed mouse or vice versa. Click on the **Start** button, then on **Settings**, then on **Control Panel**. In the Control Panel window, click on the **Mouse** icon, and use the resulting dialog box to reset your mouse's properties.

Problem: The Windows application you want to use is hidden behind several other open windows.
Solution: Click on the application's name in the Taskbar.

Problem: The SAS window you want to use is hidden behind several other open SAS windows.
Solution: Click on **Window** in the SAS System main menu, then click on the name of the window you want to see. If you have more than nine SAS windows open, click on **More windows** to see a complete list of open SAS windows; double-click on the name of the window you want to see.

Editing and Working with Files

Problem: You cannot click in the PROGRAM EDITOR window. Every time you do, your computer beeps, and the mouse pointer is an hourglass.

Solution: You may have a synchronous DOS session active or have a dialog box open waiting for input (either in the SAS session or in another Windows application).

Look at the Taskbar. If **MS-DOS Prompt** is listed, click on that task. Type EXIT at the DOS prompt to close the DOS session. To keep this from happening again, submit an OPTIONS statement in your SAS session with the NOXWAIT option.

If the Taskbar does not list any active DOS sessions, press ALT-ESC to toggle through all open windows to see if you have an open dialog box that needs input. If neither CTRL-ESC or ALT-ESC works, your Windows session may be hung—see the second problem under "Learning to Do Windows and Performing the Basic SAS Software Tasks under Windows," earlier in this appendix.

Submitting SAS Code

Problem: Your program is in an infinite loop.
Solution: Press CTRL-BREAK and click on **Y**, then click on **OK** to cancel the submitted statements.

Problem: The **Recall text** menu item does not work.
Solution: You have probably cleared the window. Try using the UNDO command repeatedly to back through your actions. If this does not work, you must retype your text or reopen the file.

Printing

Problem: Your printer output does not look like you expect.
Solution: Be sure you have selected the correct printer for your output. Also, you may have a form selected when you do not want to use forms, or the wrong form may be in effect. Check the Print Setup dialog box to see if the **Use Forms** option is checked. Use the FORMNAME command to display the current form. Also check the font and typesize settings, and check your CONFIG.SAS

file for LINESIZE, PAGESIZE, SYSPRINT, SYSPRINTFONT, and other system options that affect printer output.

As a last resort, delete the WNSPRINT.WINPRINT entry in your SASUSER.PROFILE2 catalog.

Problem: Your SAS output looks funny and things do not align.
Solution: You may have chosen a proportional font for your printer output. Change the font to a monospace font such as Courier or SAS Monospace.

Problem: You get an error message when you try to print a bitmap file.
Solution: Check your free disk space—printing large files requires some free disk space for temporary files. Delete unnecessary files to free up more disk space.

Adjusting Your Windows Environment

Problem: You cannot resize or move the SAS application workspace (AWS).
Solution: The AWS is probably maximized. Check the maximize/restore button in the upper-right corner of the AWS. If it is a single box, click on it once. Now you can resize or move the AWS.

Problem: You set colors in some SAS windows, but the next time you start the SAS System, the colors did not stick.
Solution: You may have forgotten to issue a WSAVE command from each window you changed. Make the changes again, and this time issue the WSAVE command from each window you change.

Problem: You've closed one of the main SAS System windows, such as the LOG or PROGRAM EDITOR, and want it back—but it's not listed in the **Window** menu.
Solution: Click on **Globals** in the SAS System main menu, then on the name of the window you want to see, such as **Log**.

Managing SAS Files

Problem: You have accidentally deleted a file.

Solution: If the file was deleted using the Windows Explorer, use the Recycle Bin on the Windows desktop to recover the file, as described in "Restoring Deleted Files" in Chapter 1.

If the file was deleted using the SAS System (from the DIR window, for example), the file cannot be easily restored without a third-party file restoration utility such as Norton Utilities.

Problem: You know a file exists, but you cannot remember where you stored it.

Solution: Many dialog boxes in the SAS System (such as the Open dialog box) contain a **Browse** button. Click on this button to search through your computer's drives and folders until you find the file.

Another approach is to use Window's Find feature. Right-click on the **Start** button, then click on **Find**. In the resulting dialog box, type the filename in the **Named** field. If you want to search the entire root folder, click on the down arrow next to the **Look in** field, then click on the C: drive. Click on **OK** to start the search. The results of the search are displayed in the at the bottom of the Find dialog box.

Problem: You cannot perform a file operation, such as rename, move, or delete—you get a SAS error message about "insufficient authorization."

Solution: The file is protected by either the SAS System, Windows, or both. If the file is protected by the SAS System, you must specify the READ=, WRITE=, and ALTER= data set options and their respective passwords when you access the file. If the file is protected by Windows, use the Windows Explorer to display and change the file attributes. To do this, right-click on the file's icon in Windows Explorer, then click on **Properties**. The Properties dialog box appears, showing the file attributes.

Another possibility is that the file is being used by another Windows application. For example, you may be trying to access a text file that is already open in Word. If this is the case, close the file in the other application, then try accessing it with the SAS System again.

Customizing Your Start-up Files

Problem: The SAS System displays a message during initialization that it cannot find the CONFIG.SAS file.

Solution: Add the CONFIG system option to your SAS command (e.g., at the end of the **Target** field in the Properties dialog box). Be sure to specify the full pathname for the CONFIG.SAS file.

Problem: The SAS System does not execute the AUTOEXEC.SAS file.

Solution: Add the AUTOEXEC system option to your SAS command (e.g., at the end of the **Target** field in the Properties dialog box). Be sure to specify the full pathname for the AUTOEXEC.SAS file.

Problem: The SAS System complains about not being able to read the CONFIG.SAS or AUTOEXEC.SAS files.

Solution: You may have syntax errors in these files. In the CONFIG.SAS file, precede each option name with a hyphen, and do not use equal signs between the system option name and the value. Check your AUTOEXEC.SAS file for missing semicolons, comment delimiters, and mismatched quotes.

Another possible cause of this problem is that you may have inadvertently saved the CONFIG.SAS or AUTOEXEC.SAS file in a non-ASCII format. If you have recently edited these files with a word processing program, check to see if you saved the files in a proprietary format. If so, this adds formatting characters to the file that the SAS System cannot interpret. Re-edit the files and save them as plain text (ASCII) files.

Using Batch Mode

Problem: You cannot start your SAS batch job; double-clicking on a SAS program file icon starts a display manager session.

Solution: Use the Options dialog box in the Windows Explorer to edit the default action for .SAS and .SS2 files. See "Double-Clicking on a File Icon in the Windows Explorer" in Chapter 9 for more details.

Problem: You get an error message "PATHDLL not found" or "CONFIG file not found" when you start your batch SAS job.
Solution: Try specifying the CONFIG system option in the SAS command (such as in the **Target** field in the Properties dialog box or in the **Open** field in the Run dialog box). If you already have the CONFIG option specified, be sure it references the correct pathname.

Problem: The LOG and LST files from your batch job are not where you expect.
Solution: Check your program for PROC PRINTTO statements. Also, check your CONFIG.SAS file for LOG, ALTLOG, PRINT, and ALTPRINT system options. Look in the SAS working folder and in the folder containing the batch SAS program to see if the log and list files ended up there. Also look in the folder C:\WINDOWS\DESKTOP.

Executing DOS Commands and Windows Applications from Your SAS Session

Problem: The result of the DOS command you executed via an X statement or command flashes by so fast you cannot read it.
Solution: Submit the following OPTIONS statement:

```
options xwait;
```

Now resubmit your X statement or command. To return to your SAS session, press any key.

Problem: You started a Windows application via the X statement or command but now cannot use your SAS session while the application is open.
Solution: Close the application. Now submit the following OPTIONS statement:

```
options noxsync;
```

The next time you start an application with the X statement or command, it runs independently of your SAS session.

Problem: You used the X statement or command to start a Windows application but get an error message about being out of memory.

Solution: Each application you run takes up RAM. If your machine has a small amount of RAM available (such as 4 or 8M), you may be able to run only a few Windows applications at a time. Close unnecessary applications, and try the X statement or command again.

Problem: Your program uses the X statement but generates error messages or incorrect results. You are sure your programming statements are correct.

Solution: If the results of the X statement are not available before your program continues, it will not generate correct results. Specify XWAIT in your CONFIG.SAS file, so your SAS program will not continue without your permission. Also, if you are starting another application such as Word, use the SLEEP function to pause your program long enough for the other application to start.

Sharing Data between Your SAS Session and Other Windows Applications

Problem: When using DDE, your data does not look like it should—all the data are in one cell, there are tabs where you do not expect them, or the data are truncated.

Solution: Remember that the SAS System expects tabs between variables. By default, it writes variables to separate cells when the data contain spaces. Use the NOTAB option in the FILENAME statement when you define the DDE fileref to suppress this default behavior. If the data contain spaces but is truncated, use the DLM statement option to define another delimiter.

Problem: When you submit your SAS DDE program, an error message says the SAS System cannot communicate with the other application.

Solution: Remember that the application must be open before you submit your DDE SAS program. Either manually start the application, or use the X statement or X command to start it. You may need to use the SLEEP function to pause your SAS program long enough for the application to start.

Problem: The OLE objects in your SAS/AF applications do not reflect changes.

Solution: You may have forgotten to select the **Link** option in the Paste Special dialog box, thereby creating an embedded object instead. Re-create the object, ensuring that this time you select the **Link** option.

Problem: When you open a FRAME entry containing linked objects, you get a message that the link is unavailable.

Solution: Someone may have moved the source file for the object. Use the DLGLINK command to invoke the Links dialog box. Click on the link you want to modify, then click on **Change Source**. Type the new pathname in the **Source** field, then click on **OK**. Now click on **Update Now** in the Links dialog box to update the link. Finally, close the Links dialog box by clicking on **OK**.

Using SAS/CONNECT Software

Problem: You receive errors when you try to sign on to a remote connection.

Solution: First, check the physical connection to the remote system—a cable may have jiggled loose or broken. Also, check the syntax of your script file. If your network is busy, the connection may time out before it is complete. In the script file, look for a PAUSE or similar command and increase the time.

Problem: You try to access a SAS catalog using Remote Library Services but receive error messages.

Solution: Because of how characters and numbers are internally represented by operating systems, you can access SAS catalogs through RLS from the following operating systems only: Windows 3.1 (Win32s), Windows NT, and Windows 95.

Problem: You want to transfer an external file without the automatic conversion from one operating system format to another.

Solution: Use the BINARY option in the PROC DOWNLOAD or PROC UPLOAD statement, which prevents these procedures from converting the file format.

Problem: You need to transfer a text file whose record length is more than 132 bytes.

Solution: Use the LRECL option to set the record length in both the local and remote FILENAME statements.

Problem: You try to download or upload some data, but you receive errors in the SAS log.

Solution: The DOWNLOAD and UPLOAD procedures must be remote submitted. Use either the **Remote submit** item in the **Locals** menu, or use the RSUBMIT and ENDRSUBMIT statements to remote submit your upload and download steps.

Appendix 2 | Creating a Print File

Understanding Print Files

A print file is a file with special printer codes in it. These codes can be PCL codes (Printer Control Language) or PostScript codes, depending on what printer driver you use to create the file. Because print files contain these special codes, they are not ASCII files and cannot be viewed or edited with a text editor.

Preparing to Create Print Files

Before you can create print files, you need a printer set up to print to FILE:. One way to do this is to install a Generic/Text Only printer driver by following these steps.

Note: For Windows NT users, Steps 5 and 6 are reversed, and if you are a network user, you are prompted whether the printer should be shared after Step 7. Otherwise, the steps are the same for both Windows 95 and Windows NT.

1. Close all Windows applications and locate your Windows CD-ROM.

2. Click on the **Start** button, then click on **Settings**, then click on **Printers**.

3. In the Printers window, double-click on the **Add Printer** icon.

4. The Add Printer Wizard opens; click on **Next**.

5. Double-click on **Generic** in the **Manufacturers** field, then double-click on **Generic / Text Only** in the **Printers** field.

6. Double-click on **FILE:** in the **Available ports** field.

7. The default printer name is fine—click on **Next**.

8. When asked if you would like to print a test page, click on **No**, then click on **Finish**.

9. Insert the Windows CD-ROM when prompted, and click on **OK**.

Use this printer whenever you create a print file from the SAS System.

Creating a Print File Using Display Manager

To create a print file from the SAS System, you must first set the default printer to the Generic/Text Only printer. Click on **File** in the SAS System main menu, then click on **Print setup**. Click on the down arrow by the **Printer** field, and click on **Generic / Text Only on FILE:**. Click on **OK**. Now you are ready to create the print file.

If you do not want to use the dialog boxes to set the printer, add an OPTIONS statement to your code to set the SYSPRINT system option, as in the following example:

```
options sysprint='file:' 'Generic / Text Only';
```

Printing the Contents of Windows: Click on **File** in the SAS System main menu, then on **Print**. In the Print dialog box, click on **Print to File**. A text entry field appears by this option, as shown in Figure A2.1.

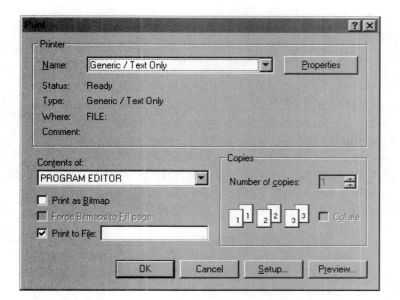

Figure A2.1
Print Dialog Box when
Creating a Print File

Type the name of the file you want to print to. If you do not want
the file stored in the SAS working folder, specify the full pathname.
You can use any extension you want, but normally you use .PRN
for non-PostScript printers and .EPS or .PS for PostScript printers.
Now click on **OK**. The SAS System creates the print file in the
directory you specified.

Printing from the DATA Step: Define a fileref, using the
PRINTER keyword, as in the following example:

```
filename myfile printer;
```

Use this fileref anytime you want to send DATA step output to a
print file. For example, the following code sends This is a
test to a print file:

```
filename myfile printer;

data _null_;
   file myfile;
   put 'this is a test';
run;
```

When you submit this code, a dialog box appears, asking for the filename of the print file. Type in the name you want to use, and click on **OK**. The print file is created.

Creating a Bitmap Print File

You can use the **Print to File** option in conjunction with the **Print as Bitmap** option to create a printer bitmap file. This does not create a bitmap file (such as the ones you open in Microsoft Paint, with an extension of .BMP); instead, it creates a file with special codes for the printer, telling it to interpret the information as a graphic. However, to make this combination work, your printer must support this technique. For example, you can use the WinFax printer driver provided with Delrina WinFax PRO 4.0 to fax bitmaps of SAS System windows.

Note: You can use this technique only from display manager.

Creating a Print File in Batch Mode

In batch mode, you do not have access to the Print dialog box. But you can still create a print file. To do so, use the SYSPRINT option to define the default printer and define a fileref using the PRINTER keyword and a filename, as in the following example:

```
options sysprint='file:' 'Generic / Text Only';

filename myfile printer 'c:\sas\print.prn';

data _null_;
      file myfile;
      put 'this is a test';
run;
```

You could also use the fileref in the PRINT= option in the PROC PRINTTO statement or in any other place in your code that creates output.

Glossary

active window: the application or part of an application that is ready to accept input.

application: a program with its attendant windows. Examples include programs such as the SAS System, Word, and Lotus 1-2-3.

application workspace (AWS): the borders within which an application operates.

click: to press a mouse button once. Unless otherwise specified, click refers to the left mouse button.

client: an application that requests data or information from another application. For example, in OLE, the SAS System is the OLE client.

Clipboard: a Windows component that is like a pegboard—a place to store something until you need it again. Typically, the Clipboard is used to store text or graphics that you want to copy somewhere else.

close: to shut down an individual window or an entire application.

Close button: an X in the upper-right corner of an application's AWS. Clicking on the Close button closes the application. Every Windows application has a Close button.

Control Panel: a Windows application that manages various aspects of your desktop, such as printers, colors, device drivers, the keyboard and mouse, etc. The Control Panel is part of the **Settings** program group accessed through the **Start** button.

DDE: see Dynamic Data Exchange.

DDE triplet: used in a FILENAME statement when you are using DDE (Dynamic Data Exchange).The DDE triplet tells the SAS System how to access data at a particular point in a file.

desktop: your screen, where all applications appear and where you do all your work with Windows.

dialog box: a type of window that solicits information from you. Usually, you must supply this information before you can continue using an application.

directory: see folder.

double-click: to quickly press the left mouse button twice in a row.

download: to move data from a remote computer to a local computer.

drag and drop: a method of using the mouse to move an object on your desktop from one place to another. You can drag and drop text, file icons, and graphics. Usually, when you drop the object, some action is taken, such as copying text or submitting a file.

Dynamic Data Exchange (DDE): a method of sharing text-based data between Windows applications.

embedded object: an OLE object that is not linked to the server application. The object and its data are stored in the client application. Embedded objects can be static or non-static. Contrast with linked object.

fileref: a nickname the SAS System uses for an external file or folder. Define filerefs with the FILENAME statement.

folder: a collection of files.

full pathname: the complete physical filename, including drive, folder, subfolder, filename, and extension. An example full pathname is C:\SAS\SASUSER\APPEND.SAS.

icon: a pictorial representation of a Windows object. Examples of objects that can be represented by icons include entire applications, individual windows, and files.

libref: a nickname the SAS System uses for a SAS data library. Define librefs with the LIBNAME statement or the Libraries dialog box.

linked object: an OLE object that is dynamically connected to its OLE server. When you paste a linked object into an OLE client application, only the object—not the data—is stored in the client application. The data remain independent of the client. Contrast with embedded object.

maximize: to cause an application or a window that is represented by an icon to restore to full size and take up the whole display.

menu: a visual method of executing commands in an application. To use the menu, click on a menu choice.

minimize: to cause an application or a window to become an icon.

mouse: the hand-held device you use to select and manipulate applications and text. The mouse activates the mouse pointer on the screen.

non-static embedded object: An OLE object that, when activated, can start its server application. Contrast with static embedded object.

object: something created by an OLE server that can be pasted into an OLE client application. Examples of objects are graphics, pieces of text, video clips, and sound files.

Object Linking and Embedding (OLE): a graphical method of sharing data between Windows applications.

OLE: see Object Linking and Embedding (OLE).

open editing: an OLE concept in which, when you edit an OLE object, the OLE server application starts in its own window, with its own menus and tool bars. Contrast with visual editing.

point: to move the mouse pointer over a particular item on the screen, such as a menu item, a word, or an icon.

popup menu: a menu that appears when you click the right mouse button.

program group: a collection of application icons in the **Start** button menu.

Remote Library Services: A method of data access used with SAS/CONNECT software. RLS accesses data directly on the remote machine, without physically transferring the data to the local machine.

right-click: to click the right mouse button once. Usually, this opens a popup menu.

RLS: see Remote Library Services.

scroll bar: a method of moving vertically or horizontally in a document. Scroll bars have arrows on which you click to move the file view.

server: an application that provides data or services to another application. For example, in OLE, Word, Excel, or Lotus 1-2-3 can be OLE servers.

shortcut: a pointer or link to any object, such as a file, program, network folder, Control Panel tool, or disk drive.

StartUp folder: A Windows program group that contains programs that start immediately as soon as Windows boots up.

static embedded object: an OLE object that is a picture. You cannot activate a static embedded object (that is, open its server application). Contrast with non-static embedded object.

subfolder: a collection of files that is part of a folder.

title bar: the horizontal element at the top of a Windows application workspace that tells you what application you are running. Individual windows inside an application also have title bars.

tool bar: a visual method of executing commands in a Windows application. Each command is represented by an icon. To execute the command, click on the appropriate icon.

upload: to move data from a local computer to a remote computer.

visual editing: an OLE concept in which, when you edit an OLE object, the OLE server application menus and tool bars meld with the OLE client's menus and tool bars. Contrast with open editing.

Windows Explorer: a Windows application that lets you move, copy, delete, rename, and otherwise manage your files. Explorer can be accessed by right-clicking on the **Start** button and clicking on **Explore**.

wizard: A Windows tool that guides you through a process, such as adding a printer to your system, or installing new software.

Index

Call your local SAS® office to order these other books and tapes available through the Books by Users℠ program:

An Array of Challenges — Test Your SAS® Skills
by **Robert Virgile**...................................Order No. A55625

Applied Multivariate Statistics with SAS® Software
by **Ravindra Khattree**
and **Dayanand N. Naik**.........................Order No. A55234

Applied Statistics and the SAS® Programming Language, Fourth Edition
by **Ronald P. Cody**
and **Jeffrey K. Smith**............................Order No. A55984

Beyond the Obvious with SAS® Screen Control Language
by **Don Stanley** ....Order No. A55073

The Cartoon Guide to Statistics
by **Larry Gonick**
and **Woollcott Smith**............................Order No. A55153

Categorical Data Analysis Using the SAS® System
by **Maura E. Stokes, Charles E. Davis,**
and **Gary G. Koch** ....Order No. A55320

Common Statistical Methods for Clinical Research with SAS® Examples
by **Glenn A. Walker**..............................Order No. A55991

Concepts and Case Studies in Data Management
by **William S. Calvert**
and **J. Meimei Ma**.................................Order No. A55220

Essential Client/Server Survival Guide, Second Edition
by **Robert Orfali, Dan Harkey,**
and **Jeri Edwards**..................................Order No. A56285

Extending SAS® Survival Analysis Techniques for Medical Research
by **Alan Cantor**.....................................Order No. A55504

A Handbook of Statistical Analyses using SAS®
by **B.S. Everitt**
and **G. Der** ....Order No. A56378

The How-To Book for SAS/GRAPH® Software
by **Thomas Miron** ....Order No. A55203

In the Know ... SAS® Tips and Techniques From Around the Globe
by **Phil Mason** ....Order No. A55513

Learning SAS® in the Computer Lab
by **Rebecca J. Elliott** ....Order No. A55273

The Little SAS® Book: A Primer
by **Lora D. Delwiche**
and **Susan J. Slaughter**.......................Order No. A55200

Mastering the SAS® System, Second Edition
by **Jay A. Jaffe** ....Order No. A55123

The Next Step: Integrating the Software Life Cycle with SAS® Programming
by **Paul Gill** ....Order No. A55697

Painless Windows 3.1: A Beginner's Handbook for SAS® Users
by **Jodie Gilmore** ....Order No. A55505

Professional SAS® Programming Secrets, Second Edition
by **Rick Aster**
and **Rhena Seidman** ....Order No. A56279

Professional SAS® User Interfaces
by **Rick Aster** ....Order No. A56197

Quick Results with SAS/GRAPH® Software
by **Arthur L. Carpenter**
and **Charles E. Shipp** ....Order No. A55127